THE

Nicky Gregson

Copyright © Nicky Gregson, 2024
All rights reserved
ISBN-13-9798326386403

To Lauren – without whom I would never have been to "Dave's"

Contents

	Page
Preface	1
Chapter One: 5.15am	17
Chapter Two: The Accidental Luthier	41
Chapter Three: Cain & Mann	67
Chapter Four: Finding a Violin	92
Chapter Five: The Fiddle Assistants	128
Chapter Six: Repair & Restoration	161
Chapter Seven: The Lutherie Club	204
Chapter Eight: The Last Commission	239
Epilogue	276
Acknowledgements	282
Further Reading	285

Illustrations

All images are © Nicky Gregson, with the following exceptions:

Thanks to Dave Mann for permission to reproduce the photographs on pages 17, 18, 19, 21, 22, 38, 42, 59 and 86; to Claire Mann for the image on p 82 and to Andreas Lassak for the image on p 80 of Claire on a Litha tour in Germany; to Elly Lucas for the image of Lauren MacColl on p 105; to Jeff Coffin for the image on p 253 of Peter Tickell on stage with Sting, taken in Atlanta, GA; and to Jack Smedley for the image on p 254. The photograph of Callers' shop window on p 29, taken in 1968, is reproduced under a Creative Commons licence from Newcastle Libraries.

Dave Mann - 2023

PREFACE

4 January, 2019. It's a cold, wet, leaden-grey day. The day when normal life has resumed after the Christmas-New Year break; and the weather seems to match most people's mood. But for me it's Christmas Day on rewind. Or, more like, the kind of Christmas Day I remember as a kid, for a mixture of excitement and apprehension abounds as I'm walking along a quaint, quirky street on the western edge of Hexham, the main market town of Northumberland. It's the kind of street that's to be found in most English market towns. Higgledy-piggledy buildings, formerly houses, now function as premises for dentists and chiropractors, computer repair shops and coin dealers. What I'm looking for though is The Violin Shop, for today's the day I'm finally going to choose my very own violin.

A few weeks previously I'd tentatively broached the question of buying an instrument with my teacher, the acclaimed Scottish fiddle player Lauren MacColl. "Give Dave a ring" she'd said. "He's in Hexham; it's near you". By then I'd been learning for less than a year, on a $100 starter instrument loaned to me by an American work colleague, Sarah Knuth. Even now I'm not sure who was really doing whom the favour, for that fiddle had travelled from the United States to Durham, England with Sarah, along with a flute. Unlike the flute, it had stayed firmly in its case. That was until one Thanksgiving meal – it must have been 2017 – when I said that I'd like to have a go at learning the fiddle. I left that Thanksgiving meal with Sarah's unplayed fiddle and life has never been the same since.

Taking up the fiddle just shy of my 60th birthday may be a personal trajectory but it's one that is widely shared. For many people approaching retirement, taking up a musical instrument, like learning a language, seems an obvious choice: a way of keeping minds active, a new challenge, a means to a wider sociality. That demand is varyingly satisfied across the UK. In countries and regions where traditional music is strong, opportunities abound. That's particularly so in Scotland, where traditional music has played a central role in the revival of Gaelic culture and heritage. Elsewhere, particularly in England's cities, opportunities are harder to come by. But in Northeast England, where I live, there is a strong culture of adult learning centred on educational programmes run at what is still known locally as "The Sage", now The Glasshouse International, on the banks of the River Tyne in Gateshead. As well as teaching adults instruments, these programmes serve to promote the playing, and hence preservation, of Northumbrian traditional music. Classes abound: ukulele, fiddle, flute, accordion, 'box' or concertina, and guitar are all catered for, along with clog dancing. Mostly, the adults in these classes are fulfilling lifelong dreams. My turn to the fiddle, though, is rather different: more a return to music than a discovery of its joys.

It's this return, combined with the career pathway that I eventually took, which has shaped this book. Without that return, the book wouldn't exist. Of that I've no doubt, for the world that I document here, and the figure who sits at is core, would have remained unknown to me; invisible but to a network of those in the know. But equally, the book's shape, form, and content are indicative of other legacies and traces. These testify to a career spent working as an academic and specifically as a social scientist. Inevitably, inexorably, in the process of research and writing I've found myself weaving together here a love of music, of musical instruments, and of the fiddle in particular with a deep commitment to ways of researching and thinking which are the hallmarks of the social sciences.

But to begin at the beginning: in primary school, now I look back at it, I must have been identified as one of those musically talented kids; not that I remember any such grandiose label being applied. I just enjoyed playing recorders, especially the treble, and singing. And by all accounts, I spent a great deal of time with a recorder in my mouth, even at 6.30 in the morning, and out in the garden! But one day I remember going to a music shop on an out-of-the way high street on the edge of Southeast London. I had been taken to buy an oboe. Or, rather, my parents bought it for me. It was a Boosey & Hawkes basic student model. I remember being blown away by the amount of metal work on it compared to my recorders. But even then the shadow of money cast long: it cost what seemed a small fortune to a cash-strapped family: £80. I must have been 11.

To this day, I cannot recall how or why I ended up playing the oboe but play this instrument I did, for several years, through grade exams, junior orchestras and wind bands. At one juncture during a lesson – I think I was 12 or 13 – my teacher broached the 'time to get a new instrument' topic, along with heading off to Royal College of Music Juniors on a Saturday. It was the summer holidays and I'd practised seriously that week; a rare event given the competing demands of school work. The results must have showed, for that evening reeds were swapped over and I was given a go on his wooden oboe and cor anglais. And they did sound fabulous! Especially when compared to my 'crappy plastic job'. I distinctly remember the not so thrilling return to playing that instrument. Temptation had clearly been placed in my way. But, there was a big but. My family didn't have any money, let alone the money required to shell out on a wooden oboe, and anyway I was much more interested in riding horses on a Saturday than going to the Royal College of Music. In retrospect that was the moment when me and the oboe started to part company. Even though it went with me to university, it was seldom played. This was because by then I'd discovered the intoxicating delights of choral singing. Handel, Verdi, Elgar, Bruckner and Brahms provided the musical accompaniment to my geography degree – or, more accurately, the degree accompanied them, for I spent more time in and around the music school than in the department where I was registered as an undergraduate student.

In all seriousness though, looking back, I doubt my attachment to the oboe was ever that strong. The first instrument I remember being enchanted by as a child is the harp. In my first year of primary school a woman brought a full-sized concert harp into the school to play for us. The sound filled the assembly hall. I loved it. And, of course, she was wearing the full-length flouncy frock. Bright red, it was just the dress to appeal to a five-year old girl. Of course, I wanted a harp; a request that strangely enough fell on deaf ears. But stringed instruments always called me. As a teenager, when I listened to classical music in the gaps between Elton John and David Bowie booming out of the stereo on full volume, it wasn't oboe music I listened to but Paul Tortelier playing the Bach Cello Suites, or Jacqueline du Pré playing the Elgar Concerto. I must have worn those vinyl records out so many times did I play them. I knew every note. For me, there was a magic about cello sound that went well beyond the possibilities of the oboe – even when playing the Marcello Concerto, which to this day I regard as the defining piece written for the instrument. By contrast, the cello was life affirming, immersive; transporting; everything that anyone could want to produce in sound. Its repertoire seemed to acknowledge those qualities. And then, staying on at school in the gap between the end of the school day and an evening concert, I remember having a surreptitious go on a friend's violin. She'd left it in its open case, no doubt to keep it adjusted to the temperature in which it would be playing. The sound of those open strings! So much more resonance, nuance, texture, colour and range than I could achieve with an oboe. What an instrument! I remember thinking 'Why wasn't I playing this?' My version of the adult learner's unfulfilled dream story, then, was to play a stringed instrument. Fast forward over forty years. With no desire to return to the grade-structured learning which defines classical music, and with the parameters of portability and sociability also to the fore, there was really only going to be one instrument to return to music with: the fiddle.

This then, an aspiring fiddler with less than a year of playing behind her but with a classical music hinterland, is the woman approaching The Violin Shop, Hexham. But what to expect? I had no idea. My sole experience of buying an instrument was the dimly remembered one of having a pre-selected, basic student instrument purchased for me. And, giving Dave a ring hadn't yielded many more clues. Evidently a Geordie – the accent was a straight giveaway – he was seemingly a man of very few words, for, when I'd rung, he'd said no more than "What's your budget?", "When do you want to come in?", and "Give me a ring when you're about to set off". Gruff, grumpy, direct, or possibly all three, I thought.

The shop found, entering in was to be transported back in retail time. A door buzzer announced my arrival and a wee, stocky guy in his late 60s or early 70s, bespectacled, wearing a scruffy jumper and jeans, emerged from a passageway which led who knows where. This, I deduced, must be Dave, though no words to establish that were exchanged. The shop was literally half the size of a front room, dominated by a huge counter, behind which hung a stretch of glass cabinets full of violins and a few violas. A few cellos hung on the side walls. But it's the counter that's attracting my attention.

Lined up on the counter is an array of three fiddles – "There you go" says the man I assume to be Dave. "Take your coat off. Here's a bow. You start playing them. Tell me which one you like the most and we'll take it from there". Hmmm, I think, taking off my coat and placing it on a chair, what to play? Any tunes that I know seem to have disappeared from my head. Spying a music stand in the corner of the shop, I ask Dave: "Do you have any music?" "No", he says and promptly disappears through the passageway from which he'd appeared. Well, I think, I might as well start off with some scales and arpeggios ... which, as they tend to do, then unlock tunes, and tunes and tunes. I play the three fiddles in turn for at least ten minutes each, identifying the one that I like the best. I give Dave a shout. To my total surprise, out he comes with another set of fiddles. "Right", he says, "put that one to one side and now play these three and see which one of these you like best". I start to realise that I might be in this shop some time ... I go through the same process, identifying the one I prefer from this set. Then Dave brings out another three. Press repeat. "Right", he says, "you've now got your top three. Your job now is to choose between them!" Off he goes again. This, I think, is decision time. I haven't asked Dave anything about them. I don't look at the relative prices, which anyway there don't appear to be on these three instruments. Instead I keep relying on my ears to tell me what kind of instrument they are, what sound they like to produce, and how that relates to the sound I want to produce eventually, when I can play rather better. I eliminate one quite quickly and summon Dave back to the shop – "What's this one?" I ask him. "German". I'm none the wiser but I'm down to the final selection. I play these two instruments for what seems an age. They're both great instruments but I keep coming back to one: it's powerful, dark but somehow still mellow and warm – all the qualities I want in sound. It works across the four strings equally, but its lower two strings are something else altogether. There's no doubt in my mind. This fiddle is it. I've found my stringed instrument. "I've decided" I say, into the passageway. Dave comes through into the shop. "Which one is it then?" I pick it up. "This one" I say. He beams: "That's one of mine", he says. "And the other?" I ask, "What's that?" "French. All show and frilly knickers!"

*

So, what is this "one of mine"? Self-evidently, this fiddle – my fiddle – is a Dave Mann fiddle. Dave had literally just completed it a few days before I'd walked in to his shop. The date inscribed on the label visible through the bass f hole is the day I bought it. But it's also, as I learnt a good few years later, on beginning the research for this book, a Dave Mann fiddle made on a Guadagnini model. This makes it relatively unusual as contemporary instruments go, for most modern luthiers favour Guarneri models for making their violins. In the course of his working life, Dave himself has made over 200 instruments, most of them on a Guarneri model. So why the change? Martin Hughes, a classical violinist, ex-second for Northern Sinfonia, a previous Head of Strings at Glasgow Conservatoire, and Director of Hexham Abbey Music Festival, takes up the story. "He'd done Guarneris. They were his domain and he was churning them out. And we were having a conversation one day and I was saying to him, 'Have you ever thought of doing something a bit like going off-piste? Like a Guadagnini?' The thing about Guadagninis for players is that they feel loud under you and they project like there's no tomorrow. Now, who's to say that when you make your first Guadagnini model that it's going to do all these things? It might not; it might be a complete flop; but none of them is. Every single one bears the same hallmarks, and some are outstanding. I remember playing Number 1 and thinking 'I want this fiddle'."

The Violin Shop

Having this fiddle in my life has transformed it, and enriched it immeasurably. It's a trite turn of phrase, but I cannot imagine life without it. I play this fiddle literally every day – usually for two hours, every morning. This isn't a chore; it's a total delight. Like writing, another activity which I do most days, I find the daily discipline of fiddle playing orders the world by suspending the world. The cognitive, embodied and emotional layers that conjoin in playing transport me to another space; a sound-body space, where the fiddle is part of me; an extension of me. And, playing this fiddle has helped me become a much better fiddle player. No question. So, when I cast my mind back to the day when I bought it, I realise that I wasn't so much buying a fiddle as being given the opportunity to find this kind of profound and emotional attachment, an attachment that comes from playing and sounding. That was Dave's gift to me. And yet, remarkably, Dave made no intervention in that process, other than to keep supplying me with fiddles to try out. That, I now realise, is part of what makes this shop unique. In the rarefied world of selling violins, where instrument value is correlated with playing ability, and where strict hierarchies determine who gets to play on what sorts of instruments, a beginner player such as I then was would not normally get a look in with this kind of instrument. Yet literally anyone can buy one of these Dave Mann instruments, if they can afford one. So, there's an inclusive quality to this shop; and it contrasts starkly with the wider violin world of which it is part, which is defined by exclusivity. That is a marker of the man whose shop it is.

*

The gift of this fiddle alone though was not what brought me to write this book. That has been a more gradual journeying. In the years that I've had this fiddle, I've made what's seemed increasingly like an annual pilgrimage back to the shop for what Dave calls the fiddle's annual MOT. This comprises a clean, polish and set-up, plus any minor repairs that might be required. For the first couple of years that I had the fiddle, this involved handing the fiddle over to Dave (often along with the bow, for a rehair) and then disappearing off into Hexham for a few hours. When I returned, the fiddle was there on the shop's counter ready for collection, smelling, as it always does when it's been back to Dave's, of a unique furniture-polish aroma. And when I played it, it would invariably sound even better than it did when it went in. "Wow Dave! What have you done?" I'd say. Ever under-stated, he would say something on the lines of "Oh, just moved the sound post a bit". That spare turn of phrase conveys much. There is an opacity about it which works to separate the world of the luthier from the world of the player. It also cloaks that differentiation in a form of magic dust. Luthier magic happens out of sight, unseen – somewhere through the passageway. It was a closely guarded world that I didn't get to see.

At some point though, I don't quite remember when, I was invited through that small passageway from which Dave had first emerged on the day when I first set foot in The Violin Shop. It was like being transported to yet another world. Lauren MacColl describes it as a passage not unlike going through the wardrobe in CS Lewis's Narnia books. If to enter the shop is to enter a bygone age of retailing, what lies beyond the passageway in the shop is to go back centuries in manufacturing time, to a world of artisanal craft production. Anyone who enters this inner sanctum for the first time, no matter who they are, or from which walk of life, responds with the same jaw dropping, "Wow"! Some liken it instantly to a scene from *Harry Potter*. The walls are lined with fiddles, in varying states of repair and disrepair. Below them, on the walls, hang what seems to be hundreds of specialist hand-crafted tools. Saws, chisels, planes, set squares, rulers. And then, there is the centrepiece of the atelier: a work bench. A chair is placed with its back to the barred window, positioned to allow the cast of natural light over the shoulder. On the bench is a strong desk light, high powered magnifying eye glasses and a jumbled mess – tiny precision tools, discarded strings and tailpieces, pencils, measuring jugs, erasers, small pieces of ebony and pine, and often wood shavings. Usually, there is something else more recognisably fiddle-like on this bench – the back, or belly of a fiddle in the making; a neck, a scroll, or a fiddle in varying stages of repair or restoration. What this is so clearly is the mess of a master craftsman at work.

Getting to see this inner sanctum is why I've increasingly felt that pilgrimage is the right word to use to describe my fiddle's annual journeys to Hexham. Just like a migratory bird, it's coming back to the place, to the very bench, where it was actually made, and to the hands of the luthier who made it. In some strange way, the fiddle seems to recognise this homecoming. When I play this fiddle in this atelier space it seems to know it's come home. It's hard to explain this, but there is, I think, something about the unique combination of the cool temperature and dry humidity of the atelier which means the wood is in what I like to think of as its sounding sweet spot; it's in what I call the fiddle's 'happy space', where it's able to resonate to full capacity. That it is perhaps is not that surprising. After all, the wood from which it's been made had been sitting in that same shop for years before it became a fiddle.

*

For such thoughts to suggest that they might take shape in book form, though, needed a catalyst. Sometime around the beginning of 2022, I happened by chance one Sunday tea time on a BBC Radio 3 programme which began to explore the question of a violin's relation to wood. It was one of Tom Service's, *The Listening Service*. Being Radio 3, the focus was on classical music, and the arc of the programme flowed back in time; to old instruments and old makers, and to wood felled centuries ago. Inexorably, it gravitated to Cremona, a city in the Lombardy region of Italy, and the centre of the golden age of violin making, to Stradivarius, and to the specific forests and trees from which these instruments – revered in the classical music world as the epitome of luthier skill - were crafted. To tell a story in this way is a variant of an 'origin story', and it is the standard trope for the literature on violins. Listening to that programme, though, set me thinking in the opposite direction.

Drawn by what I was increasingly identifying not just as a sound unique to my fiddle but to the more generic sounding quality of a Dave Mann fiddle, I had the idea of exploring the craft of contemporary fiddle making and to follow that forwards into the instruments themselves. With that thought in my head, and having dispatched to the publishers another book that I had long needed to write, in early May 2022 I set off with my fiddle on its annual pilgrimage. What followed was either serendipity or perfect timing. Sitting in the atelier in the chair opposite Dave's, 'blethering away' with him whilst he worked on the set up of my fiddle, he pointed to the arching of the table of his latest Guadagnini lying amidst the clutter on the work bench. Then he said: "This'll be me last one, me last commission". It was the kind of opening any researcher/writer needs: "In that case, Dave", I said, "I've got a proposition for you". This book is the result. But, as with all research, the book is not quite as I'd originally conceived. Whilst Dave's fiddles, and some of their players, certainly do feature, the book goes beyond them.

*

So where does this book travel that I did not originally envisage? Inevitably, there is the influence of Dave's own backstory. The 'So, how did you get into this Dave?' question might have been an obvious starting point for our discussions, but how could I have known that asking this question would have highlighted that this was a luthier with a difference? That here would be someone who hadn't followed the standard route into the profession; which is one that starts with an interest in violins and wood, and being taught at a violin-making school. Well, knowing a bit of the man, perhaps I might have guessed. Unique, idiosyncratic even are just some of the words people use to describe someone who is quintessentially working class, a proud Geordie, and who embraces that culture to the hilt, particularly its humour. But what I would never have guessed is that Dave's life-story is a journey that would take me from the familiar trajectory for working class lads of his age and born in Newcastle, of an engineering apprenticeship, to the unlikely milieu of professional drumming, to the Newcastle club scene of the 1960s and 1970s, its gangsters and villains, and to the world of *Get*

Carter. But that is Dave's life. It's a life which led thence to classic car restoration. Violins came much later; once Dave became a dad.

Then there are the effects of a social scientist at work. In conducting the research for this book, I've used the same methods that I'd deploy in academic research projects – a mix of interviews and more informal conversations, repetitive, often weekly, visits to the shop and the workshop over the course of a year to watch Dave working and being at work, photography and video recordings. Just as in other projects, that way of working discloses how things actually work, rather than how those with particular, often vested, interests tell that they work. Invariably, they also throw up the unanticipated and the unknown.

The longer I spent in this atelier, the more I came to realise the wider significance of what appears at first sight to be an innocuous, tiny shop and workshop, off the beaten track in Hexham. This was manifested first by its geographical reach. Bows arrived by post in long tubes from literally all over the UK whilst people travelled for hours from as far as London and the Southeast, or the furthest west and northerly extremities of Scotland, just to come to try out the fiddles, cellos and even the occasional double bass in Dave's shop. In my line of academic work, this is an exemplification of reputational capital; it's an indication of the regard in which Dave's professional and craft working practices are held. At the same time, The Violin Shop revealed itself to be an entry point to what I've increasingly come to think of as an ecosystem – more than that, it's a key node in it. The ecosystem comprises instruments and people, chiefly players but also other luthiers and dealers, and the networks that connect them. Shops like The Violin Shop are critical to the functioning of this ecosystem. They provide instruments for various levels of player, and they are often lynchpins in the development of young, talented musicians' careers. Even more critical is that they offer the full range of restoration, repair and maintenance services.

Unlike many other musical instruments, and as generations of parents have discovered, the violin family and their bows require a lot of maintenance and repair work to keep them playable. This goes well beyond most people's level of DIY competence. Even replacing a broken string can be a challenge; a collapsed bridge for a parent is something of a catastrophe. All string players therefore need luthiers, and professional players are dependent on them. The relationship between a professional player, especially a classical player, and a luthier is akin to that between a professional athlete and their physiotherapist. Luthiers' skills keep these instruments sounding optimally; and just like an athlete's body, these instruments need frequent attention to keep on top of the wear and tear that the demands of classical playing place on them. Yet, for all that, the essential work of contemporary luthiers remains pretty much invisible, hidden behind the veneer of great past master craftsmen, particularly Stradivarius, and books which catalogue and revere the instruments they made. This book seeks to make this contemporary work visible.

It also seeks to recognise what it is about this shop that makes it such a special place for so many people. It was on my second visit to the shop when I realised that I wasn't just dealing with a luthier with a difference but a shop with a difference, and that the two were inexorably intertwined. It was a quiet Monday afternoon in the atelier and a couple, Mick and Pauline, had popped in. What I thought would be just a short chat turned into an all afternoon conversation, in the course of which my jaw probably did hit the floor. Being a social scientist, I have colleagues who've spent much of their professional lives trying, often unsuccessfully, to get men of a certain age, many of them men like Dave, to talk about their health, mental as well as physical. Many are the discussions that I've had with these colleagues about why that is such a difficult, at times impossible, exercise. So, what I witnessed that afternoon in Dave's workshop left me flabbergasted. Here I was privy to an extended two hour, no-holds-barred, conversation about exactly that. It's a situation that I've witnessed on several subsequent occasions, with different men from all sorts of walks of life and backgrounds. Reflecting on this, I think it's to do with the ambience and the atmosphere of the workshop. Dave sits and works quietly away, surrounded by wood; those who visit sit either opposite him or against a side wall and they invariably start to open up in what is something akin to a therapeutic encounter. "Dave", I said as we left the workshop that Monday afternoon, "you're not just running a shop. You're running a drop-in centre". "Aye", he said. "I know! It all comes out here!"

Obviously, the content of those conversations is not repeated here but the openness, warmth and generosity of the sociality of this shop runs through and across many of the chapters. Like many hobby-enthusiast shops, The Violin Shop is a special space. The marker of that is that it has gathered a community – or, rather, it's the guru figure, the magician at its centre, who has done this. Not just a maker and repairer of fiddles, Dave Mann is also restorative of people and it's in recognition of that that people trek, often many hundreds of miles, to his door. They might bring a fiddle, or a bow – or they might want to buy a fiddle or bow – but they're also bringing a person, themselves, to this special space. Invariably, they leave touched by this place.

CHAPTER ONE
5.15am

Nineteen Sixty Seven
Bandit man in birdcage heaven
La Dolce Vita, Sixty Nine
All new to people of the Tyne

5.15 am: Mark Knopfler (*Shangri La*, 2004).

"So Dave", I say, "you're Benwell born and bred". "Aye, Benwell born and bred!"

David Gifford Mann, known to his friends as Dave or Davey, was born on 18 January 1951, the fourth – and third surviving – child of Ted Mann (pictured) and Hilda Duckworth, who themselves are described by him as 'Benwell born and bred'. Benwell is in the west end of the city of Newcastle upon Tyne, in Northeast England. The 'born and bred' phrase is still in common use in this part of the world, where it denotes a rootedness and connectedness with place that is inter-generational. Its close parallel is the phrase 'We don't  go far', which captures how family members continue to live in close proximity to each other; if no longer on the same street, no more than a very short drive away. Scratch the surface, though, and begin to delve into family history, and the cracks in the 'born and bred' narrative which families tell start to appear.

Like many Northeast families, the Manns and the Duckworths have not lived in Benwell for generations. Rather, they ended up living on Tyneside in the relatively recent past. This was because of work. Like many of the families who lived around them in Benwell, it was the employment opportunities afforded by industrial Tyneside in the early part of the twentieth century that drew them there, from all over Northern England.

Dave tells me about his family history: "Me dad's dad (pictured) was from Nottingham. He was a blacksmith originally. He was out shoeing horses on the front line in World War I. Me dad said he shot himself! He shot his own bloody toe off, the daft old bugger, so he could come home.

In World War II he was a sergeant major in the Home Guard. Early on in the war me dad was in his regiment, as a private. He was dishing orders out, 'Private Mann' – and me dad would say, 'Shut up you stupid old bugger'! Just like *Dad's Army!*" Further back on Dave's dad's side of the family they came from Co. Monahan in Ireland. "They were Catholic priests who ended up in Liverpool. But me mother's lot were originally from Cumbria – Penrith way. There were lots of problems when me mam and dad got married, cos me mother wasn't a Catholic. Dad was. It interfered you see. So they got married in a registry office cos me dad had a row with the priest. It split the family up. I hardly ever saw me grandma and granda Mann. But me dad's brother – me Uncle Tommy who I never met – he went to Sri Lanka in the 1930s. They had 10 kids. So I've never met any of them. Heard about them – but they all had the surname Mann. If you come across any Sri Lankans called Mann they've got to be related to me!"

When Dave was born the family lived at 109 Ellesmere Road (pictured), in a house they rented. Ellesmere Road is one of several long parallel streets in Benwell which line the north bank of the River Tyne. The streets run north-south, stretching from the West Road, which is the main arterial road west out of the city, down to the Scotswood Road, which runs parallel to the river. In the 1950s these streets comprised terraced housing – 'two-up; two downs' with a back yard. Much of this housing was demolished during waves of urban regeneration in the 1980s and 2010s.

By the 1980s Benwell was a byword for what happens when local and regional economies collapse and the social fabric and cohesion is ripped out of them. It had become an area identified with transient populations, and particularly drugs and crime. A consequence is that Benwell had become somewhere those who could left; it was the sort of place people don't choose to live in but rather are placed in by others. By the 2000s it also stood as a marker of national and regional policy failure, as programme after programme intended to reverse its fortunes failed to arrest its social and economic decline. As a consequence, it had transitioned to become a cause célèbre for generations of university undergraduates studying the social sciences – the people I taught. It was also one of the places where, in the late 1980s, I took visiting academics from the US and Canada to see some of the most deleterious effects of 'industrial restructuring' on Tyneside. So, Benwell was a place known about for all the wrong reasons and put under the microscope for precisely those same reasons.

Back in the 1950s, when Dave was born, things were very different. Benwell then is somewhere he remembers as "Nice. All the doors were open, and all your neighbours were your aunties and uncles, like Auntie Nellie and Auntie Betty". And there was plentiful employment still about. The Scotswood Road then was home to several engineering firms, including Armstrong Vickers, which manufactured tanks and ordnance, and a welter of smaller engineering 'shops' (workshops) which manufactured and supplied component parts. Further east along the river, by Walker and Wallsend, were the shipyards and allied engineering firms which had underpinned Tyneside's reputation in the late nineteenth century as 'the workshop of the world'. This was a world where men worked in heavy engineering industries and associated trades. Women's place, by contrast, was in the home. True to this pattern, exactly a year later, on 18 January 1952, Dave was followed into the world by his sister Christine: "Actually we're twins, but she's a late developer!"

The 'twins', as Dave refers to himself and his younger sister (pictured), had two much older siblings: "There's Pat – Patricia – she died recently but she was born in 1938. And then there was me older brother, Teddy – well John. He was born in 1936, but the family name was Teddy. He died when he was 56. It was an accident at work. He had his own business, a tool room turner – big lathes. And he got caught in one. His jumper got caught in it, and it strangled him. A customer found him. So I had to go and tell me mother that he was dead." That was in 1993. Many years earlier Hilda and Ted had lost another child: Doreen, who  died at two days old, at some point during World War II – Dave does not know when or why. Her short life is all he knows of her.

Dave's father Ted was a motor engineer by trade, as was his father's father, once he'd stopped shoeing horses for a living. "Dad had certificates from Rolls Royce. He had papers that gave him permission to work on Rolls Royce engines". Those qualifications led to him being sent to Rosyth for part of World War II, to repair and maintain naval vessels. "Me mam was left with the family in Benwell. I've got some of the letters he sent to her when he was away. 'Hope Teddy's ok; he'll be getting a big lad now. I do hope you're not going out with other blokes. Lots of love, Ted'. There'd be like half a page – just that, and then, 'I can't think of anything else to say – tara'!" He laughs. Sitting opposite Dave in the atelier, I can't help but think about Hilda, his mother – left not only to bring up a young family single handed during war time, but also having to cope with the death of a baby on her own.

Hilda, who was born in 1916, was evidently a woman of strength and resilience. One of Dave's close friends, the Edinburgh-based fiddle and double bass player Freddie Thompson, describes her as "An amazing woman". Freddie described to me how he was first introduced to Hilda by Dave's younger daughter Claire, at the wedding of Dave's older daughter, Sarah. He also tells me how, as an old woman, Hilda "Used to sit in her chair, and she never used to lock the front door; anyone could've come in. I'd listen to her tell stories about when she was a girl, 14 or 16 or something. She got the boat down to London 'cos the train was too expensive. She was working for people who had market stalls and stuff and she'd be going round topping up their tea and doing that kind of thing. It was either on the way down or back, but a storm broke out and they had to pull into a place for a few days and just wait the storm out before she could get back. Can you imagine a girl at that time, 16 years old?"

Hilda was also a woman who held onto her dreams. Many decades later, like many older working class women living on Tyneside, she returned to paid employment, this time working as a care assistant in an old people's home. Dave describes her as loving this, both for the money it eventually gave her and the independence. It allowed her to realise her dreams. One such dream is recounted by Freddie and concerns a dolls house. Freddie: "She told me the story about that dolls house. She insisted; it was at Sarah's wedding, 'Claire take him up and let him see me dolls house'. It was a beautiful dolls house with little pieces of furniture and all that. She had only got it fairly recently and the reason she got it was when she was a child, she'd never forgotten it – the family opposite had more money than her family and this wee girl had got a big dolls house and she wouldn't allow Dave's mum to play with it. It must have been on her mind all that time – 'when I get older, I'm getting a dolls house'. And she got her dolls house!"

The world of dolls houses was a world away from the realities of everyday living in the Benwell terraces of the 1950s. "So Dave", I say, sitting opposite him in my customary chair in the atelier watching him repair a fiddle, "it was a terrace?" "Oh aye". "Did it have an outside toilet?" "Yes - an outside toilet, and a coal house in the backyard". "Did you have hot water?" "Yes". "And presumably you had to share bedrooms?" "Oh aye. There was just the two bedrooms". As he says this I'm adding up the people and wondering how they all fitted in, especially at night. I ask, "So where did Christine go?" "Well she shared with me other sister Pat until she left. She left when she got married, but that wasn't until she was 25. So Pat was sharing with a little child really. They used to share the same bed. They had a double bed, and they both shared that". Thinking about arrangements where adult children are sharing beds with young children, I ask: "So did you have to share with Ted then?" Dave: "No, well by then he'd got someone pregnant, married and left, so I had to share me mam and dad's bedroom – I had a little Z bed!" I exclaim – "Bloody hell, Dave!" "I know, but we didn't think anything of it. All the families in the street did the same, 'cos they were all big families in them days".

Like the rest of the local kids, Dave went to Canning Street School – infants, juniors and secondary. When he was 11 he joined the local Boy's Brigade and – much miffed – was assigned to playing the bugle. "All I wanted to do was to play the drums: snare drum, side drum. But they gave us a bugle, which I didn't want. I used to annoy the neighbours of course, especially the woman next door. I was 12. I was out in the backyard of this terraced house in Benwell. We'd got this hose pipe, and I stuck the bugle mouth piece on it. Drhh-di-drhh-di-drhh-di-drrrhhh!!" He imitates the sound of the makeshift bugle. "The next door neighbour's back door bursts open. It was Mrs Temple! She grabbed the bugle off us, pulled it apart here." He mimes separating the mouthpiece from the hose. "She went hysterical! 'I'm going to tell your mother!!'"

Eventually, though, Dave did progress from the bugle to the snare and side drum. Then his dad got him a drum kit – "an Olympic – white. Bass, snare, tom on top and floor tom and a couple of high-hats. We formed a little band with kids. Someone would knock on the door, 'me mam's not in tonight, get yer drums down'." But when he was 14 things got more serious: Dave started taking lessons with a local professional, Jack Bell: "He was a good drummer but old fashioned. He played with Joe Loss' band." "Swing?" I ask. "Aye, Swing".

From the point he started lessons with Jack, Dave didn't want to do anything except play the drums. But at 15, like all his peers, Dave left Canning School, with no qualifications. "You didn't need them to be an apprentice. You went in and you could pick what you wanted – tool fitter; electrician; jig borer; miller; working on lathes. Me elder brother Teddy, he worked at Vickers. Me dad, he worked for small companies. So the natural thing to do was to follow the line and be apprenticed".

Like father, like sons. Being apprenticed into the engineering industry was the unquestioned, natural order of things for 15-year old boys living in Benwell at the time. But, whilst Teddy had been apprenticed to Vickers on the Scotswood Road, Dave followed a different route into the engineering sector: "One night me dad came in and said, 'Got you a job at British Engines – that's where you're gannin'. He got us it because he knew somebody. So that's what I did". British Engines was located in Walker, further east along the river, down near Wallsend and Tyneside's shipyards. To get to it from Benwell involved a bus journey rather than walking or cycling. A world beyond Benwell and Scotswood had begun to open up to Dave.

Unlike Vickers, British Engines is still a presence in Northeast England. At the time Dave joined its apprenticeship scheme in 1966, the company specialised in the machine tools sector and in engine repair for cars, trucks, ships and planes. It then expanded into high pressure valves used in the chemical and offshore industries. I ask Dave how they taught the apprentices back then. "They had like a school, like a class – a workshop like with machines and benches and stuff, and off that was a classroom, with a blackboard and stuff. That was just for the first year. There were two teachers who were like off the floor, given the job. We'd have like a couple of hours in the classroom every day, and you'd learn stuff and then you went out into the workshop, and you were given jobs and shown how to do them. How to use the machines and how to be careful. They had different machines – grinding, milling, lathes, capstans, borers, and you had to learn how to use each one. You were taught how to use the machine and how to clamp your jobs on and stuff and how to centre, so the cutter – you had to learn how to centre your job to like two-thousandths of an inch. That was hard, to learn how to do that on each machine."

From learning to use the machines, Dave progressed to metal pattern making, for rollings for casts in brass and bronze. By his own admission, he hated this work and was continually waiting for the clock to turn to 4.15pm and finish time. He served his apprenticed time of five years, but midway through those five years, when he was 17, his world changed completely. As a respected and well known drummer on Tyneside, Jack Bell had connections and was a go-to source in the city for all things drums. One day he was approached by the Allen James Group, the house band at a city centre night club. They were looking for a drummer and wanted to know if Jack knew of anyone suitable. Dave recounts: "Jack said 'Do you fancy doing a job at Michael's club?' I went, 'What, me?!' 'Aye, you – you can do it; get yourself down there!' So I played in a night club when I was working in a factory – 'burning both ends'. I'd get up at 6.30 to go to work; work 7.30-4.15. Get the bus home for 5/5.30. Have me tea; try to get some rest, then 10-2 at the night club, and then up again for work. I did it for a year".

Michael's was one of the first of a wave of nightclubs to open in Newcastle city centre in the mid-1960s. The city centre – unlike places like Benwell, Walker and Wallsend, which remained dominated by heavy industry – was then the site of a burgeoning leisure industry, focused on nightclubs, music, dancing and drinking. This was the beginnings of UK city centre economies shifting from a focus on manufacturing industry to the consumption of goods and services. The immediate enabler of the nightclubs was the relaxation of the licensing laws, which allowed drinking into the early hours. But the nightclubs also aligned with the modernisation ethos associated with the T. Dan Smith-led city council, which was simultaneously bulldozing and rebuilding industrial Tyneside, recasting Newcastle as 'the Venice of the North'. The clubs signified glamour and sophistication. Mary Scott, a former manager of Michael's, noted in an interview for the *Evening Chronicle*, the local Tyneside newspaper, that: "Working in a nightclub in those days was a glamorous affair. Everyone was dressed so beautifully. I always wore an evening dress on stage when I was introducing the acts." Similarly, in a piece on Newcastle as a party capital, Stanley Henry, co-owner of the Bailey Group, which owned La Dolce Vita and the Cavendish, remarked: "We brought real nightclubs into the provinces at a price ordinary folk could afford, and gave Geordies a touch of glamour they'd not had before. We appealed to them with thick carpets, sexy lighting, swoony music and they went overboard".

*

Michael's was owned by two Greek Cypriots, the Michaelidis brothers, Homer and Michael. They later became established figures in Newcastle's night-time economy, acquiring and then refurbishing what were the Old Assembly Rooms on Finkle Street into the Casino Royale, to this day one of the high-end fixtures in Newcastle's night life. Michael's was a more modest affair. It occupied the two top floors above Callers' department store on Northumberland Street, the city centre's main shopping street, on the site now occupied by JD Sports. The night club, 'Michael's Place', was run by Michael Michaelidis. It occupied the first floor; above that was the casino, run by Homer. This was Club Tiberius. Top acts were booked by an agent to play in the nightclub, with the Allen James Group, as the house band, providing the backing. The band comprised Jimmy (James) Allen on guitar, John McGarry on bass – described by Dave as "a lovely Fender bass", Ernie

Graham on organ and Dave on the drums. Looking back on those times, Dave recounts: "The sound I loved was that Hammond organ – it had a really earthy growl. That sound. I loved playing with that. When I hear the sounds of the fiddles I'm probably subconsciously going back to that – the projection. As a drummer you're riding the sound; you're part of the sound". The standout act which the Allen James Group provided backing for whilst Dave was with them was Nina Simone. "She came to Michael's. I was only about 18 or19. It was part of a tour she was doing. Mostly she did it herself; there was very little we had to do, a bit of brush work when necessary. All good fun!"

When the club finished at 2am, people would then repair upstairs to the casino. Dave: "roulette wheels, blackjack, Las Vegas style". Ernie the organist did this: "He'd be gambling – and he worked for Bells the builders, in management. He used to roll out of there at 7.30 and go straight to work! I went in once; the other lads would go only now and again to have a flutter. The blokes running the casino would say, 'Do you want to make a bet?' But the lads would be 'Don't – you've just been paid. They'll take your wages off you'. Even Ernie the organist he'd be saying "Don't son; don't"'.

As Dave recounts this, there's a strong sense of a band of older guys looking out for Dave. He was at this time a young 18 year old, an engineering apprentice whose horizons had been shaped entirely by Benwell and the experiences that define working class life. The other band members though knew exactly what was going on in Newcastle clubland in the late 1960s – a world thoroughly captured by the now cult classic film, *Get Carter*. It wasn't just the addictive qualities of gambling and 'the house always wins' that the band were protecting Dave from. These lads knew first hand that the milieu they were

The Violin Shop

working in was peopled by, some would say run by and for, organised crime – and what that meant. Dave: "I was just 18. You land here. You're sitting playing; and there are gangsters coming in. 'See him; he's a murderer; just smile ....' 'Hi guys, Want a drink?' 'Just a coke, please; or a lemonade'. They were friendly. They came to relax and chill out – 'Play such and such a tune'. But you had to be on the right side of them".

Our talk about this period of Dave's life then turned seamlessly to two events. The precipitate here was that I'd received a copy of a newspaper clipping from *The Evening Chronicle* – the local evening paper on Tyneside – from Roger Smith, the curator of the Readysteadygone website. On his website Roger pays homage to the Newcastle nightclubs of the late 1960s and early 1970s: La Dolce Vita, Grey's, Cavendish, Club A' Gogo, Marimba, The Mayfair. The clipping, however, reports on a huge fire which occurred on 30 November 1969, which is alleged to have started when a mechanical character in Callers' Christmas shop window display (pictured) burst into flames. The result was one of the worst fires in the city's history. Not only was Callers destroyed; so too was Michael's and Club Tiberius, along with some of the instruments belonging to Jimmy Allen and John McGarry.

Dave then switches to tell me an infamous story told by the Newcastle mob, of what happened when the Krays – one of the major organised crime families in London in the mid/late 1960s - came to Tyneside: "When I used to go to the Jazz Café in the 1990s and 2000s, the guy who ran it was one of the gangsters who ran Newcastle. Great bloke, dead now, but a jazz enthusiast. A hard man but a nice man. He's talking to us – 'Aye Davey; when the Krays came up here on the train', he says, 'we went out to Central Station to meet them, and they didn't get off the train. We got on and told them, 'If you get off here, you'll be going back in a coffin' – and they didn't get off the train. They went all the way to Edinburgh and we waited to when the train came back – and they didn't get off. They didn't get off because they knew what they were going to get. But Sibbert got it.'" Sibbert is Angus Sibbert, and the story of his murder is one of the inspirations behind *Get Carter*. The director of that film, Mike Hodges, recounts how the film, whilst based on the novel *Jack's Return Home* by Ted Lewis, is also underpinned by the Angus Sibbert murder: "The crime, committed two to three years earlier (in January 1967), somehow captured the sleaziness and corruption festering in the city's underbelly: it even involved a hit man, already incarcerated, but who, like Jack Carter (played by Michael Caine), had come up from London".

Dave joined the Allen James Group shortly after the Sibbert murder. After telling me the legend of what happened when the Krays tried to take over Newcastle, he then elaborated to me on the Angus Sibbert case. This case is part of Newcastle gangland folklore. It also comprises the central hook for the Mark Knopfler song, 5.15am, the centrepiece of which is the collision in the late 1960s between the Northeast's industrial past, shaped by coal mining, and a Tyneside present, shaped by nightclubs, gambling and the leisure industries. Dave: "Angus Sibbert was a fruit machine king. Of course, he was from Newcastle. He went to school with me mother, in Benwell. He was born in 1916, same age as me mother – went to Canning Street School in Benwell! Anyway, he'd moved to London and he was a gangster. He ran the fruit machine businesses for the Krays. He came back up and tried to take over up here – and he was murdered by the people up here, Michael Lavaglio and another one, Dennis Stafford. They all used to get into Michael's. It was one of Sibbert's haunts. He was found with a bullet in his head a few months before I started. The lads were saying how they were interviewed and giving evidence. They used to use Stafford's caravan. They'd borrowed – they were allowed to borrow – his caravan, at Amble or somewhere up the coast, for the weekend, and they trashed it. They got pissed and had women in and went berserk and trashed it and they had to tell him. He wasn't pleased! When the lads had to give evidence they had pressure put on them: 'Shut the fuck up'. The local mob was being investigated for the murder, 'You know nowt. You understand or you'll end up like that!'"

*

Dave left the Allen James Group a few months before the fire at Callers. He says: "I found it impossible to do the clubs, doing the nightclub, and then working all day. The others just played – that was their job, they were professional musicians". Being professional musicians, Jimmy Allen and John McGarry had another musical incarnation, as a show band. Dave: "The show band did the working men's clubs scene – as a comedy show group. We were called This, That & the Other. I was the Other!! We played pop music. We did that most nights and then we reverted to being the Allen James Group in the nightclub. It was six nights a week in the nightclub, 10 pm – 2am; and the show band before that." This, That & the Other is the group which Dave stuck with for a while, mostly because it allowed him to get a proper night's sleep ahead of work the next day.

The working men's clubs (WMCs) of the late 1960s on Tyneside were the cultural antithesis of the city centre's nightclubs. But, as Pete Brown details in his book *Clubland* (2023), the two were connected by money, through the one-armed bandit (or fruit) machines which lay at the heart of the Angus Sibbert murder. Brown recounts how Northeast organised crime operated a front company which offered finance and maintenance deals to WMCs installing the machines. The one-armed bandits appeared to offer the WMCs a guaranteed source of revenue; critical at a time when the clubs were beginning to lose share of 'the leisure pound'. Ultimately though, the machines bled the clubs of money and are one of the reasons for their eventual decline. Another is the changing nature of entertainment and the expansion of the leisure industry. As both Pete Brown and Ruth Cherrington, in her book *Not Just Beer and Bingo* (2012), show, the WMCs were founded on bingo, cheap Federation beer and snooker. They also provided a self-determined and uniquely working class form of entertainment. Often described using terms such as 'adult', the entertainment offered by 'the turns' the WMCs hired was in stark contrast to the knowingly clever, satirical and ironical humour that was increasingly coming to dominate the national comedy scene in the UK – a type of comedy that emanated from Cambridge University Footlights and thence gravitated to the national airwaves and TV screens via the BBC. The WMCs, by contrast, were unashamedly working class spaces, located in the heart of working class communities and with working class rules of engagement. Acts were no bigger than the club and its audience, and there could be no 'airs and graces' or any sense of cultural superiority. Witness the tale recounted to Pete Brown of David Bowie getting ready to play an early version of Ziggy Stardust in a Manchester WMC, and asking in that

The Violin Shop

unmistakeable Bowie voice, 'Can you direct me to the lavatory?' He was shown a sink – so he was told, used by Shirley Bassey before him.

One morning, and in an effort to find out more about this world of WMCs on Tyneside and Dave's time in the show band, I'm joined in the atelier by the well-known stand-up comedian, TV presenter, writer, actor, erstwhile band member and now fiddle player, Mickey Hutton. Mickey is one of the regulars in Dave's shop, and today he's agreed to join me for a conversation.

Mickey: "So Dave, I was trying to explain WMCs." Ever the man of few words, Dave replies with a dead pan summary: "Big room, rows of cheap tables and chairs, stage at one end and a bar at the other end!" I ask the two of them what it was like going on to play such a venue. Mickey [eating a scone]: "Horrendous! Especially on a Sunday!" Dave: "Strippers! Sunday afternoon." Mickey: "Rough strippers – but nobody took any notice of them. I remember the concert chairman saying one day at Newcastle Labour Club, 'Now calm down; if you don't calm down I'm going to bring the stripper back on'. Dave: "Aye, that was the concert chairman!" Mickey: "He was the one. He was the boss." Dave recalls how the concert chairman's role was to look after the turns. "We were called the turns."

I ask if this role ran to supplying a green room. Mickey, laughing uproariously, exclaims, "Well, there was a dressing room!" Dave: "There was a little dressing room on the side of the stage, and you had to do exactly what he [the concert chairman] said."

Evidently reflecting on changed times, Mickey says: "But you were so used to it; there wasn't a big deal that there was a stripper on." Dave: "I used to back them me!" [He mimes the drum rolls]. Mickey: "And a lot of the lads had allotments, so they had fruit and veg, and I was waiting to go on with Andy Taylor [from Duran-Duran] – this was before he became famous like – and we were sitting out the back and they were throwing this veg [at the strippers]. You wouldn't believe it now, but they were shipyard workers who'd been through the war and everything."

Warming to the memories, Dave recounts how This, That & The Other were out seven nights a week. "You wouldn't go in the same one in a year; there were hundreds of them". I ask how many turns there'd be on per night. Dave: "Maybe's two. The big one, the main act, and the support." Mickey: "We used to do two [sets] – two 45s". Dave: "If there was a band on, aye, they might do that, but other than that they'd probably have two singletons. We all had bright green suits." Mickey: "Sexy!" Dave: "It was a comedy show band." Nicky: "So what does that actually mean, a comedy show band?" Mickey: "The Barron Knights – that kind of thing." Dave: "We'd play tunes but then we'd do sketches and things. And then a comedian would come on and we'd be walking behind him and doing daft things. One of my turns was Jimmy – the comedian – before he started acting up he'd say, 'We'll do some rock stuff and then we'll do some more cultured stuff like'. And everybody's going 'What?' And my job was to jump up with a tray – a beer tray - and belt him right across the back of the head. Bang! And he'd fall off the front of the stage!! I used to really belt him. And one night he said, 'Don't catch us with the edge of the tray like you did last night 'cos it 'effin hurt. Get us in the middle of the tray!!' He fell off the stage one day and broke his leg. But, he got back up and carried on! He didn't know it was broken at the time!"

Trying to make sense of all this, I reason that the clubs are a development on in comedy terms from music hall and panto. Mickey: "That's exactly what it is. But everyone loved the bingo." Dave: "It was the biggest thing on the night – didn't matter who was playing." Mickey: "The concert chairman would come on and I'd be playing, I'd be in the middle of a really delicate solo and he'd be coming on with the bingo machine! And, 'Testing!'" Dave: "'Testing, One, Two, One Two!!!'" Mickey: "'Can you hear me in the bar?!'" Dave: "'Can you hear me downstairs!!'" After a pause for the laughter, Dave continues: "I played in Byker Quay Club for a while, resident drummer, and it was rough. You had to wipe your feet on the way out. It was at the top of Shields Road. And the secretary of the club had been accused of fiddling the one-armed bandits. And one Friday he got up on the stage – and it was packed – 'There's been allegations going on round here that me and the committee have been fiddling the one-armed bandits. It's not true and furthermore when I catch these alligators they're going to be barred from the club'!!" Cue more laughter. Mickey: "Remember that smell – beer, Federation beer, tobacco, cigarettes, sticky carpets! From the stage all you could see was a sea of fag smoke. But you didn't think anything of it in them days."

With that, Mickey leaves the atelier to go and get on with his day, but Dave – warming to the theme of the culture of the WMCs and the comedy it revered – tells me to type Bobby Thompson into the YouTube search bar on his computer. Bobby Thompson is probably the most noted of the working class comedians who plied the Northeast's WMCs circuit. Known as 'The Little Waster', his act was delivered wearing his trademark stripy gansey sweater and flat cap, together with a Woodbine tab in his mouth. His routines revolved around money, its lack and the consequences (chiefly debt); male work and domestic frictions, involving 'the wife', 'the mother in law' and neighbouring women. To this day, his is a humour which continues to appeal to Dave. We watch a couple of his sets on YouTube; Dave laughs a lot at them – me a bit. I can appreciate the talent and the capacity to capture the essence of conversation and mannerisms, but for me this is a humour that relies on a mutual appreciation of sending up a shared life. It's for, of and about Northeast working class life in the middle decades of the twentieth century – and, precisely because of that parochialism, it doesn't travel easily beyond those borders. More than that, these YouTube clips are a window on a lost world. It's not just the fashions and the ubiquitous cigarettes – literally everyone in the room, including Thompson, is smoking. Society too has moved on – most visibly in the role of, and attitudes towards, women. Watching the audience watching Thompson, I'm struck by how the women are not only invariably the butt of, and expected to laugh at, Thompson's routines but also simultaneously present in the audience only as attached to particular men. That's because, at this time, they could only go into a WMC if they were signed in by a man. This is so not my world! But in its humour at least, this is Dave's world. He tells me that he doesn't like modern comedy; that he doesn't find it funny. The humour that's to his taste is precisely this: older, what he regards as authentically working class.

The wider conversation with Mickey reverberates around my head for a few more days. Mickey and Dave are six years apart in age but they share a working class background. And both were apprenticed in the heavy engineering sector, following in the footsteps of the men in their respective families. Unlike others in their families and in the immediate neighbourhoods in which they grew up, they both rejected this pathway. Music and the burgeoning live entertainment business in the Northeast offered them a way out of the apprenticed life – and gigging the WMCs was the first step on this road. Quite apart from the personal story, theirs is an important story. This is because the wider trajectory of which their working lives are a part – of the de-industrialisation of the Northeast and the rise of Newcastle as a leisure-based party city – is one that is mostly told through the eyes of the consuming public or 'punters', as enlivening the drudgery of working class factory lives. As bringing glamour to these working class lives. What's missing in that story is that the same clubs also became an escape route for talented young musicians in the region. For some, like Dave, they offered a reliable source of work in the region itself, whilst for more than a few, like Mickey, and including such household names as Sting, Bryan Ferry, Mark Knopfler and Andy Taylor, all of whom hail from the Northeast, they were the foundation to building an international career in the music and entertainment business.

*

In 1971 Dave finished his apprenticeship at British Engines. By then, like many young men of his age, he had developed a passion for cars, and not just drums. So, he then went on a six-month spray painting course at a local skills training centre. Later, in 1976, he went on a panel beating course, on which he met another atelier regular, the harmonica player Ray Burns. Following the first of these courses, the day job for Dave became working in garages, on what's known in the motor trade as 'body work'.

In 1973 Dave got married – aged 22. He left the family home in Benwell and moved a few miles away to Westerhope, on the western edge of Newcastle. It may have only been a few miles from Benwell but this was a world away from the Benwell terraces where Dave grew up. Westerhope then offered young couples the property-owning suburban dream: "The first house I bought was 11 Bournemouth Gardens – a little Dutch bungalow. Lived there for five years – I bought it for £4950 and sold it for just under £15k, five years later, when the two girls (Sarah and Claire – pictured) were little. 1978. The house I bought wanted doing up and I got that for £18k: three bedrooms, detached and in its own grounds. It had a double wooden garage – at the back like. You had to come in and drive round. I knocked that down and built another bigger one. It was a triple garage".

In 1982 the garage where Dave was then employed burned down. "Then I thought, 'I don't want to work for anyone else'. So what I did was I kept the drums going. I was playing six sessions a week. Five nights a week and a Sunday. But during the day I worked from home. I'd built the garage purposely – bought a compressor, got all the gear. So I was buying and selling cars from home. I had room for four in there". Some of these cars were vintage restoration projects: "Ray Burns (pictured) prepped them; I did the paint and body work; me dad did the engine work – stripped them down, re-bored them, new engine, back axles. Me brother Teddy helped where he could – so if we needed anything making he'd make the parts, cos he had his own workshop with his big lathes and stuff".

Dave's first car restoration project was a MG TF. "It was black. 1954. And I restored the whole thing down to the frame. Concours condition". I ask about the seats and the interior. "We got an upholsterer to do that. We had everything off; the wings were rotten. I bought it off my old drum teacher – Jack Bell – he bought it new, 1954, and he kept it till I got it; it must've been about 1970. He had a stroke and it was sitting in his garage, rotting away. Keeping it was like looking after a baby. Every time you take it out you've got work to do on it. So you have to check everything over when you get back, wrap it all over – I had a parachute silk for it. If you took it out in the rain you'd get all the underneath dirty, so then all the chassis work had to all be cleaned".

I ask Dave what happened to the MG. "I sold it – to an enthusiast!" He adds: "I love old cars – I still do them now". It strikes me, listening to him talk, that it's not so much the cars themselves that are Dave's passion so much as repairing and restoring these cars, and dealing. As if on cue, into the atelier comes fellow vintage car enthusiast Ray

Burns, carrying a plastic bag: "Dave", he says, "I was just passing and I just had to bring this in to show you". He pulls out of the plastic bag a brass repair job that a 91-year old vintage traction engine enthusiast has just done for him. This has made good a part on his own 1908 vintage car which he'd been struggling to see how to fix. Ray places the part triumphantly on Dave's workbench, right in front of him, and the two men inspect it closely with a mixture of awe and wonder. "How on earth did he do that?" "I cannot see how he's done that". Neither can I – nor can I even see that it's been repaired. But, I muse, amidst a workplace dedicated to the repair, restoration and making of violins, those very same skills are being appreciated and celebrated, this time in relation to old cars. Ray then explains the back story to the much admired repair. It's a story of tinkering and mutual help between hobbyists. Flummoxed by the challenge of repairing this particular part, Ray had gone to the traction engine nonagenarian as something of a last resort, saying 'Don't worry if you can't sort it'. To his utter surprise, a few weeks later the guy appeared at his garage with the part. Ray had asked the 91-year old 'what do I owe you for the repair?' The reply: 'Oh nothing – you did something for me years back, this is my chance to repay that'. Ray: 'Well, thank you very much. Anything you want round here – parts and what – you just ask'. He says to me: "I think the world should be more like this". I can't help but agree.

CHAPTER TWO

The Accidental Luthier

How does a working class lad from Benwell, a drummer by night and a spray painter and panel beater by day, living and working in Westerhope in the west end of Newcastle, get to be a luthier in Hexham? To answer that question, and to account for that unlikely trajectory, requires not just delving into family history but also an excursion into the luthier profession and its manifestation in Northeast England in the 1980s.

Today the trajectory into a career as a luthier is highly likely to involve formalised training that aligns with the structures and principles of higher education. In the UK, the Newark School is the main pathway into the profession. Founded in 1972, it now offers three year degree-accredited programmes specialising in guitar, piano, violin and woodwind. There are similar programmes in other European countries, on which the Newark School is modelled – most famously at Cremona in Italy, once home to the makers regarded as achieving the epitome of violin craft – Stradivarius and Guarneri. Others are at Mittenwald in Germany, Mirecourt in France, and Brienz in Switzerland. Years ago, though, in the UK the pathways into lutherie were infinitely more varied and often less formalised. Mary Ann Alburger's book on British violin makers, written in the 1970s, reveals a multitude of routes: from players turned luthiers, to dabblers in fine art; from a host of woodworkers - joiners, cabinet makers, furniture makers and restorers to boat builders; from those who began life with a desire to become a violin luthier and who were apprenticed to violin makers, to self-taught amateur hobbyists and enthusiasts whose initial work was deemed to have promise and which gained them an entrée into a strings workshop. Within that last group of amateur enthusiasts, there are often two points of commonality: a ubiquitous reference work in the form of a 'how-to' practical guide to violin making dating from 1884, written by Edward Heron-Allen, *Violin Making as it was, and is,* and thence, attending an evening class. This, the amateur tradition, is how Dave's career as a luthier intersects with that of other luthiers. But how did he come to even be on that pathway? One lunchtime early on in my visits to the atelier, before I'd even heard about drums and gangsters, and after having watched Dave prepare a mortise joint to join the neck of his latest Guadagnini violin to its body, I ask him: "So how did you get into all this, Dave?" He pauses, stops to think and says: "Well I suppose it all goes back to the girls."

"The girls" are Dave's two daughters, Sarah and Claire. They take up the story. Sarah: "It all started when I was about eight; I started learning at school and I brought this violin home and he was quite interested in how it was put together and stuff and I think his curiosity just grew, and so he went and got a book and had a go". Claire: "He got into making when Sarah started playing. The way I remember, Sarah brought a fiddle home from school, like a Skylark [a very basic student starter instrument], and he was looking at it saying 'I wonder how you put this together?' We went to the local library in West Denton, and he got a book out of the library on how to make a violin. So he made the first violin by doing that". Sarah: "The very first one, if I remember rightly, was a red one and that was the first one he made using the plans in the book". Claire: "And I remember, when he made the purfling he used some kind of putty, like he used to repair cars! I always thought it was called Bodge! I remember it being a bright red fiddle with this like black purfling. My cousin stood on it and broke it!! It was propped up in the corner of a room and it fell over and he stood on it!" Looking back on this now, Dave describes this fiddle, his first effort at violin making, as "embarrassing". Not surprisingly, having been broken, it ended up in the bin and Dave set to work on making another violin for Sarah, again with the book borrowed from the library as his guide, and using his garage tools and what he had to hand around the house.

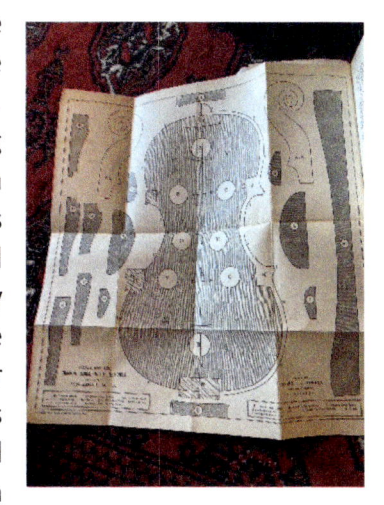

Sarah's mention of the plans is the clue as to the identity of the library book. They are one of the defining features of the Heron-Allen violin making book and, to this day, some of its most valued contents, for there are many copies of the book in existence knocking around minus their plans! Having discovered its significance to Dave's eventual trajectory to becoming a luthier, I asked him one day if he had a copy. Cue a search. Having forced his way past a laundry basket containing at least 50 'knackered bows' and through a thicket of double bass and cello cases, he reveals the existence of a book cabinet that I've never noticed before. He rummages in this, emerging eventually triumphantly to pronounce – "here it is!" Complete with a dust jacket and pages yellowed with age and with the distinctive aroma of old books, it's a second edition of the celebrated work, first published in 1884 – complete with all the plans.

*

Edward Heron-Allen (1861-1943) himself merits a short digression. A renowned polymath of the late Victorian/Edwardian age, his expertise and knowledge encompassed palmistry, Persian translation, chalk foraminifera, asparagus cultivation and the local archaeology and history of Sussex, as well as violin making. He was also a novelist, writing under the pseudonym of Christopher Blayre. Already a violin player, on leaving Harrow School he'd gone into the family firm of solicitors located in London's Soho. The family's firm clearly didn't keep him fully occupied, for it was in Soho, at 157 Wardour Street, that he made the acquaintance of one Georges Chanot III.

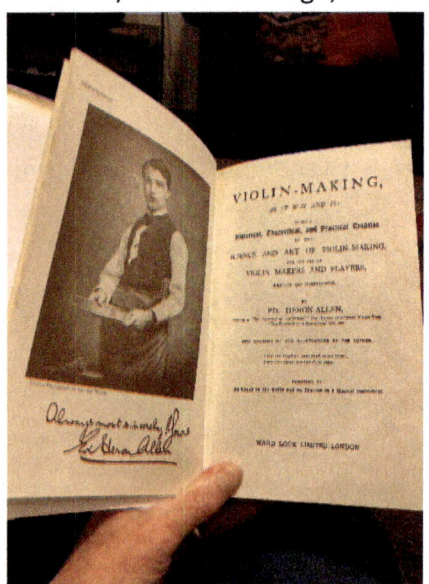

Born in Paris, Georges Chanot is part of the famous Chanot dynasty of French violin makers which traces back to the 1700s, and Mirecourt. Having served his apprenticeship with his father in Paris, Georges Chanot was sent to London to work as the assistant to Marcoutel. On the latter's retirement, he purchased the business before moving his premises to Wardour Street. The heart of London's violin quarter, Wardour Street was home to prestigious firms of violin dealers such as Beare & Goodwin and Hart & Son. The Chanots, however, were luthiers. They were known for producing fine copies of Cremonese instruments at affordable prices – although Georges Chanot III also achieved notoriety, having faked a Carlo Bergonzi label and sold the instrument as genuine. Through 1882 and 1883, Georges Chanot evidently instructed Edward Heron-Allen in the craft of lutherie – in which time Heron-Allen completed two instruments, as well as compiling the basis for the book which he was to publish in the following year. Over a hundred years later, the book is still in print.

Heron-Allen's book is one of those unique practical volumes, written for amateur enthusiasts. Like classic cookery books which seek to teach culinary cultures, rather than impart mere recipes – books, like for example, Elizabeth David's on Mediterranean food, or Madhur Jaffrey's on Indian cookery - this is a book which has its author at the side of the budding luthier throughout the making process. It works by empathising with the novice enthusiast, rather than by adopting what Richard Sennett in his book *The Craftsman* calls the technique of 'dead denotation'. This is the kind of instruction which might work as a refresher for someone who already knows how to do something but which is next to useless for someone coming to a craft practice for the first time – largely because it tells someone what to do, rather than showing how.

Heron-Allen begins the practical part of his book by stating: 'I shall proceed as if I were actually working with the reader, and he [sic] were using my moulds, models and tools' (p 219). The authorial device is certainly suggestive when we know the back story: the 'my' here is surely the substitution of Heron-Allen for Georges Chanot, whose moulds, models and tools the author will have had access to in making his two violins. Thereafter follows a detailed, intimate description of violin making, using Stradavari plans – the kind of plans that are essential to any workshop producing fine copies of Cremonese instruments. The text reads as if alongside one as one works is a guide who not only has made this their lifelong passion but who is also thoroughly committed to passing on their knowledge. This, I would suggest, is not Heron-Allen, given what's known about his interests. Rather, it's as if Heron-Allen is using the opportunity of his lutherie training to write a book which will disseminate Georges Chanot's craft knowledge widely, turning his own personal tuition into a craft treatise.

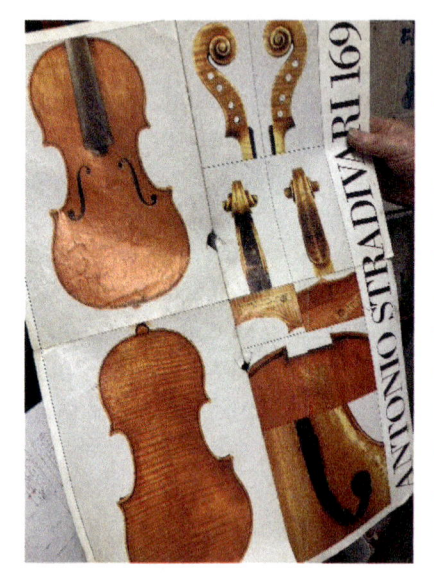

Heron-Allen also writes as if he is at his bench in front of his readers. Many is the occasion in passages in the text where he seems to be channelling Chanot's inner voice as he writes, possibly recalling his own instruction. He outlines the tasks in sequence, carefully explaining how each task is to be accomplished and with which tools, articulating the kind of tool care and attention that's required for each stage and always highlighting the pitfalls that lie ahead – how not to approach certain tasks and how not to hold certain tools, as well as how to. Alongside the voice of a highly attuned craft worker there are the meticulous hand drawn drawings and plans, which reflect Heron-Allen's amateur scientist interests and background. Highly detailed and accurate, they indicate the scale of the work, and the fine margins, which a budding luthier has to achieve – tolerances which it's worth noting would be nothing to someone, like Dave, trained as an engineering apprentice to work to two-thousandths of an inch. Here, for instance, is Heron-Allen's detailing of the positioning of the f holes in the belly of the violin: 'From B' to B", 7/16 inch; from C' to C", 1 inch; from D to D', 2 1/8 inch; from E to E', 1 7/16 inch; from F to F', 15/16 inch' (p 255). The book is an example, then, of the very best type of practical guide. And yet, there are things even Heron-Allen cannot help the budding enthusiast with.

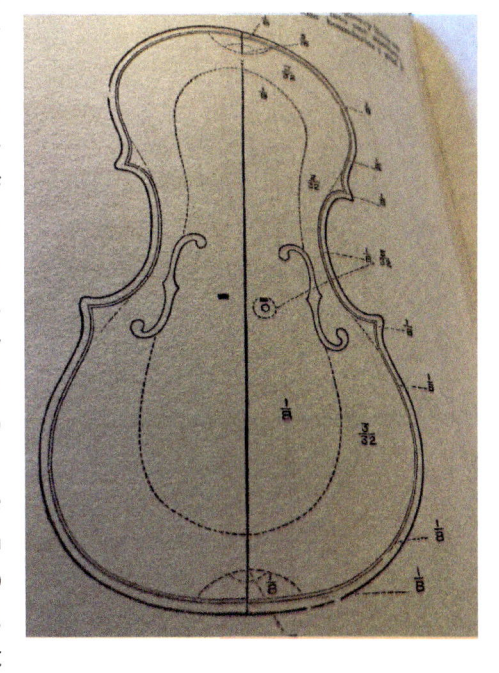

Some of this is the difficulty of particular stages – joining the two halves of the back, for example, or gouging the arching of the back and belly. In the first instance he says: 'to produce this perfect fit in curly wood like maple is a very difficult matter to an unpractised hand, and may therefore be relegated to a professional joiner' (p 240). In the second, the hobby enthusiast is told 'you will find it a great advantage if you can compare your work with a true specimen of the great master's work, for then you can check the accuracy of your guide slips and correct any errors which may creep in in tracing them from the plate' (p 243). In other words, having another violin around to copy – preferably one of top quality – and having access to skilled joiners would be advantageous!

Maybe quality instruments were readily to hand in 157 Wardour Street and London's proximate violin quarter in the latter years of the nineteenth century, but they were certainly not available via the social networks surrounding a garage in Westerhope in Newcastle in the 1980s. Neither were joiners, nor too the specialist tools which Heron-Allen begins by saying are absolutely essential for any skilled luthier work; nor was specialist material such as purfling and varnish, and then there was the very big problem of finding the right wood. Claire: "I remember him making a three-quarter size one for Sarah, and I think he made it out of an old chest, a storage chest kind of thing". Sarah: "He didn't really know much about which were the right woods, so I think he just used an old box or chest or something and cut it out of that! It was a funny angled thing but it kind of worked! I mean, I probably did my Grade 5 on it. It sounded all right. It was better than your Chinese things!"

As Sarah improved and her talent became more and more obvious, so the challenge which Dave, unbeknownst to her, had quietly set himself, to make an instrument worthy of her playing, became more difficult. With her higher grade exams looming, he'd reached the limits of what he could achieve in his garage, using his car mechanic tools and cannibalising domestic furniture. Gaining access to the right woods, to the right tools, to instruments and to the required level of violin-making expertise had now become essential. Cue his enrolling, sometime in the mid-1980s, on an evening class run by Barry Oliver, in his shop-cum-workshop in Washington, Tyne & Wear.

*

Barry Oliver is one of a handful of young British luthiers whose work is highlighted in Alburger's 1978 book on modern British violin makers. Born in 1946, he too hails from Northeast England and is five years older than Dave. Unlike Dave, his pathway into lutherie is one of lifelong fascination: by the time he was at grammar school he'd decided he wanted to be a violin maker. Already by that age he was hanging out with an amateur maker in Whitley Bay on the coast near Newcastle. This was Harry Clare. He was also dabbling in repairs and beginning to make inroads into violin dealing. Seemingly, his parents were less than keen on this career path and insisted he went to a teacher training college instead. But Barry persisted. After realising the financial impossibility of being apprenticed to the then obvious destination, Hill's workshop in London – where the cost of living even then was prohibitive for families with limited financial resources – he answered an advertisement in *The Strad* magazine and became apprenticed to Lawrence Naisby in Liverpool. Naisby had been apprenticed to George Byrom, who had worked alongside Thomas Hesketh under the Chanots in Manchester – this branch of the dynasty stemming from Georges Chanot III's son, Georges Adolphes. Barry was there for just over three years, until he had completed his apprenticeship.

On finishing, Barry was keen to broaden his knowledge of violin making. He headed for Cremona, funded by a small grant from the Northern Arts Council. There he was taught by, and worked as an assistant to, several of the top Italian master craftsmen: GB Morassi, F Bissolotti and P Sgarabotto. In his interview for Mary Alburger's book he describes how he learned "how to use my eyes, and how to control my hands with my eyes". And – as importantly – he accrued much by way of the local knowledge that comes from being in an industrial district such as Cremona. The city, then and now, is home to many small violin workshops as well as the violin-making school. Being in such a milieu has huge advantages: "you could just walk around the streets and bump into violin makers or drop into their workshops, ask questions and chat about problems". All told, Barry spent four years in Cremona, assimilating a raft of knowledge about the Italian methods and styles of violin making. On his return he worked for Ealing Strings in London for a short while before returning to his native Northeast, where he rented two units in the newly opened Biddick Arts Centre in Washington, Tyne & Wear, undertaking repair and restoration work as well as violin making.

Replicating the pathway that he had himself followed into the profession, Barry took on apprentices. One of these apprentices was Julian Batey, now a luthier/dealer in Shrewsbury. Julian was steeped in the violin business from the outset for his father, Brian Batey, was also a violin dealer. Then, in 1984, just when Julian was finishing up his apprenticeship, into Barry's workshop walked the person who was to become his next apprentice: Nial Cain - the person whom Dave was eventually to become a business partner with.

*

Born in the late 1950s, and so several years younger than Dave, Nial's pathway into lutherie starts, not with a desire to make violins, nor with a family history of working in the violin trade, but with playing musical instruments. He begins a long conversation with me by telling me that his family moved from Snowdonia in North Wales to Plockton, on the road to Skye in the Scottish Highlands, when he was 13 or 14. Those locations have more than a little to do with his father, A. C. "Ginger" Cain, being a well-known rock climber and a very fine mountain artist – see the website mountainart.co.uk. Nial goes on to mention the foundational experience for his future life and career of Glen Cottage in Torridon, now a National Trust for Scotland rental, which he describes as "a hotbed of folkie-ness" – later sending me his written memories of the first time he went to this place:

> We were not the YHA type, more van and tent-on-its-last-legs types, so I had little in the way of hostel preconceptions. The impressive large lodge house and outbuildings, dramatically placed in the lower glen looked promising for my current obsession, digging for antique bottles, and when we arrived I appreciated the way the management and clientele didn't condescend to a teenager.
>
> I'd recently started listening to music and vinyl LPs were a big deal then, treasured possessions – hard to imagine in this age of Spotify and streaming. A friend had lent me half a dozen LPs for an entire school term to play on my dad's new hi-fi. Jethro Tull, Led Zeppelin, Focus. And we'd had Clancy Brothers records playing in the background since before I could remember. So I was primed and ready for some sort of musical awakening.
>
> In the evening there was a big communal room with a blazing fire – in an old range I think but I couldn't swear to it. It was rammed with people, and many of them played music. Of course Dave and Liz, the proprietors, sang and played, but only occasionally as so many of the others pitched in with their own songs or tunes. *You Keep Going your Way and I'll Keep Going Mine* seemed to get an outing every night, and *The King comes Home in Peace Again*, which title got affectionately shortened to the king comes home pissed again. Aside from guitars and mandolins and concertinas and whistles Andy, who wasn't a guest but had somehow got to live there, had installed a home-wound pickup on an old flat play-on-the-knee zither, and at the congregation's insistence would haul out an amp, plug it in and play haunting, mesmerising airs. He was no slouch on the whistle and concertina either. He

took it very seriously, and practised during the day – you could faintly hear him in his room getting on top of some difficult tune, until he could play it through flawlessly, another little lesson to take home, practice mattered. He cut a striking figure – tall, stick-thin, a rock-god mane of hair and a leather waistcoat with an illuminated capital A from the Book of Kells covering the entire back.

What I took away from this was that being a musician wasn't some genetic gift bestowed on the privileged as a fait accompli; anyone could, with a little application, get there, and what's more the getting there might be rather fun too.

Some judicious scrounging was applied to my parents. I wanted a guitar like Dave's. And to be able to play like him, but a guitar would do for starters.

Later, a half sold card of Generation whistles arrived from my grandmother – she had a record shop in Liverpool and these had been left hanging on the wall F, B flat, G, C and D. Not a guitar, but...

The guitar had to wait till I was 15, but that's another story.

Back to our conversation: Nial recounts how he started teaching himself the tin whistle, to the point where "I got quite decent at it. I could learn jigs and reels off records". But the guitar remained the burning desire. Nonetheless, any approaches to the parents continued to be cold shouldered. "A penny whistle was about the budget really! But I was good at art at school so I was quite close to the art teacher in Plockton. He wasn't local – he was Scottish but he wasn't local. He'd been to art school and he'd made a couple of guitars – I think he'd made about three by that point. And I was moaning about this and he said, 'Well let's do it as an art project!' We were lucky. The local dump at Plockton was behind the school. Up by the airstrip there was a big dump and all sorts of stuff used to turn up there, including a piano. So we went up there one day and pulled bits off the piano. We cut the soundboard up into slices and glued them up to make a front. I think there were some bits of mahogany off of drawers as well. Apart from putting the sides on – I think I had help with that –all the rest of it I did. This guitar, it did get modified a bit. I showed it to a guitar player in a band. Alex someone, who could play very well – he was saying 'the neck's a bit wide, even for a classical'. So I brought that down a bit. And then I learnt to play on it. And a couple of years later I had a holiday job, and I bought a Yamaha steel string, because I wanted a steel string. Having learnt to play on this guitar I could play quite well by then. So that was the first thing. From then on I could always fool about setting the action on guitars and things like that. Mates would go 'Oh this is hard to play' and I'd have a go at making it easier to play."

    I ask how the transition from guitar to fiddles came about. Nial: "Well the art teacher, Austin Bankhead, he'd restored a mandolin – quite a nice round-backed mandolin. I actually have the Harrod's catalogue with it in and it was a little under a fiver in 1908. So I had a go on this mandolin and I could play jigs and reels on that – I knew some by ear from playing the whistle. And then someone locally got given a fiddle. He was in my class at school. And he leant it to my mum; she'd said she'd like to learn the fiddle. I was home for the holidays, and I was playing around with it, because the fingering is the same as the mandolin. I found I could plink out these tunes even if I couldn't actually do any of the bowing. So I nicked the fiddle off me mum and took the fiddle down to Newcastle [where he was doing a Fine Art degree] and learnt to play it, until the next holiday when I brought it back to her. And then I was in Stirling, and there was an antique's fair. By then I was playing [guitar] in a ceilidh band. And the fiddler in the ceilidh band, Rosie, she said 'if you ever see a violin with double purfling on it it's a good violin' – it's not definitively true by the way! So anyway, walking round this antique's fair in Stirling, there was this table of violins. There was a big violin scene in Stirling around then [the early 1980s]. So there was a violin with double purfling, and I liked the look of it. It was £100 – which was quite a lot in those days. And I took it back down to Newcastle. And there was a really good fiddler down there called Pete Toolan, who'd been at the same school as [the Irish fiddler] Kevin Burke. So Pete played this fiddle and he said 'This is a brilliant fiddle; I think you've done great here but it could be a lot more valuable than what you've paid for it'. And then he thought a bit more and said, 'Oh I know this violin maker. He's doing some work on my violin. Why don't you come over when I go to pick it up and bring it with you and he'll have a look at it and tell you what it is'. So I thought 'Why not?' So we went over. And the violin maker was Barry! Barry looks at this violin and he goes, 'Yeah – it's made in this little village in Germany, it's a copy of Maggini and it's made in about 1890'. 'And what about value?' 'Oh about £100!'!"

At the time of this first encounter with Barry, Nial had finished his degree and was working in a dead-end job in a warehouse: "it didn't pay well and it wasn't going anywhere." As he recollects, Barry must have mentioned at the time that his then apprentice, Julian, was coming to the end of his three years shortly, so Nial took himself off to the Central Library in Newcastle and read everything he could find there on violins and bows. "As soon as I'd done that I went back to Barry and said 'Any chance of me being your next apprentice?' So he said 'Come and try it for a week and see if we get on'. We did get on. And I think it helped that he had this dog, a basset hound, Bessie - Bessiewig Benefit the Third! And I'd had a basset hound as a kid and I really liked his basset hound."

I ask how Barry structured Nial's apprenticeship. Nial: "I think the first job he gave me was actually drawing in some purfling on a cello with a biro! A corner had been knocked off and it needed to be replaced – but it worked well enough! And the next thing he had me do was to make a cello tailpiece out of maple. I seem to remember with this tailpiece I had the holes for the strings – they need to be evenly spaced. And I measured it with a tape measure. They ended up evenly spaced but at the end he said 'How did you do these holes? With a tape measure?' 'Ah – no, you should have done it with dividers, it's much faster'. So then he showed me how to do it with dividers. So you did learn, but perhaps retrospectively sometimes. [The big plus was that] I got to see some pretty nice violins. Barry was like the only game in town. He had a pretty high profile. He'd worked for Ealing Strings. He'd worked for the three top living Italian makers at the time. He had a lot going for him. After I'd been there a bit he said, 'Oh, time you started making a violin'. So he took me through making a violin. The workmanship was very decent; the tone wasn't anything fantastic. He didn't really communicate anything at all about archings and thicknesses. And he was using a varnish that we bought off-the-peg."

On his blog, *nialcainviolinmaker*, Nial summarises his learning as an apprentice and his debts to Barry Oliver as follows: "I learned to make violin instruments within the Cremonese method and style, to restore, to set up to a level satisfying the professional and what makes a good [bow] rehair. I was also exposed to some very fine instruments which came through the shop, which developed both my eye and my expertise". But in talking with him, he goes much further, to reflect on craft working practices, and on the violin trade: "I would say – I was just thinking that, that the most important thing that Barry probably taught was care and handling tools, how to sharpen, how to work efficiently with your elbows into your sides." So, I say, summarising what I'm hearing, "he taught you how to embody being a luthier. How to inhabit a body that can work with wood in this way." What I'm thinking about here is not just the inseparability of hand, eye and tools in craft work, or what Barry described as the ability to control one's hands, and therefore one's tools, with one's eyes. It's also that to achieve that degree of control requires mastering particular ways of moving with tools, such that tools work as a seamless extension of bodily capacities and capabilities. Teaching these kinds of kinaesthetic skills is no small task. It also almost goes without saying that not everyone has the capability to be able to achieve the degrees of hand-eye-tool coordination that are required in violin making.

Nial: "But I think the other great lesson from Barry was you had to be reasonably efficient financially if you wanted to be a luthier, otherwise you wouldn't be around." Not only this, knowledge was, as it still is, king. "Some of the bad decisions [he made] were selling things without knowing enough about them. For instance, he had a cello when I was there that was certainly Italian. It was in a mess. It didn't have the right neck on it; it was really a body. And he didn't know what it was and he let it go for the price of a speculative cello. That cello – I don't know how true this is – but the chat was that that cello was Brescian. And it had subsequently been bought by the Mafia pension fund and they had one of the best fakers make a new scroll for it! I don't know how true that was but there was a lesson there. But he knew a lot about fiddles, and he was pretty free with that knowledge. And at that time, we're talking pre internet, a lot of knowledge was not shared because dealers who came round, they wanted to pick stuff up. They wouldn't tell you that a bow was French or whatever. So Barry was very good like that. He taught connoisseurship."

*

Earning a living from lutherie can be difficult. With income dependent upon sales from making and repairs and maintenance work, cash flow can often be lumpy. Evening classes were Barry's answer to this problem; every Wednesday. As Nial says, "He used to charge for them – a reasonable amount, just to pull people in. But he also wanted to spread his knowledge about a bit."

Barry's evening classes took place in his workshop. Nial describes the layout: "There were three benches and I guess there was another bit of the room that had a band saw and stuff in it. You don't always need a bench. If you're cutting a bridge or something you can just sit and cut it freehand. Barry had his own bench that he'd had made which was a very nice bench. The other two were Sjöbergs, which are off-the-peg benches."

Along with Nial as the apprentice, the class itself comprised a small but consistent group of men: amateur enthusiasts. Nial recalls the core membership: "There was Tom, who was a pitman; there was Dave, and then there was a really nice old boy, Bill Burnett, who had been a graphic artist, and his violins were excellent. His were the best. He used to come in sometimes and do work for Barry and get paid for it. He was very slow but it was very good work so he'd give him like a long restoration with lots of little pieces on it and Bill would beaver away on it. He'd also do graphic design jobs sometimes. Barry used to sell a varnish reviver and Bill designed the label and I think a cardboard box for it. And then Derek Greener came along too." As he describes this, I'm thinking that, effectively, Barry was running a lutherie club.

I ask Nial how long the classes went on for. Nial: "Two or three hours. I guess if everyone was really into something then there was no reason for it to really end. It was quite a social thing too. Possibly not everyone turned up to every class, so three benches were enough." I ask how Barry structured and supervised their work. Nial: "Sometimes Barry would work on something himself and you'd get to watch him doing that. And if you were doing something he'd probably show you the right way to do it and then leave you to it."

This classroom set-up – what would now be called a small group, student-centred learning environment – is where Dave began to hone his skills as a luthier. Reflecting on those classes not as Barry's apprentice but as a paying 'punter', Dave describes them as very 'hands-on' and Barry's teaching style as emphasising the route to perfection: "Slowly, slowly – take your time". "He wasn't satisfied with crap or mediocrity. Good enough wasn't good enough. With Barry, you'd do a certain procedure and then you'd go and show him". He picks up a fiddle and mimes Barry's inspection of corners – "'that's the best one; that's the second best; that one, nah! The next fiddle you're going to have to do better'". But the class learnt by more formalised instruction too: books, with pictures of quality instruments, were scrutinised carefully, and then there would be the opportunity to study any quality instruments that came into Barry's shop. Because he was, as Nial describes it, 'the only game in town' in the Northeast, Barry had customers with Italian instruments which they would regularly bring in for maintenance work. He emphasised measuring these instruments; studying them – inspecting rare and fine instruments, treating them as objects that could be continually learnt from. He also taught his class how to see subtleties. Dave recalls how they'd be working on necks in his workshop and then he'd stop them to show them the difference between round necks and the necks on an Italian instrument. To this day, Dave appreciates the importance of learning that degree of close observation. As he says: "I learnt everything from him; more than the basics".

It was at Barry's evening classes that Dave made his third and first full-size fiddle. This is the first that he remembers being proud of. Known in the family as 'the yellow fiddle', it was the first one he'd made from the proper woods – maple, spruce and ebony. Such was the difference between this instrument and the three-quarter sized Heron-Allen-guided salvage effort that preceded it that embarrassment ensured that instrument went in the bin. Unlike those early efforts, the yellow fiddle also had a label inside: 'Sarah's violin'. As an object, a form of material culture, it speaks to a father's love for and immense pride in his daughter. Sarah: "I got the yellow one when I was about 10 or 11 I'd say (pictured). I was asking Claire the other day – and she was saying that she was sure she remembered me playing the yellow one, and that would've been when I was about 12 or 13. I must've done Grade 6 or 7 on that one."

*

Nial finished his apprenticeship on 22 September 1987, at which point Barry took on a new apprentice: Sven. The classic problem encountered by all those apprenticed in 'one-man band' circumstances then faced Nial: how to branch out and set up on one's own. This is a readily acknowledged problem for both master and apprentice – and one of the reasons for the decline in the apprenticeship model of luthier training. For the one there is always the fear that the person you've trained will set up in close geographical proximity and take away trade, and one's livelihood; for the other, there are the challenges of finding the right premises and establishing a reputation from scratch – especially if one chooses to do this in the same geographical area in which one has trained, where one will often be competing for business directly with the established master. Nial began on this pathway at some geographical remove from Barry's workshop in Washington, by doing up a room in the flat he had in Newcastle to use as a workshop, and by using his folk music network to try to gain a toehold in to the business. It might have worked, but these were very sketchy forays and, as he readily admits, who knows what would have happened had serendipity not intervened. He explains: "One night I was at home and the phone went, and it was Bob Archbold, who had the violin shop in Hexham. I'd only met him once. I'd been and bought a bow for myself once and met him then. Bob was going to retire. He'd heard down the grapevine that I was floating about so he phoned me up and said would I like the shop?"

Bob Archbold had a background in medical instrument sales but had long had interests in antiques, particularly clocks, about which he was extremely knowledgeable. He was originally from Northumberland and had moved back there in the 1970s to open two small shops on a street called Hencotes in Hexham – one specialising in antiques, especially clocks, and the other selling violins. At that time, Hexham, like many well-heeled provincial market towns in England, was a flourishing antiques centre. Talking about this time one day in the atelier with one of Dave's regular clients, I'm told that there were at least 14 antique shops in the town in the early 1970s. The number may or may not be entirely accurate but it certainly attests to the feel of the town back then. It was the kind of place people seemingly went to either to sell cattle or sheep, or to spend an enjoyable day browsing in the antique shops looking for 'finds'. The violin shop was of the same ilk, and very occasionally, quality violins came through Bob Archbold's door. One such is currently in the ownership of Martin Hughes. It's what he calls his temperamental "Old Neapolitan" (pictured). This instrument is probably from the workshop of Gagliano, and he purchased it in 1983, after having been accosted by Bob on the street as he passed the shop – "Martin, come and have a look at what I've got!"

Nial gives more of a sense of Bob's shop's interior: "The shop where it is now is not where it was. It was two doors up. It had a certain eccentric olde-worldy charm as it were. The bit where the customers came in was tiny. You came in through the doorway and there was a space where really if three people came in that was too much. One had to go outside or you all had to breathe in! There were lots of violins hanging up. There was a rack of violins ready for sale there. A drawer and a till and a really nice Victorian gas lamp with a ribbed glass shade - the real thing, not a repro - shining down. And it had been wallpapered. So it had ambience. And it had glass behind the shelves so you could see through into the workshop which people liked."

The agreement Bob and Nial came to was that "Bob carried on owning the shop, and I rented the shop off of him. I forget what I paid for the business but it was a few grand I think. He had a load of unsold stock which he allowed me to sell on commission. I can't remember what the commission was but it meant that the shop could trundle on". Having a shop meant that violins continued to 'come through the door', as it is called in the trade – as people discover them in lofts and attics, or inherit them from people who've died, and look to cash in on their unexpected assets. Nial's ambition, though, was not to own an antique dealership-cum-shop specialising in violins. It was to turn around the shop's reputation – to shift it from being the kind of shop people went to if they were looking to buy and/or sell a violin, to being at the same time a centre of excellence for luthier craft work.

*

Back to Dave: in late 1987, shortly after Nial left Barry's and having attended the evening classes for two years and shown promise, Dave took his first steps into lutherie as paid work. He began to assist Barry. This he did alongside the new apprentice, Sven. By Dave's own admission, this was a very difficult period in the Washington workshop. Barry's health issues increasingly made it harder for him to work with his hands. Inevitably, he came to rely increasingly on Dave and Sven to do the work that was booked into the workshop as well as the work of violin making. This led to frustrations of the type that have long beset the craft work tradition, as apprentices and workshop assistants come to resent their work being presented as the work of the master craftsman. This is what Richard Sennett describes as one of the hallmarks of the workshop as a productive space in the modern era: the unresolvable conflict between authority and autonomy.

Authority in a workshop setting rests on the power of the master craftsman to set the work of others, who then complete that work according to instructions. Authority rests on, and gains its legitimacy from, the skills of the master craftsman and the acknowledged skills gap between the master, journeymen and apprentices. When the workshop first emerged as a productive space in medieval Europe, the output of the workshop was seen as that of an anonymous collective rather than the work of individuals; more than that, through the guild system, this work was attached to a particular place, not people, let alone a person. The guilds controlled where something was made, not who made it. Nonetheless, tensions emerged in these medieval workshops – between assistants, between assistants and apprentices, and between the assistants and apprentices and the master craftsman. Orhan Pamuk's wonderful novel *My Name Is Red* centres just such jealousies and rivalries and their manifestation in the work of the copyist.

By the time of the Renaissance, authority in a craft setting had become a lot more complicated. Not only was there the rise of art to contend with, but alongside that went the emergence of a sense of an artist, producing original work, and more generally a sense of the drive to self-expression as a distinctive human quality. The products of a workshop, as a consequence, changed from being a collective output to become identified with the work of an individual, or a family – an original artist, or an outstanding craft worker. These were the kind of workshops that were to be found in Cremona during the golden age of violin making. But, whilst they were identified with a particular name – most notably Stradivarius and Guarneri – the instruments that comprised the workshop's output were, almost certainly, made by more than one person. As Toby Faber writes in his exploration of the history of six Strads, *Stradivari's Genius*, by the 1670s it is clear that the instruments being produced by the Stradivari family's workshop were made by more than one hand. Richard Sennett: 'The workshop of Stradivarius […] was filled with the Stradivari family and many young male apprentices and journeymen lodgers […]. Youngsters at work usually did such preparatory labour as soaking wood in water, rough moulding and rough cutting. Journeymen higher up did finer belly cutting and neck assembly, and the master himself took charge of the ultimate installation of the parts and of varnishing'. The same practices were still to be found in in the twentieth-century craft workshops producing stringed instruments and bows – and they continue to this day. Teams of skilled workers may sit at the bench and be employed but their skills are rendered visible only as either the work of a particular workshop, or subsumed under the mark of the master craftsman heading up the workshop.

Eventually, the frustrations in the Washington workshop came to a head, and Barry, Dave and Sven parted company. A few weeks later, Dave went through from Westerhope, where he'd returned to the day job of working in his garage, to Hexham to see Nial. Nial: "And I sort of said 'What are you doing at the moment? What violins are you working on at the moment?' And he said, 'Well I'm not doing anything at the moment.' And I was thinking 'Well here I am with too much to do, maybe you should come over'. So initially Dave worked as an employee. And I was paying him maybes £100 a week. And after a bit, we're making violins together and I'm thinking 'Well this is not a master-apprentice situation'.

Dave was coming up with very good ideas and doing extremely good work on his own so I thought the fairest thing was to make it into a partnership."

In such a way, the business partnership of Cain & Mann was born. Through a series of fortuitous openings and coincidences, a violin shop and workshop in Hexham had fallen into the hands of a guitar player, luthier and fine artist in the shape of Nial Cain, who – purely by one chance meeting brought about by wanting to know more about a violin he'd happened on at an antiques fair – had found his way to becoming apprenticed to a violin luthier, Barry Oliver. Through the same sorts of social connections, this time forged through an evening class in Washington, Dave Mann, a drummer-cum-spray painter and panel beater from Benwell, inspired by his eldest daughter's talent as a violinist, found himself with the opportunity to become Nial's business partner in Hexham. Even more significant than this - the serendipitous entwining of individual life stories - is that as a direct legacy of Nial and Dave's years of training with Barry Oliver, Cremonese lutherie practices had become readily available to people living in, or near to, Hexham. Not surprisingly, the reputation of the shop and the workshop started to grow, not least amongst professional and semi-professional musicians in the area. But it also signals a wider point. Cremona's international reputation for violin making means that it doesn't just endure as a world renowned centre of teaching. Those who pass through its violin-making school and then go on to work independently elsewhere in the world – as Barry Oliver did – have the potential to constitute its diaspora. That diaspora can turn up in obvious places – currently in China, as Chinese luthiers return having studied at Cremona. But it can also turn up in the most unlikely of places. The Northeast of England for instance – where it began in

Washington (Tyne & Wear) and then expanded to the market town of Hexham.

When people ask the question, as they inevitably do, 'Why's this [kind of] shop and workshop in Hexham?' the answer is not, as might be assumed, one of business economics and rational location theory, based on the laws of market demand, business rates and rents. Rather it's about social connections and social ties – ties which led Bob Archbold to return to Hexham, open a violin shop, and then to sell a business to one Nial Cain.

CHAPTER THREE
Cain & Mann

For a while Nial and Dave continued working in what Nial now calls 'the top shop'. Then, events once again intervened. What they both call 'an insurance job' happened in another shop unit, just down the street: another fire. When the legalities had been completed and the fire damage rectified, those premises once again became available for rent. So, in 1993 Cain & Mann moved two doors down the street, to 27 Hencotes. As Nial explains, the move was a no-brainer: "The shop was way better, and there was more workshop space. OK, you couldn't see into the workshop but you could see down into the corridor. And we'd let people come in to see the workshop."

An empty shop unit provided no in situ legacy look; rather it required settling on an appropriate shop aesthetic and new fitments. Top end violin dealers gravitate to an instantly recognisable type of retail interior. This is one readily associated with the sale of 'rare and fine' goods, especially antiques: wooden floors, Persian rugs and cabinets are a pervasive presence. Frequently, such premises have rooms dedicated exclusively to playing, necessary for trying out instruments. This is an aesthetic which screams reverence for the old. It also conveys exclusivity and, of course, money. That it can be intimidating and exclusionary goes without saying. But 27 Hencotes is not this kind of shop. In atmosphere, it's altogether humbler, less reverential and a very long way from exclusive. If it has a reference point, it's more the junk shop-cum-second-hand shop than the high end antiques shop – but one stocked full of instruments rather than furniture, furnishings and collectibles. Instruments line the shop walls: cellos hang on both side walls, fiddles and the odd viola hang inside a glass-fronted cabinet on the door-facing wall, and there is usually the odd double bass knocking around on the shop floor.

The shop's ambience exudes not just from the instruments and their manner of display but also from its fitments: the glass fronted wooden display cabinets on the back wall and the counter in front of them. Dave explains their back story, "we got them from Miller's Auctions, off the Shields Road in Byker (in Newcastle); I think we paid about 80 quid for them". Nial: "We got lucky with that cabinet. It was a school bookcase, and the counter is the bottom bit of it". Dave: "The display cabinet used to stand on top of the counter – but we split it up; it looks better that way". Nial: "Stuff doesn't have to be perfect; it just has to have the right look". The Cain & Mann "right look" is the unmistakeable aesthetic of bricolage. To this day, it's reproduced on the counter, which functions as the repository of discard and stuff that needs to be to hand. This is where there are tickets and leaflets for upcoming (and past) gigs; trade catalogues, instrument tuners, dusters and bits of stuff that have been chopped off from instruments, like a chunk of ebony sawed off of a cello's fingerboard; odd strings, a cello tailpiece or two, a few pencils.

27 Hencotes, though, is more than a shop that sells violins, violas, cellos and the occasional double bass. The clue is in the window display. In the left-hand window there are artfully-arranged piles of tone wood, a few random backs and bellies of old, discarded and partly completed violins, an unfinished unvarnished violin 'in the white' and piles and piles of wood shavings, in which if one looks carefully one will find a toy mouse. The window display speaks to the shop's core purpose: the making, repair and maintenance of the instruments of the violin family. It also signals that the beating heart of this place is not the shop but rather what lies behind it: the atelier, or workshop.

*

I ask Nial about how he and Dave managed the work of making under the auspices of Cain & Mann, and the division of labour they evolved between them in the workshop. Nial: "I think at first we both worked on most of them. I would do the scrolls. Not that Dave did awful scrolls but I felt mine were that bit better. I always did the varnishing, and when it settled down I think that Dave would make the bodies to my arching ideas. He'd input ideas but I'd have the final say. Dave would show me the arching of the front say and I'd say 'It needs to be a bit lower there' or 'This time let's do a longer arch on the front'."

Dave's recollections of the same period broadly correspond. Nonetheless, they also disclose the perennial undercurrent of the authority-autonomy dynamic which pervades all workshop production spaces. As the senior partner with more experience, Nial did all the restoration work that came into the workshop, and the decorative carving work on the scrolls on each new instrument, whilst Dave did most of the actual instrument making, to Nial's satisfaction. Dave: "He did that cos it was Cain & Mann." Reflecting on those times, he acknowledges, "It used to piss me off a bit like; he liked to sit there and critique my work, but it was good because he showed me what he wanted, and I respected him cos he was good. " That incipient tensions did not boil over in the workshop was, to my mind, not just about the mutual respect between the two men but also bound up with the partnership's increasing commitment to innovation.

*

At this time, in the early-mid 1990s, Hexham was home to an emergent small cluster of luthiers. Not only was it the location of Cain & Mann; it was also where Stefan Sobell, a guitar luthier with a then growing international reputation, had his workshop. In the way of all such concentrations, the cluster provided the conditions for knowledge exchange. No matter what's actually being made, be it stringed instruments, clothing or shoes, the clustering of workshops results in the same kind of interaction – as Barry observed in relation to his time in Cremona (Chapter Two). In this instance, in Hexham it provided the opportunity for Nial and Dave to begin to experiment with mechanisation.

Like all trainee violin luthiers at the time, both Nial and Dave had been taught to make instruments entirely by hand. Whilst they had been encouraged by Barry to use a band saw to speed up the process of cutting wood, everything else was done using hand tools. This is a mode of learning that valorises the craft tradition, and which reproduces that tradition as one of working entirely with hand tools. Its effect is still visible today in those luthiers who continue to make violins entirely by hand, who insist that there is no place for mechanisation in violin making. As in everything else in the violin world, the justification for these arguments goes back to Stradivarius. Since these were the methods of the Cremonese masters, whose instruments cannot be bettered, there is no place for modern methods in violin making – at least, that's how the argument goes. In a business environment, however, especially one given over to general repair and maintenance work as well as making, there are limits to that approach. I ask Nial how many violins he and Dave were producing a year initially. Nial: "Good point! Maybe a couple a year to begin with; because it's quite hard to get on with it with repairs and so on".

Making violins entirely by hand ensures that workshop productivity remains very low. This has obvious ramifications for profitability. In a quest to increase their efficiency and output, Nial and Dave started to take a much closer interest in what guitar luthiers were doing, in so doing returning to learn from the making of the instrument that had first inspired Nial's interests in lutherie: the guitar.

As Chris Gibson and Andrew Warren show in their book, *The Guitar*, guitar luthiers have been less encumbered by the valorisation of old instruments over new than their violin counterparts. By the time Cain & Mann set up in business, even those guitar luthiers specialising in hand-built instruments, like Stefan Sobell, had begun to experiment big time with mechanisation.

Nial's telling of the story of the pathway of Cain & Mann to mechanised innovation begins with someone he calls "Young Nigel", and a book. "Young Nigel" turns out to be the now internationally renowned, Queensland-based guitar maker, Nigel Forster, and the book is Robert (Bob) Bernadetto's, *Making an Archtop Guitar*. But when I ask Nial the 'Who's 'Young Nigel' question I get a much richer story, full of characters and social connections – and one which evokes the ambience and rhythm of life in The Violin Shop at this time.

Nial: "OK. So you've got to realise that every violin shop attracts, we used to call them "nutters"! So one of the nutters – and he wasn't a nutter really – was this nice old bloke called Charlie Ferguson. Charlie used to walk by the shop. I think he lived up past the shop – and he used to stick his head in. And he'd been an old jazzer. He'd played jazz guitar. And way before my time, the Grainger Market in Newcastle had had a music shop in it. That was probably in the 1960s. And Charlie had worked there and had amassed a fantastic collection of instruments. Then he swapped them all for a single Martin guitar – Martin guitars were incredibly rare then. And he once brought in a wodge of photographs like a stack of playing cards of these things he'd had. Some of them would've been worth as much as a Martin guitar on their own now. But one thing he was left with was a Maccaferri guitar – and I don't know if you know but a Maccaferri guitar is a bit like a Strad violin. It's in that sort of league. Anyway so Charlie Ferguson, this old jazzer, comes in and talks about guitars in a violin shop probably once or twice a week. And I've never regarded talking to people who are passionate about a different instrument as a waste of time – you'd get people who knew lots about ukuleles and you'd get people who knew a lot about concertinas. You'd talk to them and you'd pick up stuff. For instance, concertina reeds vary by the year the concertina was made and some years are highly desirable. The ukulele guy had met George Harrison because he was in the Ukulele Society of Great Britain and George Harrison was. And the ukulele guy could play George Fornby solos, which let me tell you are not easy – you need to be a virtuoso. So anyway, Charlie comes in and if we'd got a guitar in he'd show us some stuff on the guitar – so we had one nutter. And then, bloody hell, did his grandson not start coming in, who was 'Young Nigel'. So he used to come in on the way home from school. So 'Young Nigel' would come in on the way home from school and maybe we'd just got rid of Charlie and be settling down and it'd be Nigel and in he'd come and talk about guitars as well! He wasn't doing well at school; he didn't fit in well at school. And another person we used to get in sometimes was Stefan Sobell. Stefan used to come in and sometimes talk to us about wood; I once went on a week-long trip to Germany with him buying wood so I ended up knowing him quite well. So Stefan came in and it was a bit like when I went to Barry's [Chapter Two]. Stefan said his assistant was going somewhere else and finishing. He didn't have an apprentice; he had an assistant. So I thought, 'Young Nigel'. So I mentioned it to both of them. And anyway 'Young Nigel' ended up going and working for Stefan".

    The strong social ties between Nigel and Nial and Dave in The Violin Shop ensured that he continued to keep on popping in to see them, even whilst he was working as Stefan's assistant. He did that from 1988-1990 and then from 1992-2003, with the break coinciding with when he did a degree. In an interview talking about those very early years at Stefan Sobell's with guitar enthusiast Terence Tan,

Nigel characterises the late 1980s and early 1990s in Stefan's workshop as mainly working by hand. But even then "We had an Inca band saw, an inaccurate planer thicknesser and a router we used for about two or three jobs". By 2003, when they went their separate ways, Nigel describes the workshop as "pretty swish". By then, Stefan had invested in dust extraction equipment, a belt linisher and table saws. Quality and efficiency underscored this workshop. The motto was 'Get it ready, Get it out' but 'it' had to be good and right first time; re-doing anything was the difference between making money on an instrument, or not. Much the same kind of thinking informed the book which Nigel brought in to The Violin Shop on making archtop guitars. Nial: "Bob Bernadetto was very mechanised. In his book he was saying 'Oh you can do this with a router and that with a router'." A result was that Nial and Dave started to think about the potential to use a router in the atelier. One of the most obvious candidate areas to consider was cutting the channels for the purfling, the decorative, yet also protective, parallel lines which run round the belly and back of a violin.

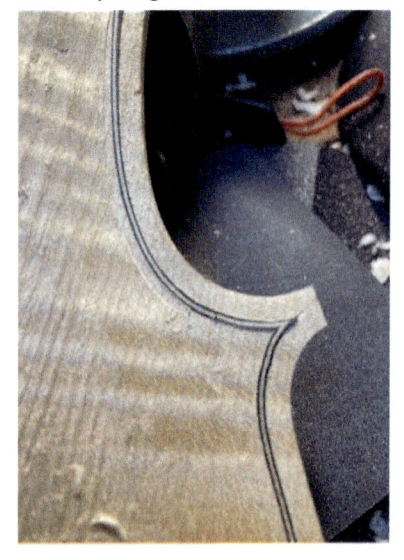

*

Purfling consists of two lines of ebony sandwiched by sycamore. It can either be bought ready-made or self-assembled by gluing together sheets of ebony, sycamore and ebony, and then cutting them into narrow slithers. The slithers are heated on a bending iron, pressed and then glued into a narrow grooved channel cut into the wood – and then cut to shape the intricate 'bee stings' which figure in each violin's corners. Dave: "We used to cut the channels by hand, and when I joined Nial we had a few to do". This was a slow job, "It was 'For Christ's sake! How can we speed this up?'" Watching Dave show me how to do this by hand one morning with the fiddle he's currently making, I can appreciate the sentiments. After using a purfling marker to place cutting guidelines in the wood on the violin's back, and then scoring into them with a sharp knife, he takes out a tool called a purfling pricker, dons his magnifying glasses and begins to demonstrate: "Where the two outer lines touch, in your corners, is going to be your bee sting. Then what you do is you've got to cut [a channel] out with your purfling pricker. So what you do is you draw down (with the pricker), each one gets deeper and deeper – the first cut you just let it follow, and it is cutting the fibres, and then you let it go a bit deeper, you don't force it, you just let it cut itself; when you get a bit deeper you can put a bit of a force into it." The only sound in the workshop is the repetitive, 'prit-prit' picking noise of the pricker. It's abundantly clear to me already that this is painstakingly slow work. It's all about feel; a conjuncture of hand, eye and the pricker combining to read

the wood fibres in the emerging channel groove. It's also obvious, watching Dave work, that the work is a continual negotiation with the fibres that happen to be in the channel; complicated by pricking on the curve against the grain, and into the corners where each bee sting is to be produced. Done like this, and with the interruptions of other shop work, I realise that it would take days to complete the task; that much is obvious. After about 10 minutes of this demonstration of his hand tool competences, Dave exhales, 'Phffft' and pronounces: "And now I'm going to show you how *I* do it"!

How Dave does this goes back to the years of experimentation with mechanisation in the Cain & Mann workshop. Initially, Nial and Dave had pushed their luck with what was available via Stefan's workshop, using this as an opportunity both to learn about what sort of equipment he had, and how it might translate to violin lutherie. Nial: "Stefan was already using a duplicating router for doing guitar fronts. We'd made a master and gone up and made a load of fronts and backs on Stefan's machine. He'd let us do that." Dave: "Stefan had routing machines and a copier for his guitar making. I'd take a few down there and spend a day in there. He didn't mind at first, but then it got to be 'You're here again!'" Having exhausted the limits of the favours available through local channels, Nial and Dave put their minds to in-house mechanisation.

That morning, in the machine-room-cum-kitchen area and toilet-cum-general dumping zone that lies out of sight behind the workshop, I get a demonstration of one of the results of their improvisation; this is how Dave does purfling channels. A router is attached to a Bosch power drill, vertically mounted on a guidepost. I ask Dave how he and Nial had worked out how to do it this way. Dave: "Eeh, well me and Nial gave it some thought. 'How can we do this quicker?! How can we save time?' It's ingenious!! Trial and error! Other people use this method as well – but we found a way to do it ourselves with what we had and what we could buy." Bricolage again, but this time with machinery; improvising with domestic power hand tools and bits sold as something else. Today, Dave has to hand numerous differently sized router attachments, suitable for preparing purfling channels for violins, violas and cellos (pictured). With evident pride he says, "When I do my purfling channels it only takes seconds!"

Looking back on that time of experimentation in the workshop, Nial says: "We were pretty ahead of the curve. But I was very fired up by the Bob Bernadetto book. Previously we'd made on the Italian system that I'd learnt from Barry; and the difference between the Italian, and let's call the other system the French system, is one is an outside mould and the other's an inside mould. With the inside mould (the Italian system) you make the sides, the ribs, on that. That's the shape that you make the front and the back to. The French system is you have an outside mould and you make a very precise set of ribs; then you're able to make the front and back to a template. And of course the whole template thing lends itself very much to the router. So instead of cutting the outline by hand with a knife you could have a template and use a router. So that idea, I came up with that, with Dave's input. I don't think he'd mind me saying that much of that was my way of thinking. Some of what we came up with didn't work. I had the idea of cutting the neck mortise with a router and you can never get that to work."

*

The effect of mechanisation in the Cain & Mann workshop was immediate: two violins a year became nearer 10. But mechanisation's traces also needed attention. Dave tells me one afternoon in the machine room, when he's making the ribs on his latest fiddle, "You're not supposed to use sandpaper when making violins!" He has just cut the rib blocks, and then six ribs with the band saw, each to 2mm thicknesses. Now he's standing in the corner of the room, cajoling a machine disk sander into life by kicking it. He says: "I'm not going to do this by hand. 2mm has got to come down to 1.2mm. I used to do it by hand but I thought 'Hang on a minute, there has to be an easier way!'" One hour later, along with huge amounts of sawdust, six ribs of the requisite dimensions have emerged. But Dave points to the finish on them: "That's too smooth; the dust from the sander fills the pores of the wood. And you can see the disk marks there; scratches. The finish I want is a scraper finish". We return to the atelier where Dave sets to work with a hand scraper he's made himself: "See where I've scraped it: it's lined and silvery. It brings out the wood and the flame". Mechanisation produces a machine finish. This may be fine for factory-made instruments, but it's certainly not acceptable for instruments, like Dave's, made in the handcraft tradition. The valorisation of handcraft in the violin world means that the trace of mechanisation has to be removed, and replaced with the patina of craft. If one uses power tools, one has to have the skills to disguise that.

*

And what of the violins that Nial and Dave made together, the Cain & Mann's? As I'm talking with Nial he mentions one of the first instruments he and Dave made together: "I don't know if Dave told you about Sarah's fiddle. We made Sarah's fiddle. It was the first fiddle we made to look like an old fiddle. I did the antiquing. I even made an almost indecipherable fake label. And when it was all together I took it over to Barry, because sometimes I'd take him over an interesting fiddle to see what he thought of it. I didn't say that we'd made it; I took it over and gave it to Barry, and he didn't clock at all that it had just been made. That was a good punch!" I ask: "So that one you say is Sarah's fiddle?" Nial: "Yes – this would've been either very late 1980s or early 1990s". Nicky: "Was it red?" Nial: "Yes; the model would've been a Guarneri". Nicky: "Ah, this is what's known as 'The Red Fiddle'.

Dave's daughter Sarah takes up the story: "The red one, I must have done my Grade 8 on it. There was a Bach piece, a piece by Elgar and something else – three very different pieces, and it did lend itself well to all of those. It was a really lovely instrument. I can't quite remember but I did a broadcast on it, to raise money to go to the Purcell School, because the fees were like ridiculous. Martin [Hughes – her then teacher] managed to get me to be on the BBC – and I think I was playing that fiddle then, and I think there's a video of me, on the TV. I got into Purcell School and I think I started off on that at the school Then they gave me something else. It was an old instrument – I don't know what it was, until I was about 21. And that's when dad made me the one I've got now."

So what happened to the red fiddle? The answer lies with Sarah's sister Claire: "The fiddle I have now (pictured) dad made for me in 2004. He'd always promised to make me my own fiddle. So that's when I got my very own hand-made fiddle by Dave Mann. Before that, though, I always got my sister's hand-me-downs! The first one that I got was a golden-coloured fiddle – a full-sized one with a quilted maple back, which had a label in it which said Sarah's Fiddle or maybe Violin. When I got that one she got another one – the next model on so to speak. When Sarah went to the Purcell School and all that, she had the red violin. And then, I think she ended up getting, where they loan out these really expensive violins, I think she got one of those and then I then got the red fiddle, which I played for years. I've still got that one up in a cupboard upstairs".

Claire's Cain & Mann Guarneri model fiddle is one of the instruments that accompanied her on her early career as a professional folk musician. One afternoon during a pause in violin making in the workshop, I ask Dave when Claire first started playing traditional Irish music. Dave: "She was seven or eight. She was learning the fiddle classically at school when she was about seven, following on from Sarah like, but she didn't like it cos she had to do what she was told! Tony Corchran – the Director of Irish culture in the Northeast. He ran Tyneside Irish Centre, and at that time he was looking for kids to come and join Comhaltas (the society for the preservation of traditional Irish music, song and dance). So that's the way she came through. She did a bit of Irish dancing, which was good cos she knew what was wanted for the music. She just loved it and she didn't do school fiddle any more. Tony, he'd have the kids in. He wasn't showing them how to play the fiddle; they'd be playing tunes, teaching by ear. The kids loved it. Kids being what kids are, after two or three weeks – derh, diddy diddy diddy. Claire just loved it; she'd be doing it at home. Tony'd be saying 'listen to Frankie Gavin, listen to Mary Birgen'. So I got the Mary Birgen, it was cassettes then in those days. And she had them on all the time. She'd be up in her bedroom. Coming home from school; getting up – first thing in the morning, 6.30 – you'd hear the whistle – 'It's too early; go back to bed!!! Go back to sleep!' Diddly diddly! Then the flute took over."

It's on the wooden flute that Claire Mann became All Ireland champion twice, in 1993 and 1994. A hugely talented multi-instrumentalist, she's also a highly accomplished folk fiddler. In 1995, after meeting the Scottish fiddle player Aidan O'Rourke, she and Aidan formed the band Tabache. The band toured extensively, including in the United States, and released two CDs (*Are You Willing* and *Waves of Rush*). 'The red fiddle' is to be heard on both recordings, along with Aidan's French Lamy.

As a band, Tabache was relatively short-lived; they disbanded in 1998. But it had a considerable buzz around it. Being young and little more than teenagers, Aidan and Claire were identified as bright young stars in the traditional music revival; a Scottish counterpart to the Irish supergroup Altan. Inevitably, the instruments which they played attracted attention in that scene. Here is Lauren MacColl talking about that time: "Claire (pictured with the red fiddle) would've been playing with Aidan in Tabache and she was also doing a lot of gigs in her own right so I first kind of met her when I went to a workshop of hers in Grantown-on-Spey, when there used to be a festival there. I loved, I still do, I absolutely loved her playing. I guess the precision of it, and all this Irish music that I'd not really heard at that point. And the sound that she made. And then I had the recordings of her and Aidan playing that hybrid of Irish and Scottish stuff – by the time I was in that workshop with her she was playing a Dave fiddle I'd say."

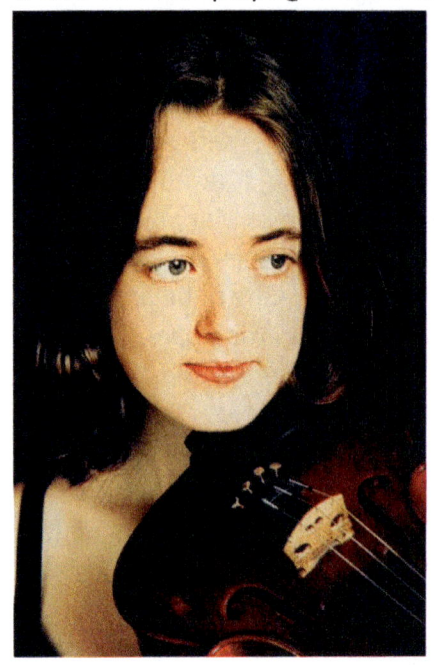

Similarly, here is Peter Tickell – a member of the band Peatbog Faeries, who played violin with Sting on two of his world tours and who also happens to be Kathryn Tickell's brother - talking about the same time, around 1998/99: "I must've been a teenage boy and I was playing at a hall in

Consett (in County Durham) and Claire was playing with Aaron Jones. My folks were in the audience and afterwards they remarked how good Claire's violin sounded." Noting that this would have been the red fiddle, I ask Peter what it was about that violin and its sound that made it stand out. Peter replies: "I think it was partly volume but also depth of tone. It had a depth that other instruments noticeably didn't have."

The red fiddle, then, is one of those violins which have the capacity to enthral and enchant those who hear it. It's a quality which many identify as peculiar to certain violins; almost as if they cast a spell over a listener. It's exactly that characteristic which provides the inspiration for Helena Atlee's book *Lev's Violin*, which journeys through the violin-making centres of Europe in search of the origins of the instrument, the Lev's Violin of her title, whose sound bewitched her. But the provenance of the red fiddle is much more transparent than her journey turned out. A handmade craft produced instrument from the Cain & Mann workshop, its sound – amplified by Claire's playing – testified to the quality of the instruments emanating from this workshop. With Claire moving to live in Edinburgh, the business partnership didn't miss an emergent opportunity to piggy-back on Claire's increasing profile in the Scottish/Irish folk scene.

Through the 1990s, the folk fiddle festival scene in Scotland provided a trade outlet for luthiers. Lauren MacColl: "I would've first encountered Dave at what is now the Scots Fiddle Festival in Edinburgh – back then they were just called Fiddle '98, Fiddle '99. So, when I was a teenager that was *the* event on the fiddle calendar. That was a whole weekend of concerts and workshops but it was also such a big hub of fiddlers who'd come from all over Scotland. And because it was such a big event it was in the Assembly

Rooms in Edinburgh. The whole of the downstairs was stalls, be it luthiers, Coda Music in Edinburgh, craft stalls, cards with fiddles on – everything. It was a proper festival of the fiddle. And Dave would've taken a stand there. So maybe when I was about 15 me and my friends would go there and try out all these fiddles on the stands. But I remember that there were other stall holders who had things that were much more cheap and cheerful and I remember not really having the confidence to ask to try Dave's. I knew he had really nice stuff; I maybe bought a shoulder rest off of him, rosin or something, and a few CDs from Coda Music!"

Dave reminisces about this time: "Everybody used to be there. I used to fill the car with fiddles – I sold a lot. There was me with a little stall; Stringers, the Glasgow shop as well; and some smaller businesses like me. And I always had a fiddle I'd made there. It used to stand on its own on a stand, with lights on it. I got one or two orders like that. They'd be mostly fiddle players who bought instruments. They'd want like the cheaper stuff. But I did take some expensive stuff – and I did sell one for £15k in 1999/2000. She was at the Royal Academy. So, there were classical people coming as well to have a look at what you'd got. And the benefit I had was Claire. She was there with all her mates, and they'd be like 'Oh there's Claire's dad'. 'Are you Dave Mann's daughter?' Are you Claire Mann's Dad?' 'Can I have a go?' 'Go and have a look and play – there you are, have a go; here's a bow'."

*

Back in the shop, during the 1990s Nial and Dave were simultaneously topping up the stock Nial had acquired from Bob Archbold and becoming known to dealers higher up the violin value chain, as somewhere where it might just pay to 'go fishing'. By way of introducing this scene Nial recounts to me: "There was a father and son pair of dealers – Tim

Toft is still going. Tim is a fantastic connoisseur and his dad, Alf, was a very good connoisseur too. Tim is a really shit hot connoisseur." He then asks me if I've seen Tim Toft's book on Hill instruments. I reply that I have indeed, that I'd been shown it in Dave's workshop by Martin Hughes, who'd also shown me the page in it dedicated to his own Hill instrument, 'Number 30'. Nial: "I think it was me who told Tim that Martin had a very good Hill! It's a belter; it's as good as they get." Having digressed, he reverts to his dealer story.

Nial: "So anyway – Toft Senior came in, and there was a seven-eighths violin that we'd got hanging there. I'd bought it from some lads who'd bought it at a car boot sale and they'd taken it to Anderson & Garland in Newcastle, and they'd said it was Mittenwald. It sort of looked like a Mittenwald at first. It had that crackled varnish like a lot of those early Mittenwalds do. Crocodile skin. Anderson & Garland had valued it at £400 – that's what they thought it'd make at a sale. The lads were in a hurry. They didn't want to wait for the sale so they asked if I wanted to buy it. So I said 'Yes'. So I bought it; hung it up. There were things about it that weren't Mittenwald. It didn't have – Mittenwalds often have a dropped saddle and a notch. The linings are a certain way as well. There are other violins that have that but it's a give-away. This didn't have that. And it was hanging up there and it was a seven-eighths. So it wasn't massively important to get in playing condition because you don't often get asked for a seven-eighths. Anyway, Alf Toft came in to have a look around and he was very keen on it – 'How much is the seven-eighths'? 'Ah; not selling it yet Alf'. 'I just like it''. 'You just like it?' 'OK! Well if I do decide to sell it I'll let you know'. And then some months later Toft Junior [Tim] comes in and says 'Have you still got that Chanot?' So the story with it is that Hill's used to buy unlabelled violins from

Chanot that were seven-eighths. And that's why it was unlabelled. I've still got it. My son got to play on it. One of the perks of being a violin dealer I had a half, a really nice three-quarters and a really nice seven-eighths".

*

At the turn of the millennium events once again intervened to shape the Cain & Mann business. Nial's parents discovered an old property for sale on a hillside in North Wales near to where they'd previously lived, complete with then derelict outbuildings. The outbuildings, once restored, appeared to offer the ideal workshop space. The property provided an opportunity for Nial to return to his native Snowdonia; one he found impossible to resist. Nial now works from his Welsh base as an independent violin luthier, making, repairing and restoring violins, and continuing to experiment with instrument making. One of his more recent projects has been to research and make a cwrth, a six-stringed traditional Welsh instrument. The result of this move, though, was that Dave (pictured in the shop at that time) became the sole owner of the business and the proprietor of the 27 Hencotes shop. The Violin Shop had become Dave Mann's shop – a shop which he has indelibly made a mark on, and which now has a national and international reputation. Yet, whilst Nial left The Violin Shop in the early 2000s, spending time in the shop and the workshop makes it abundantly clear to me that he's something of an absent presence here, albeit one very much still alive. His trace in instruments remains, even two decades on – testimony to the shop's history.

My first inkling of this comes early on in my visits to Hexham, when I'm talking to Dave about an Old Czech cello which looks like it might eventually have found a buyer. This cello has been hanging on the wall in the front of the shop since I first visited in 2019. Prompted by a sniff of an impending sale, Dave spends part of an afternoon checking the instrument over and re-tuning it, before saying that I can have a go on it. I'm like the kid in the proverbial sweet shop. I've never had the chance to have a go on a cello before but this is the sound that first got me hooked on the instruments of the violin family. It's the chance to fulfil a lifelong ambition. First, "for comparison's sake", I'm allowed to try one that's described to me as "Mittenwald – about £8k". Dave shows me how to hold the bow, and then says 'Think trombones!' to give me an idea of the kind of spacing and shifting required for recognisable notes to emerge. I stumble about with it, achieving some cello sounding notes and managing to scratch out 'Happy Birthday' – "Off we go!" he says, "Natural!" Then, he hands me the Czech cello – "My goodness", I exclaim, "No contest!" The difference between these two instruments, even for a total novice, is vast. What would it sound like to an accomplished player? Dave jests: "Got a spare 30k and it's yours!" But I'm not in the market for a cello.

The Old Czech cello is one of my first lessons in just how long instrument stock can hang around in shops. It's May 2022 when I get to play it, and the cello had been there in early 2019. But it transpires that the cello – which Dave refers to as "the Hellmer cello", after its suspected provenance - has been in Hexham for considerably longer than I'd imagined possible. That gets revealed when I ask

Dave when and how he got hold of it. Dave: "1994. Nial bought it down at Sotheby's auctions down in London for 6k; it's a 50:50 share." Later, Nial tells me that "the strategy was to use the Cain & Mann violins money to buy nice things in London". Dave: "Nial went down to Sotheby's. He's educated, with a posh accent, mixing with dealers and Japanese buyers. He's good. He can talk like a corporate barrister! But if he used that language with me I'd tell him to piss off!"

I ask Dave whether he'd restored this cello. Dave: "Aye. It was in a right bombed out state. There were edges missing, it'd been knocked about; ribs cracked – but basically that was it. It dates from about 1740." I ask Dave when he did the restoration work. Dave: "The last three years. It hung in that corner – see where that viola is. It hung there for about 20 years. Not touched. Covered in thick dust! Sawdust." I ask why it took so long to get round to doing it. Dave: "Well because your frame of mind at the beginning is, 'there's no need to do it now because there's a lot of work to do so we'll do it at a later date'. So it just hung up there. And every now and then we might get a dealer in, 'Oh, what's that? I'll give you 10k for it'. 'No'. Then we'd say, 'We'll probably have to get on and do that!' Then another 10 years later Tim Toft came in: 'You've still got that cello – I'll give you 15 for that' 'No'. And then Nial left. So it was just hanging and I'd got all this other stuff to do. And then Ralph [Plumb - another Hexham-based luthier] said, 'Why don't you get that done?' So I says, 'I will but I'll leave it till I'm getting near retirement'. So he says, 'You're there now you bloody idiot!' So I says, 'Oh Christ I am!' We always said, 'No need to hurry about it; we've got years. And the longer we keep it the more it's worth'. So I'd passed my retirement date, and Ralph's going, 'Now's the time to get it done man!' 'Aye – all right then!' It was six months' work. Ralph gave us a hand with it to push it on".

The Old Czech cello was not the only cello purchase Nial made at Sotheby's. Dave: "We've got another one. Nial's just finished the work on it; it's a Henry Lockey Hill - one of the most sought after English cellos in the world, and we've got one." Having one is one thing however; realising the asset entirely another. As Nial says: "Down here in North Wales cellos hardly get asked for. And I'm not really set up either for people coming to try stuff out in a nice surrounding, which I think is probably important. Mine isn't even as good as Dave's – it's a really untidy workshop."

*

A few months after the first initial whiff of a sale, and then it falling through, the Old Czech cello eventually found a buyer, through word of mouth and the musicians' network. Martin Hughes had put word of it out there amongst the cello-playing community through his cellist son, Lawrence. One Sunday morning at church in Hexham he was asked by another member of the congregation if he knew whether it was still available. He immediately contacted Dave: 'Yes'. In the workshop the next week Dave tells me: "It's gone to a lady. She'd tried it earlier in the year; loved it but couldn't afford it. But now she's inherited a lot of money. She bee-lined up here. She got here on Saturday. Took it – cos her mother lives in Hexham, so she was stopping there. So she took it away for the weekend, came back in again on Monday – 'I love it!!' And she picked a bow to go with it, which was £1.5k. So that was £31,500! Split two ways of course."

The same challenge of realising assets surrounds the Henry Lockey Hill cello. Dave: "Nial could bring the Henry Lockey Hill cello up here and I could have a go at selling it – because that Peter what's his name from South Africa, he knows about it. But I'd have to contact him, tell him it's in the shop, ask him when he's coming over – and then it'd be 'Oh I haven't got any plans for being over in the near future'. But it's known about, and he might talk to people – cos he's got a Henry Lockey Hill." But, even as he is saying this, Dave is coming round to the need to go in a direction trod only reluctantly: engaging other dealers. Dave: "That's 100 grand that one. But it's going to have to go up to Tim Wright in Edinburgh. He's a professional violinist and he's well known, he has lots of contacts, professional players, so he's set up his business in Edinburgh – he's looking for stuff. He was saying, 'Have you got anything else, I'm short on cellos'. So I said, 'well there's this one that Nial's just finished the work on.' So I told him what it was, a Henry Lockey Hill. So, he's asking if it's ready. So I says 'It's all done, ready to go, impeccable, I'll put you in touch with Nial'. So Nial's coming up – cos his wife's got relations up in Edinburgh. So they'll go up there, call in and drop the cello off." Assessing this, I say: "So the punt is that you're going to realise the sale that much quicker if you take it to Tim Wright's?" Dave:" Yes – 'cos he's got contacts who are looking for stuff". Nicky: "So he's working like an agent". Dave: "That's right". Tellingly, he adds "They (he means cello players in the market for this level of instrument) wouldn't trust me – an unknown luthier from Hexham Violin Shop. Snobbery. 'We don't know this guy – who is he?'"

*

Dave's invocation of snobbery and trust is an important window on the world of exchanging high value stringed instruments. It points to the geographical limits on sales: on which instruments are likely to be sold where, in which type of locations, and by whom. But what it leaves unsaid is what accompanies these high value sales: a paper trail which authenticates instruments and attests to their provenance.

Buyers at this level of the market mostly want evidence of provenance. In the absence of paperwork, which is common with instruments over two hundred years old, authentication has to be sought out. Only dealers at the apex of the violin family value chain can provide an authentication that carries trust in the trade. So, certification is not something that any luthier can supply; indeed, such an opinion is likely to be regarded as worthless. And, of course, authentication carries commission charges, typically 3% of the sale price. Knowledge and connoisseurship – the ability to be able to recognise something for what it is – may suggest the scope for investment, and an opportunity to boost the pension pot, but they alone are not enough to realise sales. In what is a closely controlled trade, the only safe means to realising high value assets is to position them for sale at the appropriate level in the value chain, which means that most of the value is captured higher up the chain. Aspirant dealers beware!

CHAPTER FOUR

Finding a Violin

"It doesn't matter who you are, you leave with a gift" – Des Dillon

For the uninitiated, a violin is something one buys, and the act of its purchase is, in some respects, like buying a car. The most obvious parallels are in financial outlay. Beyond the entry-level mass-produced instruments such as Skylarks and Stentors, which are sold as kit purchases complete with a case, bow and rosin, buying a violin entails considerable financial outlay. Like a car, it's a big-ticket purchase. Starting prices beyond entry level are of the order of £1-2k on current prices and £100-200 for an equivalent bow. £5k is the entry level for a modern hand-made instrument; a reasonable bow is of the order of £400. £10k gets you a top-quality modern hand-made instrument, whilst a quality carbon fibre bow is of the order of £1-2k. Older instruments, and the bows of venerated makers like Sartory, Tubbs and Hill, command five-figure prices and make these objects an investment class of purchase, of interest to individual investors and collectors as well as players looking to boost their pension pot. And that is before one gets to the instruments made by the Cremonese masters, Stradivarius and Guarneri: they command six and seven-figure sums and are owned by banks, pension funds and charitable foundations.

Like buying a car, buying a violin requires trying out. Playing as trying out is the equivalent of going for a test drive. Just as taking a test drive involves having one's driving put under scrutiny, so too is playing as trying out. Someone else – often more than one person – is going to be listening to you as you play, and to what you say about the particular instruments that you try. In such a way, trying out a violin becomes akin to entering a performance space. This is one of the reasons why top dealers have dedicated playing rooms, designed and furnished to provide acoustics that mimic an intimate chamber setting. But absent a playing room, in violin shops like 27 Hencotes it's the shop floor that will be transformed into a stage, whilst the proprietor and anyone else who happens to be in the shop comprise the audience. So here, it's Dave who listens – and anyone else who's around. Playing competences and capacities instantly come under the microscope, and are often intensely felt. Playing in front of unknown others may be no big deal for professional and semi-professional players, or for a good amateur player relatively confident in their capacities, but for many people – especially adult learners - this is why buying a violin can easily turn into a hugely intimidating experience. A consequence is that playing can become impossible. Many is the time in Dave's shop that I've witnessed tunes disappearing from the heads of folk fiddlers, leaving them in a complete playing vacuum. Whilst for classical players the absence of sheet music in the shop sets in train something akin to rapid-onset paralysis. And if one cannot play, how on earth is one to choose an instrument?

 Even assuming that playing itself is not a hurdle, there's the question of how to choose between instruments. It's here that the car buying analogy breaks down. Cars – or at least the cars that most people drive – are standardised manufactured goods. Different specifications differentiate between models, and there may be a choice of colour and wheels, but fundamentally consumers know what performance specification they're potentially purchasing when they go to try out a car; and mostly they're trying out that very model. Cars are also amenable to a wide range of driving competences; they'll perform as they've been manufactured to do, even for the worst of drivers. Violins – especially hand-made ones – are not like this at all. For starters, they're unique. Each is made of different woods, from different trees, by different craft workers – and unless one's buying new, there will be a playing memory in that instrument. It will have the imprint of its previous playing history in it, in ways of learnt resonance. So even instruments made by the same factory at roughly the same time will sound different, and they will respond differently to different players. Hand-made craft instruments are even more variable. Then there's the difference between driving as a skill and what I'll call the process of sounding – or, the interface of player, strings and instrument and the mutual accommodation between them which produces a violin's sound. Sounding is at the heart of choosing an instrument, and it turns a process that appears to be about buying into a process of finding. The process is dependent not just on playing and listening capacities, or about the sound that a player might want to produce; it's also iterative. It's about listening to how you and an instrument sound together – and then comparing that with other instruments, and being able to hold what are often very subtle differences in one's head.

All this has implications for how violins are bought and sold. It means that what's being bought and sold in a violin shop is not so much the object in and of itself, or the violin, but a particular sounding. The instrument is the means to the production of sound qualities. Since the sounding of each instrument will vary according to the player, this means violins have to sell themselves. Or, said another way, they can't be sold to a customer in the way of so many goods, by a knowledgeable salesperson whose role is to guide a customer to make the right purchase for them. Rather, it's the customer-player who has to actively choose, whilst the person cast in the role of the seller has to take a back seat. The most they can do is to offer choices – typically within a budget. So, more and more instruments get tried out – and the potential for aural overload and confusion becomes higher and higher.

Another implication of sounding's importance is that there is no direct correspondence between the financial value of an instrument and its value as a playing instrument to a particular player. Whilst valuation gives a guide to an instrument's quality as an object, price is no automatic guide to sounding quality. That will depend on the player. Instruments and players object to one another, even at the pinnacle of playing ability and with the highest valued of violins. As Newcastle-based international soloist and former prodigy Leia Zhu – certainly the most virtuosic violinist to walk through the door of 27 Hencotes – explained to Dave and me one day, she'd had the opportunity to play several Strads, including ones played by Jascha Heifetz and Ida Haendel, but she really didn't like them, or they didn't suit her playing style. She much preferred her current loan: an instrument of lesser financial value – a Guadagnini valued at a mere £5M.

To set out to choose a violin, then, is to embark on an uncertain and potentially fraught journey. It's a journey that people with different playing and aural competences are variably equipped to navigate. How does Dave choreograph that journey for different people? How does this process work for professional players, advanced students, or for that matter, anyone else who happens to walk in and wants to buy a violin? Tellingly, there is a space for all these players in this shop. It doesn't matter who you are, or what kind or level of a player you are, in this shop you not only have the right to choose a violin, you get to choose the violin that you want, irrespective of the price bracket it's in and your playing ability. If you can afford it, and the instrument sounds for you, then it's yours. And if you can't hear the difference between instruments, then there's ways that can be accommodated too.

Such inclusivity is rare in the violin world, where the conjuncture of violin financial value with playing styles and competences frequently aligns to produce social differentiation and exclusivity. The most obvious of these lines of differentiation is between classical players and 'the rest', chiefly traditional/folk fiddlers and jazz violinists. A consequence is that, in many violin shops, the best instruments will be reserved for classical players only to try. Folk and traditional fiddlers and jazz violinists, let alone an adult learner, can find themselves being treated as second-class citizens. The upshot is feelings of social exclusion. These distinctions do not apply in 27 Hencotes. Here, Dave's rules apply, and inclusivity rules. This is in large part what makes this shop such a special place.

*

Professional players coming to Dave's shop to try and potentially buy a violin tend to be of a type. Typically, they are young professionals, freshly out of conservatoires – and they can be both classical and folk/traditional players. There are reasons for this. The story of 'the red fiddle' in the previous chapter offers a window on why. The passage of that instrument to Dave's daughter Claire occurred when her sister Sarah was at the Purcell School in London, when she was given access to another older violin – the kind of instrument that is valued in the classical music world. Having access to this kind of instrument is the norm for conservatoire classical violin students, but the instruments are only on loan for the period of their studies. On graduation there follows the obvious problem of finding the next instrument. For those students destined to become top-level soloists and ensemble leaders, the classical music ecosystem ensures that instruments will continue to be loaned. These are the five, six and seven-figure violins owned by banks, pension funds and foundations; Leia Zhu's Guadagnini is an example. For everyone else, though, finding a replacement instrument is a huge challenge. It's also one that comes at the most financially and psychologically insecure point in a young musician's trajectory, when they're a usually impoverished freelance musician on the cusp of a career.

Some people get lucky. One day whilst I'm in the workshop, Martin Hughes is in and I take the opportunity to ask him about his instruments. This is when I get the back story to the instrument which Nial, in the previous chapter, described as "a belter of a Hill". Martin begins by telling me, "I've got a really very nice WE Hill and Sons, Number 30 – which is one of the greats". He shows me a photograph of the violin in Dave's copy of John Basford &Tim Toft's book of W E Hill & Sons instruments: "It sort of fell open at the page" he exclaims. "And the most amazing thing is the three words: there. He shows me what's written: "'An exceptional example'. And it's the only time those words are used in the book". He goes on: "That's the wonderful thing – the provenance". The players listed are: Manoug Parikian, Martin Hughes. I ask Martin when he got this instrument. Martin: "I got it in 1980 from Manoug, who'd taken an interest in me from an early stage. What happened was he had a lovely Strad and he often played the Hill because it was a lovely fiddle. Then he had a little mad moment like we all do. So off he goes to New York City, to Bellini – who was the big new thing. So Manoug said, 'I've got this amazing violin coming, which I've seen and is nearly there, and it's a copy of the Guarneri that Menuhin once owned'. I saw it the first time it appeared in Britain. The Sinfonia was going to Manchester to record in the Hallsworth Hall. `He brought it in – and everyone went 'Awhh.' It looked and sounded amazing. He said to me on that day, 'You've had a play of the Hill. I'm going to prove this to destruction; and, if I like it, you can have first refusal on the Hill ... eight months later, 'Yeah, I'm going to keep this one, and the Hill can be yours'. 42 years I've had it. It was lovely to have someone like that take such an interest."

Whilst the patronage system works for the lucky few young classical players, others have to begin a quest for the instrument, and often the bow, that's to be the means to their livelihood as a professional musician. This is a trail that is certainly national, and it can be international – as people scour violin shops searching for *the* instrument, and the perfect bow; the ones which will sound with them in the way they desire and which will enable them to achieve their career aspirations. Dave's shop is one of the stopping off points on this journey – although for some in this position it's already a familiar space.

Rebecca Howell graduated from the Performance Masters at the Royal Northern College of Music (RNCM) in Manchester in 2018. She is currently building a career as a freelance orchestral musician and violin teacher at Chetham's School of Music in Manchester. She grew up in Hexham, so Dave's shop was the obvious supplier of all her early violins – from a three-quarter size, which the family loaned, to her first full-size violin aged 11. Whilst she was still studying at the RNCM she dropped and broke her then violin, a modern Chinese instrument made by Shan Jiang in Beijing. A RNCM instrument loan filled the gap whilst the Shan Jiang was being repaired but this was enough of a prompt to think about embarking on finding a new violin. Dave's shop was her automatic first port of call. Rebecca tells me: "I went in and I just tried my luck a bit; I asked him if he had anything that would benefit from being played! He let me try two French ones – and the one I have, it's a Jean Lavest. He let me have it for a couple of months and then he let me pay for it in instalments, which was really good of him!" She goes on: "that's very different from my friends who've like travelled the entire country and tried 60 or 70 instruments, looking for the perfect instrument. The one that's really right for them".

Like Rebecca, the violist Alistair Vennart also grew up in Hexham. He is further on in his professional career than Rebecca; he's a member of Manchester Camerata, plays with Manchester Collective and is in demand as an educator and arranger. He leads the RNCM's Young Violas and is a viola tutor at Leeds University. As with Rebecca, growing up in Hexham meant that Dave's shop played a pivotal role in Alistair's early instrument history. It's where his parents bought him his first Stentor viola aged nine in 2000, and also where he purchased his first upgrade, in 2004/5, for £900: a Jay Haide 15.5" – a moment in which he describes thinking "holy crap, these instruments are ridiculously expensive". Jay Haide violas are American part-manufactured, part hand-made instruments. They are an example of the kind of instruments which Dave sources for more advanced students. This one tidied Alistair over until he went to study at the RNCM, at which point – like all other conservatoire students – he had the opportunity to loan various instruments and bows. On graduating from the Royal Northern in 2014, however, Alistair had to find his own replacements. The inevitable quest followed, all over the UK. Alistair remembers looking at what Dave had but his eventual instrument choice came from Cardiff Violins. "It's a Don Tatem, 16.5" which I got for a ridiculous price because it was on a sale/return". The ridiculous price meant that Alistair had unexpected reserves left over for a bow. So, he continued on a bow quest. The bow he eventually chose came from Dave. It's a Louis Bazin.

Other young classical professionals find their way to Dave's door from further afield and with no background with the shop. Rebecca Gardiner was coming to the end of her studies in Amsterdam in the early summer of 2023 when she first contacted Dave about 'a special violin' that she'd heard he had. She'd got wind of this violin via her parents, who live in the Tyne Valley. She was interested in trying it out as she was looking for the perfect instrument on which to do her orchestra audition demos. The 'special violin' is Dave's late seventeenth century restored Jakobs. It's an instrument which he's had for about 25 years, and is in the same pension pot category as the Lockey Hill and Old Czech cellos purchased in London [Chapter Three]. I first saw, and played, this instrument when I first came to the shop – after I'd bought mine (pictured). As I subsequently learned, it's the instrument which Dave gets out to show certain customers and visitors, and which he allows a selected few to play. It's also the instrument in the shop which dealer visitors most want to get their hands on. Rebecca booked her flight and duly arrived at the shop. Much as with the Old Czech cello, having family living relatively locally provided the opportunity for a short but intensive playing trial. When I next visited the shop, my first question to Dave was 'Well?' He beamed: the Jakobs had finally found its playing home.

Young folk fiddle professionals face the identical instrument-bow challenge as their classical counterparts. Being of the pre-conservatoire generation of traditional musicians, Aidan O'Rourke first learned of the imperative to upgrade his fiddle from a sound engineer. He says: "I was playing on a Lamy. A French Lamy – and Dave set it up really nicely". Since his days playing with Claire in Tabache, Aidan had had this fiddle maintained by Dave. Whilst recognised to be "not a patch on the red fiddle" it was set up to sound as well with Aidan's playing as it could. It served its purpose, and as Aidan says: "I was on an early 20-something's folk musician's income; my parents weren't in a position to help me out, and there was no way in the world I could afford a hand-made fiddle then". Aidan's Lamy "was an alright fiddle but there was one recording studio I used to go to regularly – the aim is to get to be in the studio exactly the same and as comfortable as you would be when you'd be practicing at home and on stage. It comes with years of practice, so you can lose that anxiety and open your soul. But I remember this engineer saying, 'You're really getting there with your recording and your vibe in the studio and your attitude to the music's great but you really do deserve a better fiddle'." This was the trigger that led him back to Dave's door in 2006 on the look for a new instrument. It was the early days of the band Lau. Since then, Aidan has played a Dave Mann fiddle.

Lauren MacColl is of the next generation of Scottish folk fiddle players, most of whom have had a conservatoire training. Like many traditional musicians, she began not with a bought fiddle but with what's known as 'the family fiddle': "To begin with, "I'd always played my great uncle's fiddle that I'd inherited". That fiddle is early 20th century French, bought second hand from an antique dealer in Tain in the Highlands of Scotland. Lauren still has 'Great Uncle Jack's fiddle'. She says: "He played entirely by ear; half the varnish is off the back because he played in very woolly jumpers so it's completely scratched. It'd been given to me so I'd never had that thing of playing other fiddles. But when I left school, before I went to the Conservatoire, I had a Saturday job for a year and saved up and got a fiddle from the Violin Shop in Glasgow, which I loved". She says: "It was great, but I outgrew it pretty quickly – I traded it in." I ask her what she means by outgrowing it. She replies: "I was putting in more than I was getting out". Lauren traded that fiddle in Stringers in Edinburgh for "this quite petite, very narrow, German Hopf fiddle – they're not very well regarded, I think, in that world but it had the most amazing dark, gorgeous quality about it, and I loved it and it was hard to part with it because it was with me through the end of college and that kind of time when you're finding your voice. So, I think I knew that I was really attracted to the really darker sound of the lower end of the fiddle but I struggled. What that fiddle, what it didn't give me was power and tone on the top strings. It just didn't have that because it wasn't a good enough instrument. So yeah, I knew that I needed something that was going to help me progress. It was the summer of 2012; I knew I just had to take a plunge, get a loan and find what that instrument was going to be".

Lauren was also looking for an instrument that was up to the more ambitious playing projects that she already had in the pipeline: "I was looking for a fiddle that was going to bring my playing to the next level. I was also at a stage musically where I was trying to, push myself is the wrong word – I don't go for pyrotechnics and I don't practice crazily hard pieces of music – but I suppose I was looking for something that was going to be with me on like more ambitious projects. Like Rant (a chamber folk fiddle quartet) was just getting off the ground. That's a project where you're really listening to the sound and matching sound and being very critical of sound. I had a good look around. I didn't sell the German one initially. I was in London for some gigs and I stayed on for a couple of days and I went to a couple of places. Didn't connect to anything – and I suppose what I had in my head was 'I'm getting a loan to pay for this anyway, so budget wasn't the thing that was steering me, it was just purely sound. I had to learn not to walk in and say 'Hello, I play folk music' and there's the cupboard with the low budget fiddles. I learnt that after the first shop – don't get me wrong, not everywhere is like that. But at this point I was still living in Glasgow and somebody – I can't remember who it was – but somebody I was chatting to said that they'd just been at Dave's getting a bow re-hair or something and that he had some nice fiddles. I didn't drive at this point – and then I thought, 'Oh, Hexham – I can get the train'. I'll do that and I'll just go for a day trip. It felt like a big deal; it was quite a big effort to coordinate to do that. And I thought as soon as I walked in, 'This is the right atmosphere for me'.

"And it was like 'C'mon in, what are you looking for?' And I said 'I don't know – I will know when I hear it and I don't want to know price, I just want to play a load of fiddles today'. Actually, he didn't say 'What's your budget?' I think he laid out about 20-25 fiddles, and of course one of them just happened to be this Cain & Mann fiddle. It was made in 1996. I kept going back to it and was saying 'well I really love this'. He was chuffed. He would be. Out of all of these things! Some of them were more expensive, some were much cheaper – and one of the other ones that I was quite attracted to it turns out was about £600! And that was the other thing. He didn't try and make me go for his one. So that, I just thought, maybe with my background [her parents were antique dealers], knowing sales and how people sell and what it takes to run a business – it wouldn't have been beneficial to him to let me buy that £600 fiddle but he let me make that decision. There was no push there."

What connected Lauren with the 1996 Cain & Mann fiddle? She says: "I think it's got - for me what I love is the balance between the woodiness – like the sound, you can really hear the wood. But there's also this beauty and refined quality to it. I just remember thinking 'this is exactly what I was looking for'. That beautiful warm end but also that E. And if you play – and at that time I'd have been playing even more – Highland music, pipe music, you're just on that E string all the time. And you're doing a lot of percussive ornamentation that lends itself to having a really nice tone first and foremost on the E. I just loved it. He'd just got it back the week before. The person who'd got them to make it was playing in the Northern Sinfonia but they'd got really bad arthritis and had to retire. They sold it back to Dave. It was a case of 'right place, right time'".

Reflecting on her experience of trying and sounding violins at Dave's Lauren says: "There's an openness of 'Let's work with you to find the best thing for you as a musician'. Rather than in the other places it was 'How much money have you got to spend, and here's an instrument that fits in that category'. Here's three instruments that are in your budget and these are the ones that you're allowed to try and you're not allowed to touch other options. With Dave there's a certain holistic element. Put a few things out on the table and hear how the player sounds and what sound they're capable of - because everybody's physicality is so different. Like are they just a gentle player that needs a big resonant instrument to make a decent sound? Are they a huge person who's just going to destroy a really fragile instrument because they've got too much power in their hands? And responding to how that person plays the first one or two probably then influences what he puts in the pot. It's an honest way of working – responding to the connection that individual has with an instrument, rather than 'that instrument fits your price range'".

*

Lauren's journey with violins highlights one of the key differences between classical conservatoire and traditional music students. For the latter there are no instrument loans; rather, students have to rely on the market to find the instrument which accompanies them through their degree programme. The establishment of the Folk and Traditional Music Degree at Newcastle University in 2001 provided Dave with a steady supply of such students looking for instruments, which continues to this day. The shop became part of the degree's ecosystem. Carly Bain and Paul Knox are two graduates from that degree programme.

Carly is from Kelso, in the Scottish Borders, and played in ceilidh bands before heading to Newcastle for the Folk Degree. When she finished the degree, she was part of the Monster Ceilidh Band, and has toured extensively with them. She is a regular session musician and ceilidh band player and taught the Tuesday night Folkworks class at the Sage in Gateshead before moving to Edinburgh. She's also taught on Durham Folkworks and has a number of private pupils of all ages.

Being relatively local to Hexham, like Rebecca and Alistair, Carly has grown up with Dave's shop. It's been a constant presence in her life, right from the earliest days of playing in ceilidh bands at the Hexham Gathering as a school kid. The band gravitated to the shop, having heard about it – and would go in and be "the typical teenagers, pestering and annoying Dave and maybe buying the occasional string set". Since those days she's progressed to buying instruments and bows from Dave. Carly's first fiddle, which saw her through her school years, she thinks had to have come from Dave but she has no memory of its purchase. The instrument-bow progression happened once she was on the Folk degree. When she arrived, the first thing she was told by her tutor was that she 'needed a decent bow'. At the time she was playing with a £100 job. The upgrade was huge – she went to a £2k Hill bow, which she got from Dave. The next year her tutor was Catriona Macdonald, who said to her that it was time to start thinking about a better instrument. Back Carly went to Dave's. She settled on one, which Dave let her take away for a week or so. But, when she went back to the shop, he said to her to try another – this was more in her style, louder, and sharper. This was a German 'trade' fiddle.

Paul Knox spent a number of years post degree, teaching music in schools in Newcastle and Hexham. He then trained for the priesthood and in 2022 he started serving his curacy in the parishes of Bamburgh, Belfold and Lucker, in Northumberland. Originally, he's from Walker in the East end of Newcastle, the very same area where both Dave and Mickey Hutton served their time as apprentices (Chapter One). Paul: "It turns out that Mickey Hutton knew a lot of my family when he was growing up. He grew up with my second cousins, so we know a lot of the same people". Paul himself is a classically trained violinist: "When I started playing violin it was just a cheap, crappy one from China. So, when I got towards Grade 2 or 3 the violin teacher said 'Go and get yourself a better violin'. So, I went and got a Stentor 2. And then I went and got a violin from Handmade Music in Whitley Bay, which was a specialist violin shop – a guy and his wife used to set them up and look after them. So, I got a decent violin – still a student one; nothing hand made. And we used to go to the Hexham Gathering with school, and Hexham was miles away from Newcastle, socially and geographically. And we used to wander up to the Violin

Shop and annoy Dave by saying 'Can I have a look at; can I have a try?!!' I'd have been about 11, 12, 13. So we used to go and annoy him."

Like many who start on a classical music trajectory, Paul gave up with it at the Grade 7/8 transition: "I couldn't be bothered because it was A-Levels at the same time, and I hated the theory. And by then I'd also started on the Northumbrian pipes; I started playing them when I was 15/16; went for lessons". That change in musical direction led to him applying and being offered a place on the Folk Degree. "I realised that my crappy student fiddle wasn't going to cut the mustard. So, my uncle took me to the Violin Shop to get a good violin for university. So, this was in the summer to start in the September of 2005. I had a budget that I was allowed to spend - £1k I think. And the violin I got I think was £560 – it was a German fiddle; hand-made, I really loved it. And then of course I had to have a bow to go with it, and the bow was £450, so – 'thank you very much'. And Dave was very – he was very grumpy!"

In the 2020s the same imperative to get a better instrument and bow is felt by the current generation of Folk and Traditional Music degree students. One afternoon when I was in the shop one of these students was scheduled to come into Dave's looking for just such an instrument. Whilst he was getting a range of violins out of the glass display cabinet for her to try, and I was giving them a play-over check, Dave said to me, "She rang last week. I asked her what her budget was: £5-8k. So, we may be in luck here". Dave's reference to luck relates to an instrument of his that had been commissioned but had recently been returned to the workshop and which was now available for re-sale. This fiddle's return was causing him a considerable degree of distress for he could find absolutely nothing wrong with it. And as Martin Hughes had declared earlier that morning, after filling the shop with the sound of the opening movement of the Bach Partita in D minor on it, "it's really a very good fiddle indeed". As he's tuning up another fiddle for playing/trying, Dave says to me: "If she likes it, I'll maybe let her have it for £6-7k".

When the young woman arrived at the shop, she had brought with her not her current fiddle but rather an instrument from another violin shop, which she had tried and liked. She had this instrument on trial and was now journeying around the violin shops of the country seeing if she could find something she liked even better; another version of the quest for the perfect instrument. Dave asked to have a look at this instrument and then handed her his returned fiddle. Without saying anything more about it, he says: "Try that". Of course, she liked it, but there was a problem: the price. Rather than being able to stretch to £8k, it turned out that her entire instrument-bow budget was £5k. Dave's returned fiddle, even at a bargain price, was out of her price range. And there was another problem. She tells him that the price of the currently loaned instrument had been agreed at £4.7k, meaning she only had £300 left for a bow. We leave the young woman in the shop trying the range of instruments that had been prepared for her and retreat to the workshop, out of her ear shot. Dave puffs out his cheeks and emits a 'Pffffh': "Did you see the state of that thing? Rough! Chipped corners; rough edges; I wouldn't let anything like that go out of the workshop. What's gone on there is she's said 'My budget's £5k and they've gone, 'Got a young lass coming in – her budget's £5k. Put some strings on that one and tell her she can have it for £4.7k'. Opportunity to get shot of it without doing any work. If she goes back and says she wants the repair work done on it, which she will, because she'll want it looking perfect like, they'll tell her that's the trade price. If she wants something in showroom condition it'll be another £2-3k. So, either she finds another £2-3k or she's got to play a bashed about violin".

20 minutes or so pass by and then Dave returns to the shop to ask the young woman how she's getting on. In that time, she's been playing one D-major reel on a few of these instruments. Dave comes back to the workshop where I'm sitting: "Eeeh", he goes. "She's trying ones that are about £1-2k less than the one she's got with her but she cannot hear any difference between the fiddles; she likes them all. Dearie me". I offer to go through and try to help her hear the different sounds and to act as a listening ear, for how a fiddle sounds under you is different again from how it projects to a listener. I start by suggesting that she could perhaps try playing a few different pieces in different keys and at different tempi to hear the range of colour and tone possible with each instrument. Aside from demonstrating to me the range of capacities to hear sounding, the experience is déjà vu with a difference for me, for back in my youth I used to have Saturday jobs working in retail sales. This is retail sales like nothing else I've encountered: I realise, it's the violin that has to sell itself, and the only way it's going to do that is by connecting in sound and feel with who's playing it. There's nothing that a sales advisor can do to shape that, other than comment on the sound they're hearing.

An hour and a half later the young woman left the shop. Nothing she played that was within her budget was connecting with her any better than the instrument she'd arrived with. Dave's parting comment is to say to her: "You really do need to say to them when you go back that you want those repairs dealt with; it's not in good condition". Reflecting on the whole experience later I say to Dave: "I wouldn't have been confident buying something like this for that kind of money at 19/20, Dave; would you?" I'm thinking that the degree of financial savviness required to set out to buy a violin in this price bracket is clearly high – and I definitely didn't have that at that age. "No! No way!!" he exclaims.

The quest for the perfect instrument, then, can be as much a financial minefield as it is an odyssey in sounding, requiring a knowledge of 'sharp' trading practices that is beyond many student musicians. The scope for them to be unknowingly ripped off in the course of their journey for *the perfect* instrument, the one they hope is going to put them on the pathway to a successful professional career, is high. It's a journey full of potential jeopardy. In this regard, Dave's honesty and care in the luthier business stand out. I reflect; it's as if he knows and understands the naiveté he's encountering, and – in response - is trying to educate people about wider business practices. In no small part, I decide, this degree of empathy is because he's been around young folk musicians for decades. Through Claire, and then Aidan, and his own immersion in the traditional music scene, Dave has come to know these people so well he knows them like family. And like family, he wants only the best for them. Tellingly, the same ethos of care and concern applies to an altogether different category of buyer: the adult learner player.

*

Violins for adult learners are the 'bread and butter' instrument sales in a violin shop like 27 Hencotes. People local to the Hexham area will come to Dave's shop for the basic starter kits, but those living elsewhere in the Northeast conurbation are likely to have gravitated to where Paul Knox got his first fiddle: Windows, located in the Central Arcade in Newcastle city centre. Or, increasingly, they'll buy one online. Dave's, by contrast, is the kind of shop reserved for an instrument upgrade; it's where those who've decided they're committed to learning to play the violin come to treat themselves – or to be treated by others, just like Paul was by his uncle. No matter the level of playing ability, they each receive a warm welcome and experience the same routine. Invariably it goes something like this.

Having established that their budget is in the £1-2k range, Dave will have laid out a choice of three to five fiddles on the counter in the shop. Usually, he will have got whoever is around in the shop to lend him a hand in this process, by giving them a play-over, just to wake them up a bit, for he himself doesn't play. When they arrive, the customer will be welcomed, told to take off their coat/jacket and handed a bow – and then left to get on with the playing-as-trying-out exercise. Some arrive with partners, or a friend, in tow; in which case they're told to 'take a seat'! Some are on their own. Most though are exceptionally nervous. As a result, trying/playing often is little more than a very cautious drawing of the bow over the open strings, or the occasional scale.

A case in point: one day just before Christmas 2022, a woman and her partner come into the shop to choose a fiddle, with a budget ceiling of £2k. As they come in, Dave says to the woman: "Put your fiddle there on a chair and take your coat off". Then, to her partner, "And you'd better take a seat – this might take a while!" The woman says to Dave: "Can I ask you a question? A concert violinist, if they played my £300 one, could they make my £300 one sound as good as their £30k one?" Dave: "They'd make it sound better! But no, it wouldn't sound concert level". The woman replies: "Mind I paid that 27 year ago for that". Dave: "Aye that's as maybe – but you just have yourself a go on these two and see which one you like. I'll just pop out the back – and you just give me a shout if you need me". Dave retreats to the workshop where I'm sitting drinking tea. He sits down in his chair and reverts to the repair job that he's working on.

From the workshop we can hear the woman tentatively strike the open strings with short, glancing bow strokes. She then asks her partner what he thinks: "I don't know", he says, "it's your job to choose!" Less than ten minutes pass before she calls out 'Hello' to summon Dave back to the shop – "I think I've decided on this one". He says, "Well now you need to compare that with the next one" handing her a German trade fiddle which he's adding to the mix. "But", he says, with a degree of understatement, "try some longer bows and play them for a bit longer, cos really you're not getting the best out of them". He comes back into the workshop and rolls his eyes. Another five minutes pass before she calls him back again. She admits: "I really can't hear any difference between these – they're all nice. I don't know how to choose". Dave does what he always does in these circumstances, where there's someone else to help proceedings along. Addressing the partner sitting on a chair, he says: "You turn round and listen to her playing them, and then you decide which is the best – after all, you're the one who's got to listen to this". They rearrange the chairs and then go through this version of a blind trial. The woman's partner decides that he likes the German trade fiddle best. "There you go!" says Dave. The woman's partner then buys her a bow as a Christmas present, on the grounds that a new instrument demands a new bow, and then a case, as they realise that they can't walk out of the shop carrying a violin and a bow. As they're settling up, Dave says: "Right; very good then. Your next step is *Britain's Got Talent*" Woman: "On no, I'm way too old for that!" She then proceeds to tell him how years ago she and two friends won a prize at a fete in Hartlepool – "We played an Irish jig –

mind we practised and practised for that". Her parting gesture is to ask Dave if he knows of anyone who teaches violin. She says, "I need a violin teacher so I can progress with my studies; you're never too old to learn. I'm 57 and I want to master this instrument – I've been playing 30 years". With a few phone numbers scribbled on a piece of paper, she leaves the shop with her Christmas present.

Mostly, the adult learners who come to Dave's shop to buy a violin have had a few more formal lessons. Retired GP Kevin Jones gives an indication of the kinds of back stories that are to be found. He begins by telling me: "I'm an instrumental idiot – without any doubt! When I was in my 30s I remember saying to someone, 'I have two regrets in life that I can talk about. One is not speaking another language; the other was I didn't play an instrument'. My parents were not musical; there was very little music in the house. My father did have an audiogram that I remember and when I was a teenager my mother had only two responses when I put a record on: one was 'that's awful – switch it off!' And the other was 'that's not too bad – switch it off'! When I was 11 or 12, I went to grammar school. We were in this big hall and we were all lined up and this enormous man, the head teacher, stood over me and said 'Sing, boy!!' Then he said, 'You're tone deaf; get out!' So that was my music education. We had music lessons after that which were dictated notes on the lives of the great composers. In my 30s, whoever it was who I spoke to said 'Well if it bothers you so much, do something about it'. I dabbled with a number of things. Then probably about 15 years ago I started playing ukulele with a guy called Ray Cowell who, he doesn't do it now, he made ukuleles".

I ask Kevin how he came to choose the ukulele. Kevin: "We used to go to Minsteracres for church, and we were running a stall one summer fete, and this ukulele band came and set up around us and I started singing with them. A number of them said 'I didn't even start till I was 70', so I started playing ukulele. I played with them for quite a few years; joined their band. I still play ukulele now – and I've got two lovely instruments made from the wood of the Olympic, the Titanic's sister ship. So, I've got two instruments made from wood that's at least a hundred years old. At least. They're very fine. Then I started going to Folkworks. Initially they had one of those taster days, and my wife said, there were six possibilities – 'You can do any of them you like apart from clog dancing! Please don't do the clog dancing!' I did tin whistle and graduated gradually onto flute, and I still play flute. Another of their taster days was a Saturday just on fiddle. And everyone always says the fiddle is very hard to learn, which it is, but I remember going to this taster day and thinking, well it's hard but it's not quite impossible. They had instruments they loaned you for the day. I came away thinking 'that was alright'. So, I thought, 'Maybe I'll buy a fiddle'. We're in Hexham, so I came to Dave's and I bought I think it was one of those Primavero ones. Then I joined some of the Folkworks things on the fiddle. When did I actually start? I'm not completely sure. I remember I started having lessons with Malcom Bushby in 2015 – so I've certainly been playing eight years; flute longer than that; ukulele longer than that".

He goes on: "I can't remember exactly when but I decided it was time to upgrade my fiddle. I came along to Dave and I gave him a budget and he said he'd prepare four or five fiddles. It was quite funny; I was having lessons with Malcolm at the time. And I'd said, 'instead of the lesson today, can you come to the shop and help me choose a fiddle'. I made the arrangement with Dave, and that day Malcolm was confined to bed, so he couldn't come. And I thought, 'Well Dave will have prepared these, I'll go along but not make a decision'. I came into the shop and Charlotte was here and Tom McConville was also here". Charlotte is Charlotte Hawes. She plays violin in the English National Ballet orchestra at London's Coliseum for part of the week, and for the other half teaches in local schools. She's also spent about twenty years helping Dave out in the shop. Tom McConville is a well-known folk fiddle player from Newcastle. Kevin: "So they said, 'Oh we'll help you choose a fiddle!' And Dave said, 'I've prepared four or five but I know which one you'll buy before you even start. So, I thought 'Oh, alright!' Tom said: 'Well I'll help because that'll mean I can have a go on it when you've chosen it!' And Charlotte said, 'Well I'll play both your existing fiddle and all these fiddles – and with your back turned. Then you can say whether you like it or not'. So, we carried on like that (with Charlotte playing the fiddles for Kevin to choose). And I said, 'Well I hope I'm being consistent!' And she went, 'Hmm – a little!' It was very interesting listening to a good person play because some of the fiddles sounded great in the lower register and some great in the highest, and one sounded good in both. And Dave said, 'that's the one I knew you were going to buy; as soon as people come in the shop, they buy them'. So that Gewa's the one I bought."

Kevin describes himself as "in the playing slow lane" with regards to learning traditional fiddle. But regardless of his playing ability he is now fulfilling a life ambition to play musical instruments, and he loves coming to the shop. As he says, "Dave has always made me very welcome". That is testimony to the inclusivity of the shop. It really doesn't matter whether you're a top folk fiddle professional like Aidan O'Rourke or Lauren MacColl, or a Kevin – the welcome will be the same. And ways can be found to help you choose an instrument, even if you can't play well enough to make that choice.

*

As he tells it, the beginnings of Kevin's fiddle playing journey lie, like so many adult learners in the Northeast region, with the beginner and lower intermediate classes run by Folkworks at The Sage in Gateshead – the very classes taught at one time by Carly Bain. Like much else in the Northeast traditional music scene, these classes trace back to the inspirational figure of Alistair Anderson, the English concertina and Northumbrian pipes player. It is Anderson who promoted the revival in Northumbrian folk music; who was a catalyst for the foundation of the Folk and Traditional Music Degree at Newcastle University, and who was a founder of Folkworks – a programme of activity which is the means to young people and adults discovering traditional music, initially through having access to try out playing instruments and then dedicated group-based instrument classes. Mickey Hutton (Chapter One) and his pal, Michael, met through these fiddle classes. Like Kevin, and many others, they have trodden the path to Dave's shop to buy a sequence of violins, from a basic starter kit through to a £1-2k instrument. They too are keen to share their stories with me.

    I begin talking with Mickey by asking him if he had always wanted to play fiddle: "Yes – but I'd never got time for it. I was always playing guitar. I went to London when I was 20 to play guitar". He shows me the Gibson he bought when he was 17: "my grannie lent me £250 to buy it and I've been all over the world with it." He then pulls down his Fender Stratocaster. I admire them and then ask: "So where did the desire to play fiddle come from?" Mickey: "Well, I come from a family of fiddle players apparently, but they're in New York. A grandad apparently – he was Irish. I'm not going to go 'Oh Bejesus '– you know. Not like the Americans, but the area I come from in Newcastle, it's very Irish. I look Irish. But what happened was, I was doing a guitar session for a well-known record producer. And I was chatting to him – actually, I'd done a mandolin session for him. So instead of paying me for the session he gave me this." Mickey shows me a Yamaha electric fiddle. "It's worth about a grand. He gave me this, and of course this doesn't make a noise. So, I played it when I was in hotels, and I was in hotels every night. I was entirely self-taught".

Decades later, and after having acquired a standard fiddle from someone else but with his fiddle playing having slipped into abeyance, Mickey and his wife Lesley returned to the Northeast, to live in the Tyne Valley. A casualty of the move was this fiddle. Mickey: "What happened was that Lesley dropped something on it – and the sound post went through the front and I didn't realise! She took it into Dave's shop to see if he could repair it and he went 'Nah; not worth it!' So that was that with that fiddle. And then what happened was, I was sitting here in my office one day, and this leaflet came through and it was for this thing at The Sage (it was an advertisement for the Folkworks classes). I used to go, well not quite on a run, but I went past Dave's and I thought 'Oh there's a fiddle shop there'. And I just went in. I had to pluck up courage to go in mind. I said I wanted a cheap fiddle to go to The Sage with and I got the starter one, which was shiny. And then I got another one for 600 quid, just to go to the lessons. Just to make sure I wanted to do it. But this is the fiddle I finally got off Dave; it's about 100 years old. It's a Jolley. He said, 'Take it home to try' – because by then I'd known Dave for a while – and I liked it."

The conversation turns to Michael's instrument-buying experience. I ask him what kind of instrument he's got. Mickey: "Well what happened was I went in with him. It was about 2019". Michael: "It's Russian. When I went in, he said 'How much do you want to spend?' And I said, 'Oh, about £1k'. And he brought out these three fiddles. 'Try them – try them with a bow'. And this one stood out, didn't it Mickey? Mickey: "Aye – straight away, because we both played it. It's a great fiddle". Michael: "And it feels great. And it's so easy to play".

I ask Michael and Mickey about going along together, and why that was. Mickey: "I think that was because I knew Dave a bit better". Michael: "I'd been in before, because I'd bought my first fiddle there – it was a lot cheaper! But I'd also been in because my daughter plays the cello, so we'd been in to get a new bow and strings and so on. But I didn't really know him." Mickey: "So I knew he wanted a new fiddle, so I said, 'Well look we'll both just go in'. And we went for a drink afterwards!" I say: "Well you've got to celebrate getting a new fiddle – it's a big day". They both agree. Michael smiles and nods, whilst Mickey says: "It is a big day!"

*

Someone else for whom going to Dave's was a big day is Des Dillon. Des is an internationally acclaimed writer of fiction, short stories, poetry and for TV, screen and radio. He's Irish-Scottish, from Coatbridge, on the outskirts of Glasgow, and is now living in Dumfries & Galloway. Whilst chatting with him recapitulates many of the points made by Kevin, Mickey and Michael, Des inevitably brings a writer's eye, perspicacity and turn of phrase to the experience of buying a violin at Dave's. Of all the people I've talked with about this, it's Des who manages to capture and bottle in words not just the uniqueness of that experience but also the magic. For Des – as for so many adults – going to Dave's, and coming out of there with a violin, his violin, has been life affirming and life transforming. The experience is not simply about fulfilling a life's ambition to play the fiddle, it changes lives.

We begin talking. Des describes himself as a musician in terms of 'level': as "a 'beginner/intermediate – folk fiddle. Irish. It's in my DNA. I'm from Coatbridge on the outskirts of Glasgow and it's got the biggest Irish population outside of Ireland. We all came from Donegal – and specifically central Donegal. Not even Donegal generally; central Donegal. Basically because of my Irish roots, I thought 'I'm going to learn how to play some of that music'. I thought, if I could play *Wild Mountain Thyme* that'd be enough for me. If I could play that one tune." I ask if he grew up around Irish music. Des: "No. That was lost by the time I was born. But I did hear what's 'mouth music' – all the women used to go, 'Hey-diddly diddly-diddly' when they were bouncing the kids and stuff. I thought nothing of it. And me auntie used to say, 'the words of every one of them, no matter what they say are My Auntie Mary had a Canary!' And every time I play a jig or a reel, I hear that line".

I ask Des when he first got a fiddle. Des: "I bought a fiddle when I was 50-odd. I thought, 'I want to take up an instrument' but it was a big mistake really because the fiddle's the hardest thing to play. I took lessons and I took my Grade 1 and Grade 2 with some eight-year-old girl. But what happened to me, I found that was stressing me out. I felt like I was being judged all the time. I'd got all prepared for Grade 3; I'd learnt all the tunes and that but I just could'nae be bothered, you know what I mean. I moved on to Grade 4 myself and then it kind of plateaued out. After eight years. Basically, I'm a working-class writer; and I was feeling that I shouldn't be doing this kind of music. Not that I shouldn't be doing it but that I should be concentrating on folk music. So, I sold the fiddle – it had cost me £1k".

Des's experience as an adult coming to formal lessons is a common one. The majority of violin teachers focus on classical tuition and organise their teaching by preparing students for the classical grade exams. Student progression is measured by those grades. It's a system designed to identify people who have the ability, discipline and temperament to go on to study at conservatoires – not for adult learners like Des. Sitting waiting for an exam alongside primary school age children, an adult can often feel like the proverbial square peg in a round hole; as not belonging, or worse, as Des articulates, as not having the right to play this kind of music. It's classic imposter-syndrome turf.

Des continues: "So, anyway, I sold the fiddle and then a few years later, I felt as though I needed a fiddle. I'd had three or four years of not playing and then there was this guy I know who's a windsurfer and I swapped him a board for a cheap fiddle. And I started playing that again. And then just as that happened, Claire's The Vault Project opened up." Claire is Dave's daughter Claire. The Vault Arts Centre is a community-run live music venue in Newton Stewart in Dumfries & Galloway in Scotland. The name comes from its being re-purposed from the building that previously housed a bank but which had long lain unused. The Vault is also a mini-version of Folkworks at The Sage, offering group classes in a range of traditional instruments – fiddle, tin whistle, flute, bodhran, guitar, mandolin, pipes etc. It was through Claire that I'd been put in contact with Des. I'd assumed that this was how Des had come to know about

Dave's, through Claire's recommendation. But no. Des: "That's not how I found out about Dave. I found out about Dave via a guy I know, who's a fiddler from Stranraer. I said to him, 'I need to get myself a better fiddle when I get back into it again'. And he said to me, 'the place to go is Hexham'". I ask Des how this guy had heard about The Violin Shop. Des: "I don't know but he said 'that's the place to go' and he's had two fiddles out of him. He said, 'he'll lay the fiddles out for you to try, and he knows your price bracket and he'll help you choose – and he doesn't go by the most expensive one'. And that's what I'd done before. I couldn't tell so I just picked the most expensive one. And then it was only about five or six weeks of going to Claire's classes that I suddenly realised, 'Hang on a minute; her name's Claire Mann!' 'Is that your dad?' And it was her dad!"

Word-of-mouth recommendation has always been one of the primary routes through which people come to Dave's door seeking to try, and potentially buy, a fiddle. Some of this is peer-to-peer recommendation amongst professional players, as with Lauren MacColl; some of it is about local area social networks, of teacher-pupil, like Kevin; or of people who meet through group fiddle classes at The Sage, like Mickey and Michael. But Des adds another dimension to this: from Stranraer to Hexham is no small distance to travel for an amateur player who is not on the quest for the perfect instrument; it's a good three-hour drive, often longer. Yet, Des is advised 'the place to go is Hexham'. It's a turn of phrase which indicates not just the geographical reach of 27 Hencotes but also the workings of insider fiddler knowledge – that people in-the-know know about this special place in Hexham.

Like Michael, Des took someone else with him to help him choose a fiddle: "I went down with a Zen Buddhist monk that I know, because he goes to a monastery down that way. Found the shop; it looked innocuous from the outside. Goes in; sees the fiddles hanging. It was like going back in time a hundred years. And then I went to the toilet – and that cemented it. I said to Claire, 'If you were looking for a film for a movie set, that's the place!' My father was a joiner; not that intricate [as luthier work] but he worked with wood. It's in my veins. It's the mess of a master craftsman; you know immediately that this is the mess of a master craftsman. The toilet was like going back in time too. He'd laid the fiddles out. My budget was up to £2k – and I couldn't play a thing. I couldn't even remember a tune. So, he said, 'I'll go through the back and you can just get on with it'. I picked the first fiddle – I played the G and when I played the G and the A strings it just rang. It rang out, sounded amazing. So, I put that one aside and tried these other ones. The Zen Buddhist guy, he was saying, 'Des, just play the same tune'. I managed to get something going. I think I played *The Rolling Waves*. And then I managed to play a bit better and a bit better. So, I eventually picked this fiddle – it was £1.25k; I think my budget was £1.5k actually. And I said, 'Well I might as well get a bow'. So, he laid some bows out. And I got a couple of those out and immediately I was playing better with one of those bows. And he was telling me about how you strike the bow, and how it resonates along the string – and I'd had like a big carbon bow. He came back out and said, 'You're a better fiddle player already'. He could hear the difference. So that gave me confidence and got me going."

In broad outline, Des's experience of trying-and-buying a violin at Dave's follows pretty much the same course as every other adult learner fiddle player I've observed in the shop. But he also highlights the importance of confidence to the choosing experience. Des recognises that it is Dave's unique style of engaging with people, through absence initially, which allows them to relax sufficiently to play well enough to be able to choose an instrument. In withdrawing from the shop, Dave removes any sense of performance from the space, allowing it to revert to a practice playing space, where one plays either alone, or with known others. I suggest this to Des: "Definitely. I felt stressed out to begin with but I left totally relaxed. In fact, I left the fiddles there to go and get something to eat. And even the Zen Buddhist was saying it felt very Zen. He didn't even need to go to the monastery! He could've stayed in the shop!" I ask Des what his friend had meant by what he'd said. Des replies: "He just meant ... I've spent a lot of time in monasteries, like this other guy has. When I walked into that shop, I got exactly the same kind of feeling. There's a sense of peace. Initially, I'd been quite apprehensive, because I knew I was going to have to play in front of somebody. That's why I was stressed out. But Dave's not there trying to sell you a violin. He's there to help you find a violin – that's what he does. That's his whole ethos. He said to me: 'You'll find the violin for you. You'll pick out one of these violins and it'll be yours'. And I picked up this one, it just felt great under my chin, and when I played it, it rang out. And it was the second cheapest one of the five he'd laid out." The fiddle Des chose is a German trade fiddle.

Reflecting further on his experience, Des says: "You get in that shop and you feel as if there's a kind of magic about that shop". I tell Des that he's not the first person to say this to me, and then ask him where he'd locate this magic quality. Des replies instantly: "Oh, it's in the wee guy who walks out. You could put another person in there in that shop and it isn't going to work. All that shop, it fell out of him. Every piece of that shop fell out of him. Every bit of that shop is an extension of who he is. That's how I feel in that shop".

I ask Des if he has ever been in another shop like this? He says: "Yes – once in my life. A shop in Kilsyth. Two old women ran it, and people used to go just to see the shop. They'd opened it in the 1930s and they were in their 90s. One was nearly 100. And they still worked the shop in the same way with the old till and that. They sold haberdashery. Socks, vests and stuff. Like Dave again, it wasn't what they sold though, it was them that made the shop what it was. It was a trip back in time."

Des reflects further on Dave: "That guy, you could put him anywhere. He has no aura or sense of ego. He's like a man with a certain power but no ego. He's almost a guru type of person. He's like the mentor you meet – he's the kind of guy who changes your life. In one pivotal moment you change direction. He's like a conveyor belt of spirituality. People come into his shop and they leave as a better human being in some way. I'd gone in there stressed out and I felt as if I could've stayed in there and played tunes all night. It's as if he's in some kind of fairy tale, and you leave there with a gift. The shop's a place of possibilities. It's like one of these Twilight Zone movies. And you come out with some kind of thing you didn't expect. I came out with the confidence to go forward with fiddle, which I didn't expect. It was a gift. In the six months I've had that fiddle I've become twice the fiddle player. Having that bow has made me a better fiddle player. Claire taught us a Tommy People's reel the other day, and I can play it now just like Tommy People's plays it. On my last fiddle, especially with that bow, it just wouldn't respond. I actually feel that now I'm a fiddle player. I walked in there and it was like opening up another road – Go Down There. That's what he's done. I play the fiddle for two hours a day. It's something I do every day; I love it; it's not something I even have to think about doing."

*

From the outside, 27 Hencotes may look like a shop; it's one shop in a row of other shops. But to see it as a shop that sells violins, violas, the occasional cello, bows and accessories, is to miss the point. Talking with those who go there to find a violin, it emerges more as a temporary staging post in the biographical and social life of these stringed instruments. The instruments located here are for sale, so technically they are goods, or commodities, just as with any other shop. But the instruments here are not just goods. They are all waiting to be found by the person for whom they sound, and with whom they connect – at which point they'll enter another phase of their social life, with that person, typically transforming that person's life. Dave is the custodian of these instruments. It's his task not to sell violins but to create the conditions in which people can find the instrument which sounds for them – whether they are looking for a sound which is an authentic extension or expression of themselves as a violinist or fiddler; whether they see that sound as a connection with their heritage and identity; or, whether their production of that sound is simply a means to fulfilling a lifelong ambition to play an instrument.

How Dave creates these conditions is by making a space outside of the ordinary world; where ordinary life with all its distinctions and social differences is suspended. Des uses the words 'mysticism' and 'spirituality' to sum up how he thinks of Dave's shop. He says to me: "You'll be aware of Simone Weil. She spoke of a place above evil and above conflict and all that, where people can communicate, where you can get an idea for say like a short story because someone else has had that idea; it's in the ether. It's a place where people can communicate in spite of their differences. Well not even in spite of, more beyond their differences. I felt that kind of thing in the shop. It didn't matter how bad or how good I was on the fiddle, all that mattered was that I played the fiddle". And that, I feel, is exactly what the shop is. It's a space dedicated to everyone who loves to play and appreciate the sound of the fiddle, regardless of who they are and what music they play; regardless of their abilities as a player; which gathers those people to it, and which creates often lifelong attachments between people and fiddles. And at its heart is its curator/magician; a working class lad from Benwell, a drummer and accidental luthier, who doesn't play. Go figure!

Nicky Gregson

CHAPTER FIVE

The Fiddle Assistants

Sales assistants in violin shops are retail assistants with a difference. Since violins sell themselves, through sounding with a particular person, an assistant is not there to sell these goods. At most, they might demonstrate them to someone who is uncertain in their capacities to choose – as with Kevin in the previous chapter. Mostly though, these assistants are there to play the violins that are in a shop; they are part of a stock care and maintenance regime – for, unlike all manner of retail goods that are held as stock in shops, typically in boxes, packaging and containers, violins are goods that need active tending.

Violins for sale may be placed in glass cases and in cabinets, in the manner of curated museum objects, or hung on racks, like clothing or bikes, but they are goods that cannot just be left as displayed stock – at least, not without consequences. This is because violins are tantamount to living things. They're not quite that, of course, for trees felled are dead wood, but there is an unmistakeable element of caring going on in all violin shops. It's not just that, like all wooden things, violins react to the temperature and humidity changes in a shop and to the changing seasons, expanding and contracting accordingly. It's also that instruments for sale are kept under tension, ready to play. This means that they need to resonate, which means that instrument stock needs to be played. More than this, these instruments need to be played fairly often. If they're not played, they will 'go to sleep', as it's called by players –

or, shut down, become less responsive, and generally not sound as well as they might. This will potentially affect sales for, if it is to connect with a potential buyer, generally an instrument needs to be sounding well. This is one of the main reasons why major dealerships employ playing assistants.

Not being a player himself, Dave has always needed playing assistants to keep his fiddle stock sounding well. Even if he was a player, he'd probably still need them, such is the volume of luthier work coming in to the shop, be that making fiddles, repairing and maintaining ones that are brought in, and restoring them. But non-playing luthiers certainly do need playing assistants to support their workshops. From basic annual maintenance work, through set-ups to minor repairs, and thence to major repairs, the work of the workshop needs to be checked over for its effects on instrument sounding. Whilst it's possible to hear some of the effects by plucking the individual strings and by drawing a bow across open strings, ultimately, assessing the effect of repair and maintenance work on sounding can only be done through playing. Then there are the much bigger workshop projects – the restoration jobs, and making a fiddle. In both cases, players are necessary to initiate a fiddle's journey to, or return to, resonance. Players are needed to answer the question: 'what kind of instrument is this?' Not as an object but as a sounding thing.

*

The importance of having playing assistants around to answer those questions is well to the fore one day in the shop. This was a day on which Dave had arranged to go and collect his new car from a garage in Newcastle, a task which would occupy a good couple of hours. To keep the shop open, he left myself and his friend Freddie Thompson in charge – or, as he called it, "promoted to temporary shop assistants". Earlier that morning, Dave had just finished completing the annual maintenance and set-up of Kevin Jone's fiddle. A few years after purchasing his Gewa fiddle (Chapter Four), Kevin had come into some money and had decided he wanted to use that money to purchase a Dave Mann fiddle. Kevin explains: "I think it's very important to have an instrument that you know who made it. It's particularly good to have instruments where you know, or have a connection with, the maker". So, just as with his flutes and whistles, Kevin decided to commission a fiddle from Dave. Like mine, it's made on Dave's Guadagnini model and he got it in 2019.

Before he left the shop to head to the garage, Dave handed me Kevin's fiddle, saying "here, have a go on this. See what you think of this one". As I started playing it there was something clearly not right with this fiddle; it wasn't sounding to me like a Dave Mann fiddle normally sounds, and certainly nothing like my own. Dave looked at me as I started to make a face and then said, "It's not happy; it's not sounding". Dave evidently agreed, but with no time to hang around, he grabbed his car keys and went out the door, saying "just thrash it!" Freddie and I took Dave literally at his word. For well over two hours we took it in turns to give Kevin's fiddle a thorough work out, switching between vigorous Scottish strathspeys and Django Reinhart jazz style. Initially, we were perplexed. Freddie: "Normally, I like Dave's fiddles but I wouldn't choose this one" he says. I agree with him, as we start comparing this instrument up against Freddie's fiddle. It's currently no contest; we'd both choose Freddie's. Eventually, after an hour or so has passed, it begins to dawn on me what's up with it. Mulling over what's in my mind, I say: "You know what Freddie, I don't think this fiddle has ever really been played. It's just not resonating. It's as if it doesn't know how to". Freddie pauses for a moment to think and says: "I think you're right. You've hit the nail on the head there!" Rather than thrashing it, I change tack with the fiddle thinking – 'right, you need to learn how to sound'.

Kevin's Dave Mann fiddle is an example of what happens to a fiddle that has never really come alive through play. Because Kevin, by his own admission, is "in the playing slow lane", it's never yet been played in a way which asks it to resonate fully. So, when Freddie and I took turns on it, it was being asked questions that it wasn't really sure that it knew how to answer. It felt if not exactly new, more unawakened.

Another version of the same problem exists with fiddles which have been played in the past, but which have lain unplayed for years. These instruments, once they are played again, sound initially as if they've been dormant or in hibernation. "Sleepy" (or, slow and unresponsive) is a term players sometimes use to describe this state and playing – a lot of playing - is the means to their re-awakening. But these instruments also carry a memory of having been played in a particular way, and having learnt to resonate in a particular way. Whilst they will work for another, it's as if they carry within them a pattern of playing and resonating that is their playing history. Kevin's fiddle was not like this; because of how it had been played it was almost as if it didn't yet have a playing history.

Eventually, by the time Dave returned to the shop, the fiddle was finally starting to open up a bit. I played it for Dave. He then immediately moved the sound post over to the AE side of the fiddle, and "bingo – there you go!" The fiddle started to sound more like a Dave Mann fiddle can.ABve, evidently relieved, says: "Right, now I can ring Dr Dolittle (his nickname for Kevin) to tell him his fiddle is ready for collection". Five minutes later and Kevin comes in to the shop. Dave tells him: "These two have been giving your fiddle a bit of a work-out. Give it a go and see how it sounds now!" He picks it up but, minus any music, and with an audience, struggles to think of anything to play. Freddie picks up his fiddle and starts to help things along before trying to teach him some new tunes, in so doing turning the shop space, as he often does, into a session space (pictured). For 40 minutes Kevin had Freddie's undivided attention – playing away with him whilst Dave and I retreated to the workshop, and yet another repair job. Kevin's parting gesture, as he left the shop to make sure he hadn't got a parking ticket, was to say "Crikey, look at the time. I said to my wife I'd only be 10 minutes; she'll be wondering where on earth I've got to!"

*

Freddie and I are examples of Dave's casual playing assistants. We are just some of the regulars who come into the shop currently whom he can ask to play whatever job he's finished off in the workshop. We get a cup of tea, a biscuit and a chat and – in return – we give whatever it is that's come off the workbench a bit of a work out. Or, we play a selection of instruments to wake them up ahead of a customer coming in to buy a violin. This is an instance of a highly social, non-monetised, economy; one in which Dave's warmth and hospitality is exchanged for access to our playing skills. Over the years, though, there have been way more accomplished players than either myself or Freddie who've performed the same role, and in a paid capacity –as casual, 'flexible' labour. Who are these assistants? What type of players are they? What did Dave get them to do in the shop? And how has working in this capacity for Dave affected their lives?

*

Dave's chief playing assistant for the past several years has been someone who is not really an assistant at all. Rather, Martin Hughes describes himself as "the test pilot". The phrase captures precisely his playing role in the shop, for Martin doesn't play any old instrument that happens to be in the shop. Instead, Martin only plays the significant violins that come out of the workshop. He has played every single one of the Guadagnini copies which Dave has made since 2018. He also plays the discoveries, or 'finds' – the rare violins that find their way through the shop door. And he plays Dave's major violin restoration projects.

But, when he plays these instruments, Martin isn't really playing. He's in test pilot mode. Having witnessed such a test with Dave's latest Guadagnini copy, I later ask him what he's seeking to find in subjecting an instrument to the test regimen. He says: "the basic requirements are 'Does this violin pass muster?' You look at F – first finger E; third finger A; second finger D – and then, 'How far does it go up [the E string]?' You want to see if it goes right up to the top". He describes it as a regimen that's "a thorough test of any instrument". Playing here, then, isn't what most people would understand by playing. Rather, it is a test of an instrument's full capacities in sounding. So, the instrument is positioned in a regime which is about finding its limits in sound; or, said another way, it's tested to find its point of failure. We are back with Manoug Parikian and proving his Bellini Guarneri copy to destruction (Chapter Four).

Playing as testing is not about seeking connection with an instrument. Instead, it's all about establishing whether an instrument is up to the exacting performance demands that will be placed on it by a classical soloist/leader. Only if that's answered in the affirmative can the qualities of connection begin to be admitted. Is it any wonder, then, that on the day that Martin was due to come in to play the latest Guadagnini copy to come out of the workshop, Dave was apprehensive? He knew what lay in store for it. "The proof of the pudding", he'd always said to me whilst he was making this instrument "is will it play? Everything can look good from my perspective, me arches and that can look great, but it's no good if it doesn't sound right. If it doesn't sound right it might as well go in the bin". He'd given me the fiddle to play first – a real honour – "but the ultimate test will be when Martin arrives. We'll see what he says". A while later Martin walks into the shop. He takes a bow out of the bow cabinet. Dave looks on, doing a passable imitation of any parent watching powerless whilst their child attempts something for the first time. Such is the pressure, he almost cannot bear to watch and hear. The verdict? Martin: "That's a really good test for anything. I walked in here reckoning 'I know how it'll be', and that hasn't been shaken. It works – very much so. It's balanced and it's going to be good". Dave visibly relaxes; his work for the last year and a half has passed the test pilot's examination.

The intensity of the playing examination for the various 'finds' and restoration projects is exactly the same. But tellingly, for Dave the intensity on these occasions is way less felt than occurs when his own instruments are being put to the test. This is because the work Dave invests in these instruments is all about seeking to return to playing condition something that has already been made. It's about salvage and rescue, not making something new. Such work will always bear the trace of the original maker; it's never fully Dave's – and indeed, post-restoration it will always be known by the name of its original maker, or at the very least its area of provenance. Witness the Old Bohemian and Henry Lockey Hill cellos in Chapter Three. The restorer here is rendered invisible by the act of restoration. Then, there is always the 'get out' – that the restoration might not be fully successful. This much is known. As Martin says in relation to an early Degani restoration project of Nial and Dave's, "I couldn't make it work, and they couldn't get it to play. That's always the risk with restoration projects".

To see Martin simply as Dave's test pilot, though, would be wrong. As someone who has spent most of his life playing and living with violins, Martin is also the ultimate connoisseur-enthusiast. What comes into Dave's shop therefore is the source of continual interest and pleasure; it's a means both to satisfy his enthusiasm and to grow his already expansive knowledge about violins as objects. Many hours are occupied in what he calls "disappearing down the rabbit hole of instrument and bow identification". Talking with him, he describes the pleasure he took in "a recent quarry". Martin: "We had one here for about four or five weeks. Was it, or was it not, a Joseph Rocker? For all the world it said Rocker. I went online and looked at all the labels and to be honest there wasn't one that looked like that. I'm naturally suspicious – I had a little bit of form with

Rockers and non-Rockers. There was one that turned up in Stockton and became known as the Stockton Rocker, which wasn't – but it looked like one. I decided this Rocker wasn't a Rocker. It plays very well, although there's an element of 'wolf' where you didn't want it. Dave did some tweaks, but I wouldn't trust it". Martin's reference to trust here is double-edged. He wouldn't trust this violin as a playing instrument, and he didn't trust what it purported to be as a violin. It's a disposition that is well attuned to the violin world's issues with fakes and copies. Less uncertain in its identification was a violin that came into the shop a few months later.

One quiet morning in the shop, Dave starts telling me about "a woman who's posing me a bit of a dilemma". He begins by explaining that the woman's children are both taught by Martin. "One's doing Grade 5 and one's doing Grade 8, and they're both doing very well but there's a big but. She came in on Saturday with that one [a basic kit violin that's now on the front desk of the shop] but she also brought in another two violins that she has. There's one that belonged to her mother and then there's another one that belonged to the grandmother. And the one that belonged to the grandmother is a Johannes Cuypers (known as the Dutch Stradivarius). I had one. I bought it off this fella, a box of like 70 pieces, all disintegrated; like a jigsaw. The back and the belly were in two separate halves, so I rebuilt it – a complete restoration. I give him £4k, about 20 years ago. I sold it four years ago for £45k. But they haven't got a clue." It being a quiet day we start scouring the internet looking at images of Cuypers violins. As we do so, Dave is comparing the images on the screen with pictures in his head, of the one he had and of the one that came into the shop the previous Saturday, and which he had only had a quick look at.

As we look, I'm acutely aware of just how little I'm seeing in these images compared to Dave. Whereas I see only the broadest of differences, he's seeing miniscule ones, even with images that are intentionally put up under low resolution – a necessity to foil copyists. Dave: "When I get the fiddle back in the shop I need to check. This is different. See the bee stings on hers go straight through ... I need to see the f holes, and the scrolls are very distinctive. They're very rough on a Cuypers. See that's different to the one I had. Now, this one (on the Christie's site) is similar to the one I had. Mine didn't have long corners like that though. This one is a Johannes Theodoros ... Mine was like that – similar type of varnish, like that; 1790s. This one (on another site) is 1804." Still not quite satisfied, Dave then turns to a Dutch website. "Blunt corners – that's it! And there's the sting going straight to the edge. The fs are similar. This is like what I saw the other day but I didn't say anything. I'll wait till I get it back in and check it against this one. Same label – handwritten, and mine was handwritten. Aye – and a dropped saddle – theirs has got a dropped saddle. So aye – I think it is. Eeee, moral dilemmas! She said [to me], 'out of the two which one would you pick for her?' And then she's got another one as well. So I said, 'bring them all in'. I don't even know what the third one is. It might be something even better! They're bringing the lassie in – so I might say 'pick what you like'. And then they might just say, 'get rid of the other two'; and then what do you do? At the end of the day it's got a crack under the bass bar. Dilemma! I'll just have to play it by ear! When they brought it in and I saw the scroll, I thought 'Christ! That looks familiar'. And I looked at the f holes and stuff, 'Hmm'. And then I looked inside – Johannes Cuypers"!

A week or so later, on my next visit to Dave's, the Cuypers is in the workshop, along with the other violin, but both of the instruments had come in via Martin. With the general busy-ness of choreographing family life, getting to the shop had got too complicated, so the violins had made it as far as the lessons – and Martin, acting as the courier, did the rest. Looking at it, Dave is now certain of its authenticity: "It's not a copy – I've got to set it up, put a new bridge on and then Martin will play it. Obviously, we'll need a second opinion. I'll send pictures, either to Tim Toft or one of the auction houses." Dave gets the Cuypers out of its case for me to see. What interests me as much as the violin is the papers that are accompanying it. They start to fill in the social and biographical life of this instrument. This is something that also interests Martin, and together we begin to research how this instrument, made in 1797, came to be in the hands of this family. It's a story that connects a jute magnate in Dundee with warehouses in Amsterdam. As so often with violins it's about lines of trade and commerce, for a significant maker's violins, like art, follow money. Tracing those connections doesn't just bring to life the back story of this violin; it gives further credence to its identification as a Cuypers. And then there are the papers that testify to the violin's more recent life. I point these out to Martin one day when he's come into the shop, as a displacement activity from practising. They're old concert programmes from

The Violin Shop

private schools and academies – of concerts that this violin has evidently been played in, for he recognises the mother's mother's name amongst the lists of orchestra string players. But there are other names too that are familiar to him: "Well, well, well!" he exclaims, as the connections between people he's known as players and certain private schools comes to light.

Martin's role as the violin research assistant for Dave's shop is well to the fore in the Cuypers story, where his passion and enthusiasm for violins complements the eagle-eye of Dave, who sees the same instrument but entirely through lutherie craft and financial value. Its social and biographical life is of no interest to him. With the repairs completed, though, it's back to test pilot mode for Martin – but for once this is conducted at Martin's, as the family decide to keep the fiddle for the daughter to play, rather than sell it. Martin reports back: "Does it play! But you left a fair amount of wood in the bridge". Dave: "I did. Yes – it's me new technique!" Martin: "it works! It sounds beautiful." And then the two men switch to the next fiddle in the family's collection, which is now sitting on Dave's workbench. Martin: "What is it?" Dave: "It's nice; it might be old English". Martin: "Is that a new neck?" Dave: "it's had a new - no, it hasn't had a new neck" Martin: "I think it's had a new neck". Dave disagrees. Inspecting the instrument more closely, he pronounces: "The neck's been out, and they've smashed the button, and they've thought, 'Oh we'll inlay a new ebony piece in here'". And so it goes on – an endless cycle of curiosity, fascination and speculation, fuelled by the latest significant instrument to be lying on the bench.

*

Whereas Martin brings a lifetime's knowledge and experience to bear to playing and listening in test-pilot mode, Dave has had a number of playing assistants over the years who have been at the very start of their careers as classical violinists. Some of them have been Saturday assistants – the equivalent of the Saturday sales assistants which the retail sector has long relied on. Some have worked a regular week day for a few years, and others have been at the shop for short periods of 'work experience'. Talking with just some of these individuals brings home just how significant working as a playing assistant for Dave has been for them, in terms not just of their career development but also wider lives.

Rebecca Howell (Chapter Four) worked at Dave's during Sixth form, on Saturdays. "It was casual work; very informal. He said, 'Just come in for a couple of Saturdays (a month)' and he'd give me a £20 note at the end of the day". Her tasks included cleaning the shop and going to Greggs (a Northeast institution) to buy Dave his lunch of choice: "Sausage rolls! Or a ham and pease pudding sandwich from Cranstons, the butchers! And I played the violins when customers came in. Often when they'd chosen one he'd make them turn around and I'd play their selection again without them being able to see which violin was which".

Abigail Strike is mostly a classical player – "violin and cello in the main". She also toured with the Sunderland band, *Futureheads*: "You'll find a Guardian article on it. The lead singer did some solo work and composed some music for stringed instruments, and we toured in 2016 around festivals and things like that. After that I went into the teaching, schools and privately". Abigail also plays for weddings. Previously though, "from when I was about 18 I used to go in the shop all the time. And one day Dave said 'I need an extra hand'. So I used to go in one day a week, for maybe a couple of years. I'd do anything he asked me to do, like go to the shop and buy some milk. He'd often get me to play the violins; to play them in. To check if there were any wolf notes or things that weren't sounding right on them. He knew I'd check them and the fingerboard to see if there were any dud notes that weren't sounding properly. And then he'd always get a tool out and if there was something that didn't sound right he'd always change the sound post."

I asked Rebecca about her experience of playing different violins in Dave's. Rebecca: "I suppose when I was 16 I hadn't really played many different violins. I didn't really know what sound I liked at all. I hadn't tried my violin before I bought it; it was just what I had. At the time I remember thinking out of all the violins I'd played at Dave's, I still liked the one I had. So it gave me confidence in that. But I'd never thought about the difference between a dark sound or a bright sound. I also think that the other thing that I hadn't really thought about until being there was how important the balance of the sound across the instrument is. It could have a really bright E string which didn't blend with the sound across the rest of the violin. Or a really gritty G string or something".

At the same time as playing, Dave involved both Rebecca and Abigail in everyday violin care. Abigail: "After watching him do lots of instruments he'd give me simple little jobs like 'clean this in between this peg'." Rebecca: "I remember once cleaning all the violins hanging in the front of the shop and he gave me like a tub full of soapy water and a paint brush! Even now, if we're playing outside, and there are three spots of rain, all my friends will put their violins away, that's what I think about. Scrubbing them all with water! So if I get three specks of water on my violin I'm not worrying about it, because I've seen what Dave does with them! I became much less precious about violins as a result of working there." Abigail: "And then there's his polish that he puts on at the end. That's got a really interesting smell, but it brings the violins up really well. But it's always secret. He'd bring the batches out and say, 'can you mix this up from these little tiny bottles'. And I'd say, 'What's in it?' And he'd say, 'That's for me to know!' (pictured – Dave mixing his "potions"). Abigail continues: "I sit here and think 'My violin never looks as good as when it's just come out of Dave's with this fresh polish on and it's all clean'. He's got his own really quirky methods; I think it's brilliant."

Watching Dave work was also an opportunity for both Rebecca and Abigail to ask questions and to reflect on his working practices. Abigail: "I was always asking questions. I'd take lots of tips and I'd ask him lots of questions about why he was doing certain things; I must have asked him millions of questions to the point I sent him insane!" Rebecca: "I remember his problem solving. I remember thinking that there was this standard way of repairing violins, of doing cracks. But I remember him saying 'What can I do with this?' And him using random bits of wood shavings lying on the floor. 'Will this fit in the gap?' I think that has definitely affected my relationship with my violin. I just don't feel as delicate about it. I almost don't want to say that because everyone else is so precious about them."

Whereas Rebecca worked for Dave as a Saturday assistant before heading to university, for Abigail time spent working for Dave was more open-ended. She characterises her time with Dave as "mostly something to do at a time when I was still really young and working out what I wanted to do with my life." In the same way that Des Dillon (Chapter Four) identified the shop's other-wordly, transcendent qualities, working at Dave's gave Abigail the space and time to work that out; as it has done for many young musicians. Abigail: "He was very, very kind to me when I was younger. He was always very kind and very, very generous and it was just nice. My favourite thing was when he'd get violins out and I'd play them and I'd say 'How much is this?' '£250k!' Ah well that's a shame!"

It was through the shop that Abigail met Peter Tickell (Chapter Two), whom she later married. Reflecting back, she says: "I then moved away from the shop, and more into a life I suppose!" Talking separately with Peter, he tells me: "I met my wife through Dave, through The Violin Shop! We didn't actually meet in The Violin Shop but we wouldn't have met without that – so I met my wife thanks to Dave! She was working in the shop helping Dave." Laughing, Abigail tells me: "I used to help clean up Peter's violin. After most of his tours he'd have it serviced. And Dave used to get me to take all the pegs out and clean it up. And once I'd cleaned it all he'd put the bridge back on and the strings back on and the tailpiece. Then he'd get me to try it out to make sure it sounded alright. And I remember one day he said, 'Well what do you think?' And I didn't know anything about this violin. He knew I was always brutally honest and I said 'I don't like it'. And he said 'You don't like it?! It's Peter Tickell's!' And I said, 'Who's he?' 'Who's he?!! He plays with Sting!!' And I went – 'Oh! Oh right!!' And he said, 'And you still don't like the violin?' And I said, 'No; it's too chunky. I don't like it.'"

Abigail and Rebecca both spent the best part of two years working for Dave. By contrast, Magdalena Loth Hill only had a week's work experience there, whilst she was at secondary school, but the influence of Dave's is no less profound. Magdalena is now based in London and plays baroque and modern violin, as both a soloist and ensemble player. She plays and tours extensively with the critically acclaimed Consone String Quartet.

Magdalena hails originally from Cumbria. She tells me: "I grew up between Hexham and Carlisle – near Brampton. I had a local teacher, Carol Head. Just before my fifth birthday I got a violin and I started with her, and I stayed with her up until about 11. She knew Dave – I don't know how. I suppose it's a small world. Originally we went to Mick Johnson [a well-known luthier in Penrith]. I started off getting all my violins and bows from him, and then he tragically died in a cycling accident. And then Carol had started going to Dave, and so I went along, for various things. I had a Mirecourt violin from Mick Johnson that I was still using and then Carol very kindly lent me a Forster violin that she had. I was playing on that for a while, and at that stage I didn't need a new instrument." What Magdalena did need, though, was a better bow – one that would match with this instrument. By then she was studying at Chetham's in Manchester, but she still went to Dave's to find the bow: a Walter Violet. Magdalena: "I just went into Dave's shop and said, 'I need a bow!' And he was very kind and I was able to take it away for a while to try it and it turned out that that was the bow that worked best with that violin. I really liked it. I learnt a lot from that bow actually".

It was through a short period of work experience in the shop, though, that Magdalena feels that she learnt the most from Dave. She begins describing this by saying: "I just had a really nice week with a great person". A good, fun experience is what Dave tries to give all work experience students. Magdalena elaborates: "I mostly played the violins! It was a real privilege actually. I got to play some lovely instruments; I polished some instruments and I went next door to the sandwich shop to get our lunch." As with Rebecca, playing so many instruments proved formative: "I don't know if I played everything but I did play quite a few of those hanging in the cabinets. That was interesting actually because I hadn't played many different violins, so to have that opportunity was incredibly educational. To have the opportunity to play a lot of different instruments; you learn so much. It opens up your ears to the whole possibility of different sounds. Otherwise you just think, 'My violin – that's how a violin sounds'. But no. There are so many more options – and actually there were more sounds that I could discover on my own violin, having played all of these instruments. It was hugely educational. At that point in my learning that was really eye opening for me. It was very useful. I did benefit from that. It's often the case that if you borrow a violin from the college say, or from a foundation, you're just given that violin and that's the violin that you use and you don't really have the opportunity to try different violins. But the opportunity to be able to try different violins is really inspiring actually."

Rebecca and Magdalena highlight how playing a variety of instruments isn't something that most people encounter when learning the violin. Rather, the common experience is to play just the instrument one plays on. Down the line, I would argue, this has effects. Sound becomes tone, but tone becomes seen as the product of the player. It's about what they are seen to 'get out of' an instrument. This is often a relation of dominance, and a celebration of human agency, and it comes to its peak expression in virtuosity. What can get lost here, I think, is what can be termed fiddle agency, and the accommodation of instrument and player in that sound production. An early appreciation of the difference between different violins, however, affords the development of a more accommodative and collaborative approach to sounding. This is what Magdalena is recognising as having gained in her work experience. Having the opportunity to play all these violins is not just educational in itself. It also opens up to her a world of different sounding possibilities. Her work experience sets her off on what I would term a dialogic encounter; one that's not just about exploring the possibilities afforded by these multiple instruments but about experimenting with her own instrument's sound world/colour as a result of that. My sense is that this, in turn, lays the foundations for her later ensemble work, where it's not so much just what this or that instrument can (and can't) do that matters, but how this instrument compares with, and folds with, others' sound worlds. Being a playing assistant in Dave's, then, is a means to sensitising ears to becoming a better all-round musician.

Reflecting even more about her experience, Magdalena emphasises how much just being in the shop also taught her. She feels this has reaped dividends as her professional career has developed. She says: "I just watched Dave work, and how he interacted with people as well. I think that's a big part too; even of being a performing musician. It's how you interact with people. How you form those kinds of relationships. I think I learnt a lot by just watching him work; just the kind of warmth and just being very ready to talk to anybody. That made an impression on me. And the investment in the community; really being present and a part of what's going on locally is so important, I think. Even things as simple as leaflets put up in his window. That kind of thing – I thought it was so nice. And so many people see those things and it's a great way of interacting with the community and supporting the people around you".

Magdalena pinpoints here the intangible, soft skills of being able to make meaningful connections with all types of different people from different walks of life – skills which she feels have transferred across to her performance career. She also clocks the shop's presence as a hub in the local community. Yet what sticks most for her, lingering in her memory, is the shop's unique smells. She says: "There's just something about a luthier shop – the smell; fresh wood. And Dave makes this amazing varnish reviver. I'm eking it out; it's the best! I've never found anything that works as well. That stuff is amazing. It's the bottled smell of an amazing luthier. It's like a potion place! I just find it such a magical place. He's so calm and he's just such a great guy. He's so patient and meticulous. And he's also so approachable. Anyone can talk to him about anything. That atmosphere is the shop, I think"

*

For other young classical violinists, assisting in Dave's shop has provided them with a perhaps more predictable step on the way to a professional career. It's been the means to finding *that* instrument; the one which will help them to stand out from a host of other supremely talented students. Competition at conservatoire level is intense, and – like any high performance activity – margins of differentiation between students are fine. This is something Dave knows well, through his daughter Sarah having attended the Purcell School and then the Guildhall. Having a good instrument isn't just desirable; it's essential. It's not just that such an instrument (and bow) is likely to produce marginal gains in performance; it will also command attention from tutors – for, just as in Dave's workshop so too in conservatoires. Rare and fine instruments inexorably attract curiosity and interest; the very best of them are fetishised. And then, having access to a good instrument also solves the post-conservatoire instrument problem (Chapter Four). So, for budding professional players, working as a Saturday assistant in a violin shop makes a huge amount of sense – it's a way to potentially luck-out in the instrument stakes.

Rhiannon and Clemmie Germaine are two sisters who - like Rebecca, Abigail and Magdalena - grew up in relative geographical proximity to the shop, in their case in rural Northumberland. Both worked in Dave's as Saturday assistants. Subsequently, both have gone on to study in London, at the Royal College of Music and the Guildhall respectively – in both cases playing instruments that they have on loan from Dave, who restored both instruments. In Rhiannon's case, the violin is a Calcunius [1706-9]. Clemmie's, though, is of uncertain provenance. Dave tells me: "Nobody knows what it is, but it's mid-to-late 18th century, like Bavarian on the borders with Italy type of thing. It's very Italian but the experts say it's not Italian! So, because it's over the border it's only worth £20-30k; if it had been over the border it would've been worth way more. That's the game! It stood in the back machine shop for 20 years, in bits like – a bit like the cello (Chapter Three). Then when I'd restored it, Martin was 'What is it? It's fantastic!' We thought it was a Camillo Camili – Old Italian, £300k. But it isn't. But it does sound like very expensive Old Italian. Clemmie took it down to the Guildhall, and her teachers – all of them on half a million pound jobs - are saying 'What's this? It plays better than mine!"

Since Clemmie was snowed under with 'uni work' when I was doing the interviews for this book, it was just Rhiannon I talked with about her time in the shop. This began when she was very small, around five, when she was sent by her first teacher, Magdalena Reid, to get an instrument. Her first proper violin was a half-sized; then came a three-quarter, both of them on loan from Dave. These less-than-full-sized quality instruments have served a generation of talented child violinists in the Northeast. They've been important stepping stones in a trajectory towards advanced study. Subsequently, once she needed a full-sized violin, Rhiannon progressed to instruments loaned from the Benslow Trust, which gives talented young UK musicians affordable access to high quality instruments. By this stage in her life, Dave's shop had become a constant presence.

Rhiannon's fascination with violins meant that she had begun to hang out at Dave's from the time that she first went to middle school in Hexham, aged nine. Dave's shop, rather than the corner of the street or the sweet shop, or the park, would be where she would wait to be picked up after school – and it could be anything from 20 minutes to a two-hour wait. So for her at this time Dave's was a glorified after-school club. Whilst Rhiannon was there she'd play the violins, and give Dave her opinion on them. At 14, Rhiannon

– like Magdalena – went to Chetham's, in Manchester, as a boarder. But she came home at weekends, later working as a Saturday assistant, just like Rebecca. As well as playing the violins, she'd demonstrate them for customers, and Dave began to teach her the basics of cleaning, instrument maintenance and bow re-hairing.

Unsurprisingly, this degree of hanging out has led to close social ties. Rhiannon describes Dave as "My honorary grandad". She says: "I've spent more time with him than with my actual grandparents". And so central was Dave, and the shop, in her young life, that she invited both him and Charlotte Hawes (Chapter Four) to her tenth birthday party, held in a big barn in rural Northumberland. This special relationship – what sociologists and anthropologists call 'pseudo kin' – manifests in the instrument which Rhiannon currently plays, and in one of the gifts which the Germaine sisters have received.

Rhiannon tells me about how one day, when she was in the shop, Dave had her trying once again to impose a degree of order on what is generally recognised, even by Dave, to be organised chaos or disorganised mess. She had been set to work on a tangled web of bows. Many such piles continue to lie around the shop. These bows currently reside in a laundry basket behind the shop counter; on top of every filing cabinet in the workshop, and on all the side benches. There are hundreds and hundreds of them. Many is the time when I've been in the shop, or the workshop, tasked with looking for something when these bows literally start cascading everywhere – to the point where I'll exclaim: "Dave, it's raining bows!" So, Rhiannon's task for that day was a familiar one. But as she was sorting through these bows, disentangling them from one another, she discovered something that was in her words "a find". This was a really good bow, which Dave, typically, had long forgotten he'd got. Such discoveries have happened more than once. Rhiannon says: "At the time, Clem needed a good bow. So what does Dave do? He says I can have it – as a gift for Clemmie. No charge!"

Rhiannon's own special gift is the loan of Dave's restored Calcunius. She describes herself as "beyond fortunate to have been loaned this instrument, which she could never have afforded", and regards it as an instrument to which she has a special attachment. Violins, she says, especially these sorts of violins, require you to play with them, not expect them to play as you want them to. They require a partnership, an approach that is accommodative and exploring of possibilities, rather than dominating and demanding. For Rhiannon, the bond between her and this instrument goes even deeper because she's been its player post its restoration. Although Dave's playing assistants all tried it and liked it, it was Rhiannon for whom the instrument first really worked, once it had been reassembled from bits. She is the person who has played it back to life, and with whom it's learnt to resonate again, beginning at Chetham's. At the time she still had an Old English violin on loan from the Benslow Trust, but it was playing the Bach Partitas for her tutor there which cemented the bond with the Calcunius once and for all. Rhiannon tells me that her tutor played the instrument first and wasn't sure about it. There are issues of balance, in that it has a really sweet, outstanding E, which is not matched by the lower strings. Rhiannon tells how her tutor handed the Calcunius back to her to play. She played the solo Bach for him, and that was it. Apparently, he smiled and said to her: "Just take the OE back to Benslow"!

*

Whilst teenage classical players have comprised the majority of Dave's Saturday playing assistants, the role on weekdays has been filled mostly by adults. Being freelancers, professional musicians, especially those nearer the base of the performance pyramid, often need a regular source of income on days of the week where income from other sources is harder to come by – either that, or they need a respite from teaching. Some have combined the role of playing assistant with teaching commitments; others have done it on days of the week when they've not been away gigging or playing in an orchestra. Some have done it for a few years; others for more than a few, decades in one instance. Most of the people who've worked in this role remain regular visitors to the shop, dropping in if not weekly certainly monthly. They are part of an extended fiddle family; but this is less a family well known to one another, more a distributed social network, one which has been fashioned by the shop and the workshop, its fiddles, and by the figure at its centre, Dave.

Talking with just some of the people who've filled this role over the years throws up significant differences between adult playing assistants and those who were either school-aged students or very young adults when they worked for Dave. What's missing here is all the talk about what the opportunity to play multiple instruments affords. There is also much less said about the relativities of instruments and bows as the means to sound production. Instead, when instruments – and particularly bows – figure, this is as a means to trade. With performing, playing and other commitments, established professional musicians have very little time available to traipse round the violin shops of the country, in the manner of the post-conservatoire quest for an instrument and bow. But a trusted professional colleague with contacts with a shop can be charged with having a look on their behalf at something that they're in the market for, trying it out, and potentially negotiating its trial loan. Intermediaries, then, are an important way in which the network of professional musicians interfaces with the stock of instruments and bows held in the country's violin shops. So, working a day a week in a violin shop can have obvious benefits for those who do it.

An example: one lunch-time on a day that I was in the shop, Charlotte Hawes (Chapter Four) popped in. She was on her way to the High School to sort out her autumn schedule of teaching, which needed to be accommodated around the upcoming autumn tour of English Ballet. It's a continual juggling act. Prior to the Covid-19 pandemic, Charlotte had worked every Friday in the shop, for over 20 years. She'd helped Dave out doing bridges and minor repairs on student instruments. Post pandemic he's seen less of her. Dave tells me: "She was here every week, every Friday for 20 years. I showed her how to do pegs and she'd do the bridges on the cheap school fiddles and set them up. When Covid struck that was it. She said she wasn't going to bother any more. So I said, 'fair enough'. But she still comes in for a cup of tea and a chat."

What brings Charlotte in to the shop today is less a chat and more that she's on the search for a Hill bow for a colleague who plays in the pit at the Coliseum. Dave brings out a case of his "special bows". The best one, which Dave starts with, is £6.5k. Charlotte knows that this is too expensive for this colleague. She says immediately that her top limit is £5k. She moves on to another that is in the price range. Quick scrutiny of the frog, ferrule, head but especially the provenance in the form of the maker's inscription, leads her to settle on this Derek Wilson bow. Dave checks Derek Wilson out in his reference work of English bow makers, and reports on what it has to say for Charlotte: "Derek Wilson - worked for Hills from 1978. So it's a modern one. It has his name on it so it's made after he left there. It might tell you when he left. He is an authority now." Dave then starts looking for a book by Derek Wilson on bows. He has a copy somewhere, but – true to form - he can't find it. Charlotte opines that the colleague can do some research.

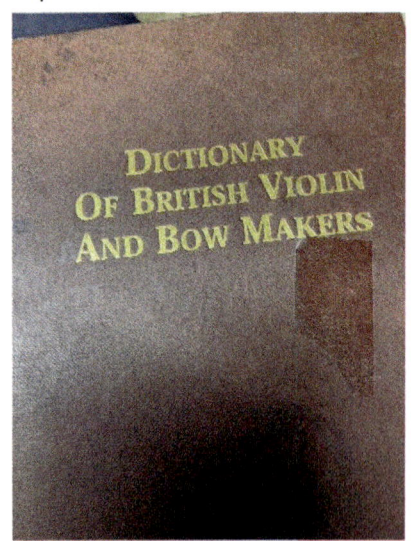

Summarising where his delving has got to, Dave says: "Tell her 'ex-Hill, top modern bow maker'".

Charlotte picks out a fiddle from the workshop and tries the bow out, declaring that it needs a re-hair. Dave and Charlotte then establish the price her colleague will be offered it for, and Charlotte's commission, if the colleague buys it. Later she tells me: "The leader of our orchestra has a bow from here. I'd taken it down for somebody else and he ended up trying it and he really liked it". Dave asks her: "Was that a Hill bow?" Charlotte: "No it wasn't. I can't remember what it was". She then tells us the background to this potential sale. The colleague's bow went in to be re-haired. "She hadn't got a spare, so she borrowed one and it was a Hill, and she really, really liked it. She said it made such a difference. She's been trying a Frank Napier one; that was 1910." Then, she asks Dave: "So does this Wilson one belong to you or are you selling it for someone?" Dave: "It's mine". Charlotte: "What weight's this one?" Dave puts it on his scales – "its 62g". He then tells her, "It came from the Leader of Opera North". Charlotte heads off with the bow, but later that same afternoon rings back to check the name of who it came from. She'd been ringing the potential buyer, who wanted to know whose bow it was. Charlotte: "Did that bow belong to David Green? That's the leader of Opera North". Dave tells her: "No. I've forgotten his name. Don't tell them names, because she'll get onto them. They must have changed leaders, cos that was about five years ago. Just say a former leader … OK". He rings off, abruptly and says to me: "Pfffhhh! She always does that and I hate it when they do that. Cos then they ring them up, and then they say, 'Oh I got rid of that bow – it was shit. I traded it in'. She always does that with her pals!"

*

Someone who overlapped with Charlotte as an assistant for several years is Paul Knox (Chapter Four); or "The Vicar" as Dave now calls him. After graduating from the Newcastle Folk and Traditional Music degree, like many, Paul went into teaching: "mostly classical. I was getting kids through their grades, and I did a few bands. I did the junior string band in Hexham. I was teaching at St Mary's middle school, and Corbridge, Brough and Humshaugh – all places around about Hexham. Mostly little ones. And then I started teaching them piano as well; very basic piano. And I'd go to The Violin Shop just to hang out. I started teaching for the Music Service in 2011-12 and I would've been going in from about 2014/15. To begin with it was just casual wandering in, wandering out, when I had the odd hour or so to fill between lessons. And then Charlotte did Friday and I think I did either a Monday or a Tuesday, because it fitted in with my teaching. I could go to Dave's till 4.30pm and then go off and do my teaching from the late afternoon".

Paul describes his role as "basically a shop assistant: cleaning; tidying the place up! And talking to customers; answering the phone." He tells me: "The shop was a mess – as you know. You've seen the back shop. It used to drive me nuts. So once I got my feet under the table I moved everything around." I suggest, tongue firmly in cheek: "I bet he loved that!" Paul: "No he did not! And I was saying, 'This doesn't look good. When you come in it needs to look good!' So I moved all the stuff; tidied everything up; Charlotte helped. We put the cellos where they are now, and the drawers underneath; the cellos on one side, with the basses. And it looked a bit better. And we did that display with the wood shavings. When we did it he hated it. And I said, 'Just throw the shavings on it'". He was going: 'Why do you want to make a mess?' 'Because people will like it. When they walk past the shop they'll go 'Oh' and they'll stop and look'". Paul was right; passers-by regularly stop and look in the shop window. Paul: "And then he put the little mouse amongst the shavings – and I thought, 'well – whatever!'"

As well as reordering the shop interior, just as others, Paul also assumed the role of the playing assistant: "Dave would send us out. And he'd say 'He's going to play these instruments, and you can listen. Which one do you like the best?' It was helpful to have a musician in the shop for Dave because when I was in myself to buy a violin I just did it myself. He found that really helpful, I think."

Now a full-time vicar, Paul no longer has the time to work in the shop but he continues to pop in on days off, or when he is on his way over to play with musician friends in Cumbria. As we talk, he reflects on how his relationship with Dave and the shop has evolved over the years, from one of "A scary, grumpy man who didn't want you in the shop" to being "a special place with, at its heart, a very special guy." Paul: "He's so generous with his time, with his knowledge, with his money – he's the most generous man. I think a lot of people don't appreciate or know about the many wonderful things Dave has done and the many people he's encouraged. [On the lutherie side] there's Lucasz who's from Slovakia – he's really encouraged him. There's been people from Italy – Pontedoro. Loads of English people he's encouraged – they come into the shop; he teaches them what he knows, and free of charge! Jeremy, Sophie, Charlotte. Ralph Plumb. He's just so generous with his time. Then there are the players. There's Rhiannon and her sister, Clemmie; there's Leia Zhu – she's always had her bows re-haired by Dave and I think she hired a really decent instrument at the beginning. He's always been nothing but really encouraging. He's so keen to encourage people, but only if he likes them! But I think people disregard him because he's in the middle of Hexham, he's a Geordie, and he shouldn't know anything about lutherie." Our conversation turns inevitably to the class prejudices of the classical music world. Paul: "A lot of the top players, the Sinfonia – they won't use him. 'Oh, we only use the London shops' Or, 'We only go to Edinburgh'." But, as he says: "The thing is, we know that this is a special place. And once you know, you know, why would you go anywhere else?"

Paul draws parallels between Dave's shop and a leather shop in Newcastle. They offer a window on why prejudices persist, even in the face of Dave's skill and expertise, pointing to the conjuncture of working class cultures and particularly cultures of masculinity in generating the kinds of differences that result in prejudice. These differences are not insuperable, but they require a willingness to recognise and work with and through. He says: "I used to do a bit of leather work. There, in that shop, you go in. There are a lot of burly men who don't really want to serve you, and who *really* don't want to serve you if you don't know what you're talking about. You've got to get past that. But me again, I kept going, and we became friends and they invited me round the back for a coffee. But initially it's that same stand-offish-ness." He thinks aloud: "It's funny. I wonder if it's something about the Northeast?" Ruminating further about how Dave comes across, especially to the predominantly middle class classical music world, he says: "Dave's a funny one; because there's a lot of love. But he doesn't suffer fools and you've got to get through the barrier. And I think even then there's still this sort of reticence. I think that's how he's grown up and the life he's led; he's a man of his time - it's a sort of cantankerous endearing! Bless him!"

*

The geographical spread of instruments and bows emanating from a particular violin shop is perhaps the most obvious evidence of its reach in the wider violin world. But the fiddle assistants of 27 Hencotes testify to a less visible, softer, form of influence: of shops on players, and particularly on the musical development and growth of younger players. To a casual onlooker, or even someone coming in to buy a violin, Dave's assistants may look like a just another shop assistant. They are not. Rather, they're all – the adults just as much as young people - part of an ecosystem which has at its apex performance space. Typically, what gets emphasised in the development of performing musicians is key teachers and key institutions, whose role is to ensure the sustainability of the profession, at every level. Without wanting to deny those influences in any way, this is to overlook how the development of violinists as performing musicians can also benefit from an engagement with retail lutherie. To my mind it is telling that those who worked in their formative years as fiddle assistants for Dave tell a consistent story: of how working here, in this shop, with Dave, took them beyond the instrument that they then 'just played', to a wider appreciation of the diverse universe of violins and their sounding world. It opened up their eyes and ears to the violin as a highly variable sounding object, one which –

depending on the violin - is more, or less, open to the exploration of potentialities in sound. And, simultaneously, it led to a fuller understanding of their role in the production of that sound, as a collaborative, listening, always attentive co-partner. The influence of that learning on these fiddle assistants, many of them now established performers in their own right, is felt in wider projects and collaborations; as is Dave himself. It's not just that the people who've worked here in this way in this shop learnt to work well with fiddles — that would happen with any encounter between a violinist and lutherie. Rather, through engaging with "the magical wee guy", as Des Dillon described him, they also learnt the intangible skills of interpersonal communication; of communicating across, or even beyond, social and cultural difference, and the importance of an honest, open, authentic form of communication. Those are life skills, but they are skills that are also central in musical performance and to connecting with a listening audience. No amount of teaching performance or stagecraft can create this kind of connection; it has to come from within.

In being just Dave, Dave has not just been a mentor to the young people who've come through his shop, he's given them the gift of showing them how to become better musicians. Is it any wonder that their appreciation of him is so heartfelt and that they return to visit him whenever their schedules allow?

CHAPTER SIX

Repair & Restoration

To all intents and purposes, 27 Hencotes looks and sounds like a violin shop. Violins are what you see when you walk through the door. But really the phrase 'violin shop' is something of a misnomer, for actually, this is mostly a repair shop.

That realisation happened very early on in my visits, when Dave was focusing on showing me the making of his latest fiddle. Every time I went to the shop, either nothing much had happened to the make in the intervening days, or whatever Dave was planning on showing me had to be squeezed into the odd couple of hours at most. What was taking precedence in the workshop was a seemingly never-ending backlog of repair jobs. Aside from the fiddles lined up in the workshop requiring his attention, barely a visit went by when there wasn't a cello lying on the shop counter or clamped up on the shop floor. And that's without the bow rehairs, of which there are typically at least six per week. Seemingly, as fast as one job went out of the workshop another, or others, came in to replace it. Still thinking at this time that luthiers were a kind of craft worker who mostly made violins, I asked Dave about the division between making and repair and maintenance work in the shop. He told me by his reckoning it's 90:10 in favour of repair, a balance borne out by my observations. He then went on to say that, in his experience, it's impossible for a luthier to make a regular living from making and dealing in violins alone. Sales – even when one's work, like Dave's, is in high demand and when one has a stock of good quality trade instruments – are too unpredictable, especially if one has a family to support. Business economics, then, mean that a violin shop, first and foremost, has to be a repair shop.

For an academic who has spent much of their professional working life engaged in researching waste, reuse and recycling and its relation to consumption, the realisation that what I'd thought was a violin shop was actually a repair shop made Dave's shop an even more intriguing place than it already was. Who would have thought it? Here, tucked away on a nondescript street on the outskirts of Hexham, I'd found a shop which for over 30 years has been demonstrating the principles of what the policy world now calls the circular economy. There, in the policy world, it's a desired ideal: a model of the future which functions as a means to move economies onto a more sustainable footing. Specifically, it's a concept that is used to seek to steer economic activity away from the norm of what's called the 'take-make-dispose' attitude to resources, goods and materials, and its counterpart in consumption, throwaway cultures, to focus on the repair of goods and the recycling of materials.

The circular economy being a desired ideal, or a vision of the future, meant that, when it started to become a fashionable term, no one was looking for evidence of its actual existence out in the real world. But, if they had been, Dave's shop is as good a place as any to start. Equally, though, it's important to recognise that no one in 27 Hencotes was trying to impose a new economic order with repair as its fulcrum. This was not and never has been a business modelled on promoting sustainability. Instead, what's been going on for the past 30-plus years in the workshop is what the policy world calls 'business as usual'. That it is 'business as usual' is because, in the violin world, the repair and maintenance of instruments and bows has long been valorised over the production of the new. Here repair and maintenance are the natural order of things. Why is this so?

As with so much in the violin world, part of the answer lies with the reverence displayed towards old instruments and the work of key master craft workers over the modern and the new. This applies not just to the obvious names of Stradivarius, Guarneri and Guadagnini but to names that have figured in previous chapters, such as Cuypers, Jakobs and Degani. In general terms, repair and restoration go hand-in-hand with rare and fine goods; they allow their perpetuity. But in the violin world, repair and maintenance work is essential. It ensures that highly valued old instruments, such as Leia Zhu's Guadagnini (Chapter Four), are kept in tip-top playing condition. It's for this reason that the top dealers and foundations have dedicated networks of repairers and restorers on hand, either in their workshops or at a distance, to whom they can outsource work. A dedicated repair network is there to maintain the instruments under the ownership and stewardship of the foundations and dealerships. This network is what underpins the violin world's reverence for the old, for without craft repairers these instruments would not remain in playing condition. In 27 Hencotes, though, the valorisation of repair over replacement doesn't just apply to instruments the trade and connoisseurs deem of high value. It applies to instruments all the way down the violin value chain.

Time and time again when in the shop, I would see customers come in to see if even the most basic of kit violins could be repaired - things like Skylarks and Stentors. Mostly, these were violins of high sentimental value. Typically, they were instruments which the customer had played as a child, often many decades ago, and which they now wanted rekindled for a grandchild to begin to learn to play. And true to form, Dave would always give such an instrument his standard set-up treatment – a thorough clean, new strings, a new bridge, new pegs if necessary - even though this work cost more than the financial worth of the instrument. It also meant that such instruments always left the workshop sounding way better than they'd ever previously done.

At the level of the £1-2k violins that the adult learners in Chapter Four are buying, repair and maintenance work is all about keeping 'their violin' – the one they found, which sounded for them – playing in the way which first enchanted them. It's about keeping, or even renewing, the bond between instrument and player-owner. And then there are Dave's own instruments; the one's he's made – fiddles in the £8-10k bracket. Every single one of those instruments leaves the workshop with the instruction to bring it back every year for the fiddle equivalent of a service and MOT, done free of charge. It's a lifetime guarantee which signals the bond between an instrument and its maker, and which simultaneously uses the ethos of care to incorporate the purchaser into Dave's extended fiddle family. The gift of free servicing means the fiddles – and their owners – keep on returning to visit the workshop.

Regardless of where they are in the violin value chain, then, violins are possessions and attachments. They are not the sort of objects which people look to cast out and replace anew with a substitute, in the way one replaces a car or a washing machine. Rather for most people they are what's termed life objects – or what anthropologists refer to as biographical objects. This is the category of objects that are with a person until such time as they either pass them on by gifting them to a significant other, or die. When this happens with violins a relative will typically come into Dave's shop, looking to either trade it in or – if it's a violin of a low trade-in value - give it away. It's because violins, and for that matter violas, cellos and double basses, are life objects that people are continually seeking to have them repaired. This is one of the reasons why repair and maintenance work sits at the heart of 27 Hencotes.

Yet the desire to have something repaired doesn't always translate to its possibility. For proponents of the circular economy, one of the bugbears of modern manufacturing techniques is that planned obsolescence and proprietary technologies combine to make it either hard to disassemble goods without breaking the whole or impossible to replace parts. Think of an iPhone. People might want to repair goods but the brutal reality in many instances is that repair is a physical impossibility.

The violin family is not like this at all. Rather, it's almost as if these instruments are made to be repaired. It's not just that they're made from wood — the holy trinity of spruce, maple (or sycamore) and ebony. Although that certainly does help, for it means that techniques of grafting are possible as well as, in extremis, fabricating a new part entirely, like a new neck or a new back or belly. It's not just that they're made using hand tools and adaptable, rather than proprietary, machine technologies (Chapter Three), so the capacity to repair is not restricted to the original manufacturer. It's also in what holds the violin sound box together and in what fixes the fingerboard to the neck – or, it's all in the glue.

I had an early lesson in glue's importance with my Dave Mann fiddle a few years before this book was even a thought. One evening, whilst playing, I'd stopped to do something else at the computer and propped my fiddle up against a waste paper basket. As I did the something else the fiddle decided to slip from its hold against the basket, and slid onto the carpeted floor. Catastrophe! The fingerboard detached itself from the neck. I was due to be playing something that night. With no spare fiddle to hand, it was a case of find some wood-glue and glue the fingerboard back in, lightly. It was a temporary fix, one that worked sufficiently to enable playing. I rang Dave the next morning, aware that the fiddle needed to attend the equivalent of A&E. "Bring it in" he said, and then exclaimed when I explained what I'd done, "You haven't glued it with wood glue!!! Eeeeh!! Woman!! It might not come off! I'll have to see what I can do!" An hour later I'd got the fiddle to the shop. I handed the fiddle over to Dave, who took it off backstage into the workshop – a place mostly unknown to me then. I went off into Hexham, rueing my stupidity and hoping for the best. When I returned to the shop, ever the magician, Dave had managed to prise the fingerboard off without wrecking the neck and had then re-glued it. Order was restored. But it was to be a good couple of years before I fully realised the secret of the glue, its importance to fiddle repair and maintenance and the potential for my temporary fix to have turned really catastrophic. The realisation went like this.

One day early on in the research, when I arrived at the workshop Dave was gluing the neck into the body of his current fiddle-in-the make. I'd thought he had been going to do this earlier in the week and that day we'd be onto the wetting and sanding phase. But no; true to form, other jobs had intervened – and, as Dave said later, he hasn't got a timescale for finishing it. The fiddle will be ready when it's ready. Instead, with gluing work in progress, Dave's glue pot was on – on a low heat, cooking.

The configuration of Dave's glue pot (pictured) looks like something from the 1930s, or possibly even earlier. I gasp at it, and Dave laughs and says "It's Old Bob's!" He means Bob Archbold (Chapter Two). So, the glue pot – like other things in this workshop, like Dave's bending iron – predates Nial and Dave's arrival in 27 Hencotes. Old technologies make little concession to health and safety. After being in the workshop for some 15 minutes, it's obvious that open cooking is resulting in a heady concoction. Glue is one of the many noxious smells that fill the workshop from time to time and which lead to it being termed by many as "a potion place". Glue sniffing, I deduce, is an occupational hazard of being a luthier – not to mention of visiting the workshop. I ask if the glue is a secret concoction. Dave says: "Well not really but it's rabbit skin; that's what they used in Strad's day. It comes from London" (pictured). I ask, 'why rabbit skin glue?' Dave says: "Because the violins are worth such a lot of money. If you have an accident and you've got to take them apart, you can put the knife in, move it apart and dissolve it with warm water, and it comes off without any damage. But if you use the new, epoxy resin glues – like guitars, they're made with the epoxy resin glues. So, if you have an accident with them, they're scrapped because you cannot get them apart without damaging the instrument. So, violin luthiers use different techniques. I've got to make them so that down the line if there are any problems for me, or for anyone else, it's got to be able to come apart."

Hand-made violins, then, are assembled to come apart. This goes beyond the current vogue for modular design, which rests on the easy substitution and replacement of parts. Instead, the key to violin repairability rests in the materials that hold these things together and the capacity for those bonds to be dissolved with minimal stress to the instrument itself. Significant too in what Dave tells me is that violins are not imagined as becoming obsolete or as being scrapped. Rather a future repairer/restorer is imagined in their making. Violins then, or at least the hand-crafted violins that emerge from this workshop, are being fabricated for repairability. Their durability lies not in the strength of the materials that are used to make them but in the dissolvability of what holds them together. This is how they're made to enable repeated repair: their durability rests on dissolvability.

That so much repair and maintenance work comes through the shop door, though, is not just about the intrinsic repairability of the violin family. It's also in no small part testimony to Dave's skill and considerable reputation as a repairer. What underpins this? How are the skills of a master repairer manifested to others? And what are the wider effects of a master repairer's practice?

*

My first lesson in Dave's repair skills with my own fiddle are typical of those who visit the shop with a damaged instrument. The instrument is handed over, with Dave saying little more than "I'll see what I can do" – and that's it.

What happens to it is entirely backstage; something most people never get to see. All they see when they come to collect the instrument is the result: abracadabra! This is what Peter Tickell defines as "the mysterious magic" of Dave's workshop. Peter is someone who wants to preserve the workshop as a place of mystery and magic. So, he likes to "go in, give him my violins and bows and disappear and then come back and they'll be done!" He says: "I'm not a fixer, a do-er, or a mender", in so doing reciting a well-worn distinction that is often drawn between practical or 'how-to' knowledge and skills and more academic or creative capacities. Dave though most definitely is a fixer, a do-er and a mender. To see those skills in action requires spending time in the workshop. Doing this may destabilise the sense of magic that many locate in the workshop. But it heightens appreciation of the work of repair and restoration, the skills it entails and Dave's undoubted capacities in this regard. Whilst it demystifies the workshop it continues to preserve a sense of the magician who is at its heart.

My first inkling of being in the presence of a magician of repair came not with violins, cellos and bows but perhaps surprisingly with a piece of ornamental porcelain. One day when I'd gone over to the shop, Dave's friend Freddie Thompson (Chapter One, pictured) was sitting in the workshop. Dave was in his customary seat at his workbench and had started working on what looked to me to be a thoroughly wrecked fiddle. The fiddle was in bits all over the bench. Freddie and I looked on, drinking tea and talking. Suddenly, Freddie piped up: "Dave, let's do *The Repair Shop* gag!" Dave: "Oh aye". I had no idea what the two of them were talking about – other than that *The Repair Shop* is a popular British BBC TV programme. It features a team of expert repairers, who each week is set the challenge of rekindling a range of objects, ones which typically are of high sentimental value rather than of any great financial value.

The two men set about staging the routine. Freddie disappears from the workshop into the shop, whilst Dave rummages around in the kitchen for a tea cloth and then uses the cloth to pick up something that's lying on one of the side benches amongst piles of bashed about violin backs and bellies, wrecked bows, a fiddle in the white and, I notice, the fiddle in the make. He places it on his work bench, covering it with the cloth and then says to Freddie: "You can come in now". Freddie returns to the workshop, at which point Dave does 'the big reveal', slipping the tea cloth off his work bench to disclose a cheeky looking porcelain robin. "Oh!!" exclaims Freddie, "just look at that! How did you do that? It's just as it was; you'd never know it'd been broken!" It's the typical response of all those who feature on *The Repair Shop*; a 'gosh' moment, which captures the capacity of a skilled repairer to restore a cherished object to its original condition. Except here, Freddie's exclamations relate to an object which he'd happened on the previous day in a charity shop in Hexham, and purchased for £3. The robin was chipped and had a broken wing but it had appealed to Freddie – and, looking at its stance and eye, I could see exactly why. Knowing that Dave would be able to repair it, he'd bought it, taking it back to the workshop. At which point it became yet another repair job for Dave. But sitting on the workbench in front of us wasn't the kind of repair to be found in a host of ornamental cats, dogs and horses in my house. All those things are childhood mementos but, in most instances, tell-tale lines of glue disclose all too visibly a history of breakages, whilst chipped ears betray the knocks of things in everyday domestic life. Looking at Freddie's robin one would never know that it had been in anything other than pristine condition. This – what Dave calls "deceiving the eye" – is the hallmark of his repair work, regardless of the object. His repairs are always invisible.

Martin Hughes is perhaps the first violinist to have appreciated these exceptional repair skills. Martin tells me: "One day when I was over at the house in Westerhope teaching [Dave's daughter] Sarah, Dave introduced me to the notion that at the bottom of the garden there was something special, in his garage. He took me down to see this thing – and honestly, I was blown away. And I've remained blown away by the sight of that very old MG (Chapter One). He had basically taken a pretty shabby and partly wrecked car – it needed to be rebuilt from within. So, Dave being a sheet metal worker, but not only a sheet metal worker but a wonderful paint sprayer. Here's the big thing. Dave possesses – I could call this a dead eye, but don't get me wrong, it's not 'dead' it's more an eagle eye. He sees things and is able to reproduce them absolutely faithfully and unbelievably. On Jack's old MG, there was a need for new panels to be made – so Dave set about making new wing panels in exactly the same grade of steel as had been used. As far as I know all he'd done is looked at - this might not be quite accurate – but now I know what he's able to do, it's possible that he just looked at them and made them. He's capable of that. And then, as if that wasn't enough, the paintwork – the spray paintwork – which of course had to be the proper thing, the right paint, the right shade – it was on another level. I'm interested in cars and I've had spray jobs done and thought 'Hmm it looks like it's been done with a yard broom'. So, it was a car that made me think, 'My Goodness'."

Over the ensuing years, Dave has done a number of repair/restoration jobs for Martin, especially in relation to bows. Martin: "I have four good bows --- beautiful bows!" He shows me them. "That one", he tells me, "suffered a break there – you can just see. He's done the most unbelievable repair. It's a classic bow, a beautiful bow – we think it's something very special." And then, Dave also repaired a Chanot bow for Martin's grand-daughter: "She split the wood of the stick through over-tightening. Dave did this most amazing repair. You couldn't see any of it; he'd repaired it from inside out; he'd investigated the reason why everything wasn't quite right."

*

Martin's telling of the car story is, at one level, a tale of two car enthusiasts and an appreciation of the quality of Dave's restorative work on an MG. But it pinpoints the wider significance of Dave's sheet metal and panel beating skills and the eye of the master craft repairer. Metal and panel beating skills are part of the accidental luthier story (Chapter Two) but they're also significant to the repair and restoration work of a violin luthier. I get an indication of their connection six months on from talking with Martin. I'm in the workshop when a violin dealer is in the shop checking in on what Dave has in stock. Towards the end of his visit, Dave says to him: "Did I ever show you me tortoiseshell cello bow restoration?" He gets it out of one of his special bow cases. The dealer, looking at the bow's frog, says: "God, you've blended it well; you cannot see it." Dave tells him: "It's two different powders mixed together – you can't see it can you?" It is impossible to tell with the naked eye that it's ever been repaired; to see that would require X-ray and/or scanning technology. Dave says: "That's for sale – you can make us an offer. I just had an idea and had a few goes at getting me colours right. What do you think?" The dealer says: "English". Dave: "Yes". Dealer: "But what?" Dave: "Silver mounted." Dealer: "Nice head. I bet it plays well". Dave: "I'm asking a couple of thousand". Dealer: "Do you think the adjuster's a bit later?" Dave: "I'm not quite sure. It could be, but that's a talking point." Dealer: "Not Dodd, but nice. It could be a bit later. But that's all original." He leaves, thinking about it but without making an offer.

Still bowled over by the quality of this tortoiseshell restoration, I ask Dave: "How is it you see this, do you think? Is it because you work with these materials all the time? Or, do you think this has anything to do with car restoration practices?" Dave thinks a while and then says: "It's something to do with being a lateral thinker." I persist with my line of thought: "But isn't it also something to do with the way you see repairs. If all that you've done in your life is repair fiddles and bows, you wouldn't have all that knowledge". Dave: "You're not consciously aware. I look at it and suddenly there's a picture." I continue: "Aye – and when you're trying to restore a car body what you're doing is bring that body back to what it was like as new. That's what you've done with that cello bow." Seeing this work, it's pretty clear to me that the ability to picture something which Dave refers to is strongly connected with his previous life in car body work restoration. There everything is about restoring the surface to pristine, showroom condition. That's what's behind the rebuilding of the frog on the cello bow. Dave is not only able to see the three-dimensional surface shape that has to be rebuilt; he can work out what materials, in what mix, will do that rebuilding and achieve that finish aesthetically. This is 'deceiving the eye' as he calls it.

Deception underpins the work of a magician. But it would be a mistake to see Dave's repair work exclusively through this lens. At the same time as the tortoiseshell cello bow manifests the invisibility of Dave's repair work, it is also a lesson in the importance of problem solving and experimentation, or tinkering, to how he approaches repair and restoration.

*

The best illustration of problem solving at work in repair and restoration in my time in the workshop came with the thoroughly wrecked fiddle sitting on the workbench at the time of the robin *Repair Shop* gag. Having finished their routine, Freddie put the kettle on for another cup of tea, and I got to hear the back story to how this fiddle had arrived in the workshop. The previous Monday, a woman had brought it into the shop. She'd come in a few months previously to say she'd got an old violin that had belonged to her mother, who'd recently died. The violin, in her words, had 'fallen apart'. Ever aware of the opportunities that might be lurking in such fiddles, Dave had said to the woman to bring it in for him to have a look at. She did so, and Dave agreed a price with her for it.

I ask Dave what he thinks the fiddle is. Dave: "It's German, about 1780 – probably Leopold Widhalm. It's highly arched; typical of that period really. I've got to take the back off. That's got to come out; same with the belly – it's a bit warped. And I've got to take the neck off – this one went in about 100 years ago. After 1860; once they went over to modern tuning. But I've got to take that off and put a new one on, and then put it all back together again. But the basic violin is good. Nice varnishing and everything. There's not much wrong with it really." Freddie and I look at the fiddle: the gap between Dave's 'there's not much wrong with it really' and what's in front of our eyes is huge. Most people would call this a wreck.

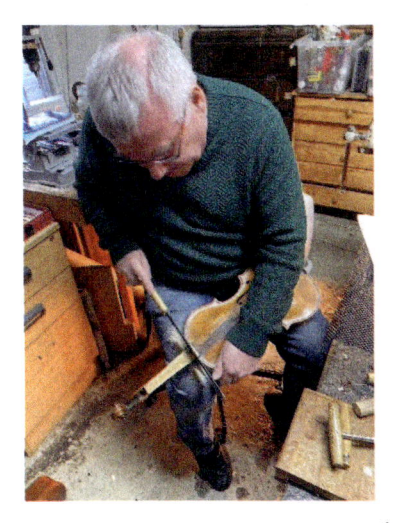

As he sits at the bench, I ask Dave how he's making a start on restoring the fiddle. He describes what he's doing as "just tickling on with it", or what I'd call tinkering, that is beginning to play around with it and to get to know it. To begin with, Dave's making the bushing for each of the four peg holes in the scroll. This will make the yet-to-be-made new neck look like one piece of wood. 'Tickling', it turns out is key to 'deceiving the eye', but it's also – I think – about starting to think through the possible courses of action ahead. Then, as Freddie continues to tell stories and reminisce, Dave starts work on the neck. He gets a saw out to get the neck root out, saying to me as he saws away: "I'm chopping that out, and now you can see the original mortise. I mustn't damage that, 'cos that's where the new neck has got to go". When all of this has been done, and the neck is off the fiddle, he takes a cold kitchen knife, slides it between the back and the ribs and carefully removes the back, in so doing illustrating the secret in the glue (pictured). He says, as he's doing this: "some of them are absolute nightmares but this is coming off easy". The fiddle is now in bits, spread over the workshop bench (pictured). However, taking the fiddle apart gives no further clue as to its origins. Any label it might once have had is no longer there. So, for the remainder of the morning, I'm set to work on the task of fiddle identification.

In a book cabinet on one wall of the workshop are shelves full of violin reference works; over-sized, hardback, collectors' books, full of illustrations. I'm instructed to get the German books out – three hefty volumes - and to start trying to match the scroll and the f-holes on this fiddle to the various photographs in the books. I start with Widhalm, Leopold. But what quickly emerges from my first inspection is that this fiddle isn't a Leopold Widhalm. Yes, it has the right shaped Stainer-influenced arching of the table, and the scroll is right, but the shape of the f-holes definitely isn't right. I check with Dave. He agrees, and sighs: "This is what happens. It all starts to become very time consuming" – and time spent searching is obviously time not spent repairing, hence my use. I carry on, buried in the books, for another hour or so, but the only reward for this labour is that all we can say is that the fiddle is definitely German, definitely 1760-80, and made in a workshop that has probably had some connection with Widhalm.

A few months later what is now called "The Old Bavarian" on account of its indeterminate provenance now has the back and belly together again. I ask Dave: "When you first looked at it, Dave, did you have a clear plan in your head as to what you were going to do with it?" He laughs and jests: "Well, repair it!!" But then, more seriously, he relates how problem solving relates to repair: "You assess the damage – whatever's happened. 'Cos it had fallen apart. What did I do? Well, I had to take the back off to sort the ribs out – but then the bass bar issue came into view. When the back was off, I removed the block; fitted a new block and got the ribs to match up and go flush, while the belly was still attached to the ribs. If I'd have taken both the back and the belly off it would've just sprung out all over the place; you'd have a much bigger job. So, that's the easiest way to do that. So, when I'd done that, I put the back back on and it's married together perfectly. And then I took the belly off. And I was inside it again – so bass bar; corrected the warpage and do any repairs; and then the saddle. And made a new neck at the same time." From Dave's description, it's clear that the thoroughly wrecked fiddle has had what amounts to a partial rebuild.

Dave continues: "All that was twisted out. The bottom block. It's all gone back in nice. I had to trim it a bit to get it go flush, but that's nothing really. And I've got the saddle somewhere; that's got to fit in there. So, I've got to put that in now. Got to put me glue pot on [which he does] – and this [the new neck, which he has made, which is to one side on the workbench] has got to be fitted. I'm repairing the mortise (pictured). I've put a piece in there, because when that slides in that all has to be in line. You see that – that's where the neck has to come spot on with that. But you can see what the problem is; there's a big gap. So, I've got to put a piece in there and then recut the mortise". I say: "So, you're like packing basically?" Dave: "Yes, because the old neck was undercut too much. I've had to pack that, and then this line here is going to match perfectly with that one. When they fitted the new neck for the previous neck graft, which would've been around a hundred years ago, he's overcut that and it hasn't joined. So, he's had to faff around. Instead of faffing around, I'll just put a piece in there and get it to fit, straight in".

Thinking back to the sunken belly of the fiddle sitting on the workbench when I'd first seen it, I ask Dave how he'd transformed this to the perfect shape sitting in front of us. Dave: "How did I do it?" He rummages around and slaps down on the bench something that looks like a hand-sized bean bag (pictured), but which, when I pick it up, weighs a ton. Laughing, I exclaim: "Bloody hell, Dave. What is it?!" Dave: "It's abrasive shot blasting grit. I put it in the microwave and get it hot! What do you do? You've got to think. Lateral thinking. The deformation wasn't there when it was made. But it's been faffed around with, and it's had another bass bar fitted, which can't have fitted. They've clamped it and then pulled it down to fit the fit of the bass bar, which wasn't the right shape. It deformed it". Summarising that situation, I say: "So some cack-handed repairer's been at it?" Dave: "Aye. Most of them are! So: deformed. But it's going to go back into shape if you know how to do it. So, you heat the sandbag up, and put a damp piece of paper on there, and then you put the hot bag on it, and it like steams it, and it just comes back into shape (pictured). I learnt that myself. Heat and damp, that's what'll shift it, because heat and damp causes problems all the time with wood. In the summer you get your doors expanding

and stuff. So that's what I did. And, as soon as I did that, I fitted a new bass bar, which is holding it, and that'll stop it ever going back into a bad shape".

The Old Bavarian is an exemplification of Dave's skills in repair and restoration. It shows an ability to read an instrument for its repair history to work out why certain problems have manifested, and then to choreograph a restorative sequence that will both sort out the problems and return the fiddle to its original state. Underpinning the restorative sequence that Dave devises is the knowledge of making, for in attending to the bass bar and the table first, and then reassembling the sound box of the fiddle, before making and then fitting a new neck and fingerboard, Dave has followed the order of fiddle making.

A few visits later, and the Old Bavarian has left the workshop. Dave tells me that Martin Hughes came in and tried it out when it had been finished and then set-up. He'd subjected it to his usual test regimen (Chapter Five) and liked it a lot. A few days later, Martin had told Dave that he'd be bringing his grand-daughter into the shop to choose a fiddle. Martin told Dave to line up a selection of violins in the price bracket for her to try (Chapter Four), including the Old Bavarian. But, as Dave says, "It was no contest. She picked it out straight away!" So now, Martin's grand-daughter has a restored Old Bavarian violin to go with her repaired Chanot bow; both of them testimony to the skills of a repair magician.

*

The Old Bavarian is at one end of the spectrum of the restorative and repair work that goes on in the workshop; it's akin to the Calcunius and Old Italian violins which Dave restored and which are now with the Germaine sisters (Chapter Five). At the other end of the spectrum are the more minor repairs that are an inevitable consequence of fiddles living in everyday life – where they get dropped; things get spilt on them, or they get knocked, or even sat on. Just as with the Old Bavarian, this type of repair shows exactly the same combination of problem solving with 'deceiving the eye'. One day when I came into the workshop, Dave was sitting at the bench with his magnifying glasses on and with the belly of a fiddle in front of him. I thought this was the belly of the Old Bavarian – but no. Dave removes the magnifying glasses to make it easier to see to talk to me, he tells me: "It's 'Dr Jeremy's' Andrea Pontedoro fiddle. He had an accident with it last week". "Dr Jeremy" is a retired consultant anaesthetist and GP, a good amateur player, an amateur luthier and a collector of violins. He's a regular in Dave's workshop. Dave then starts explaining to me what he's doing: "You see that hollow there (pictured) – that's the damage. So, I've used that gouger to get that shape. I took a gouge out of there" He shows me on the reverse side of the

belly. "The same shape, to get that shape to fit." He then gets what he calls his 'filler pot'. Looking at the powder in the pot, I say: "So this is filler; it's not baking powder is it?" Dave: "Don't be daft! It's bicarb but you *can* use baking powder." He starts putting the bicarb into the hollow (pictured). "Right – hmmmm – where did the piece go?" He rummages on the bench for the gouged piece. "It's that one. Where's the goggles? 'Cos I've got to get the grain lines to run right". He puts the googles back on and starts aligning the tiny gouged insert into the hollow. "Yes. Perfect." He starts whistling and puts some hot glue into the hollow, before carefully placing the insert into it (pictured). Dave: "I'm not bothered about it oozing out; that's good if it oozes". He then holds it firmly down, whilst I tear off kitchen paper for him to clean off the excess glue. At this point Dave asks me: "Why have I had to do it like that; any idea why? You've seen how I've taken it from that side". Nicky: "Well I suppose you wouldn't be able to cut anything else fine enough; it's like a graft." Dave: "It's a graft, yes. But why didn't I take it from that piece of wood

[he picks up a block]" Thinking about the possibilities, I say: "Because it wouldn't match the grain." Dave: "Mmm". Nicky: "Not totally?" As my understanding of what's going on here continues to be tested, Dave carries on working. I ask him: "So how do you get it to be flush when you've got it in? Ohh! Perspex, and a bit of pressure." Dave says: "Yes. Right, now you come round here and screw that down." I turn the lever on the clamp which is now applying pressure through the Perspex sheet to the area of the inlay . Dave declares: "That's it. So that should do it, I hope". Still thinking about Dave's question, I say: "I mean you'd always take a graft from the inside because it's the same wood with the same grain line." Dave: "It's the same wood, same grain line. But I couldn't take it off this side because this is two halves. So, you have to take it off in the exact opposite place so it'll match. Because [the wood for the belly] originally it was one piece." Nicky: "Aye – and you opened it like a book!" Dave: "You opened it like that. So, the bit I've cut out that fits is the opposite side. It's the same side that's going to be showing out, so I'll get the same effect when I do the varnishing. If I put anything else in, or if I put it in the wrong way round, it would've been reversed and it'd show. It would be the back side sticking out." Thinking about what I've seen of the early making process, I say: "You've got to think 'mirrors'". Dave: "You've got to think mirrors. Exactly!" He continues, thinking ahead to what remains to be done: "So, when that's dry, I can cut a

piece of that out of there [another piece of wood] and fill that in there [the gouged hollow from which the inlay has been removed] – 'cos that doesn't matter. I'll just glue it in and dress it up and put some more orange over the top."

Here we see how the invisibility of repair is produced. It is insufficient to simply cut a gouge that will fit the hollow, and shape that such that it is perfectly flush and then varnish it. The grain itself has to match identically. If it doesn't, all the repair will do is advertise its presence as a repair visually; in so doing becoming no more than a temporary fix, or a bodged job. To make an invisible repair, then, requires that the repairer also knows how to make a fiddle, and that they can read the construction of the fiddle they're repairing.

I'm in the shop when "Dr Jeremy" comes through to collect his fiddle. "Dave", he exclaims, "you've surpassed yourself. You cannot see it!"

*

The Old Bavarian and "Dr Jeremy's" fiddle are just two examples of the quality of repair work that I had the privilege of observing in Dave's workshop. There were many, many more. As I watched, I was left in little doubt that I was in the presence not just of a master maker of hand-crafted violins but a master repairer – and that this kind of repair work is very much a craft practice. In his book *The Craftsman*, Richard Sennett includes Stradivarius' workshop as an exemplar of craft production and craft work. He defines craftsmanship as the skill of making things well, highlighting within that the importance of the relationship between hand and head, and its evolution into habits of recursive problem finding and problem solving. Sennett shows how these same relationships and rhythms are to be found across multiple domains, from cooking and design to computer programming. They also figure centrally in making a hand-made violin. But, as is evident from the repair work that goes on in this workshop, and from the examples of the Old Bavarian and "Dr Jeremy's" fiddle, exactly the same habits of problem finding and problem solving, married to the intimate connection of hand and head, characterise Dave's repair and restoration work. Craft work, then, is not just about the making of things. It's also about being able to rekindle what has already been made – or to repair it well. Those who repair well are master repairers – and Dave, most certainly, is one. The result is that people come from near and far to have work done by him in his workshop.

*

For professional and amateur players living in and around Hexham and the Tynedale area, Dave's is the obvious place to go to for maintaining and – if need be - repairing their instruments.

Martin Hughes has four instruments: the Hill, the Old Neapolitan, a baroque violin and a viola. I ask him how often they're in the workshop. Martin laughs and says: "He [meaning Dave] will say, 'Here they come again'! That one [the Old Neapolitan] is in much more than the other [the Hill]. Actually, the other day it was "being croaky". The weather was on the turn, but it had settled down by yesterday. But they are worse than humans. So, it went in and he has a little tinker with it."

In so far as Martin's instruments are concerned, Dave likens his workshop to a Formula 1 car garage. He sees Martin as the equivalent of a Formula 1 driver, with his instruments having to perform at that level of precision and high-performance perfection. Martin also recognises that himself. Things have to work perfectly for him and he knows instinctively when they're a little off. But there's also an element of the instruments not just needing to sound perfect; they need to look perfect too. And it's here that the Old Neapolitan is an interesting case, indicating the limits Dave places on repair work. Martin tells me: "There's an element of wanting that fiddle [the Old Neapolitan] to be cleaned up on the back. It had a beetle, a worm attack. You can see something had almost eaten through it." He shows me it, and yes one can see and feel it. Martin continues: "Nial stabilised it. He ended up putting in some epoxy resins, because it has generally the same sound quality as the wood. It sorted it – but the thing was in such a mess when I got it from Bob." Martin now wants Dave to repair the back. He has broached it but – so Martin tells me - Dave is saying 'leave well alone'. In other words, he's reluctant to do anything with it.

Later, I ask Dave about the Old Neapolitan, wondering aloud whether what he's concerned about is taking the back off of it. Dave tells me: "That's not a problem. It's more when you start interfering with where the beetle has been. Probably there's no need to take the back off. It depends. But you've got the chance of making it worse. You can see it through the varnish on the back, and that's the problem; interfering with that. You might make it look worse, cosmetically. I might have a look at it but I'm not in a frame of mind. That's what I'm frightened of; cocking it up." I ask Dave what frame of mind he would need to be in to have a go at something like the Old Neapolitan. He tells me: "Well you've got to be perfectly clear; no trauma or anything. Focused, looking forward to doing it and knowing that you're going to make a good job of it. At the minute I'm not." Knowing something of the degrees of stress he's under, I say: "And you're not in that space". Dave: "I'm not there". Recognising the fluctuating nature of head spaces, I ask: "But would you do it Dave? If it's playing perfectly, why would you want to mess about with it?" Dave replies: "Well, this is it. That's it; that's why I tell him, leave well alone."

Martin is by no means the only professional string player to use Dave's for everyday maintenance work. One lunchtime when I was in the workshop, the international solo cellist and teacher Deborah Thorne rings up. I'd first met Debbie in the workshop, when she came in to buy some violin strings for a Ukrainian family living in Corbridge. They'd arrived in June 2022. She tells me: "They're two sisters and a mother. An 11-year-old violinist and a 17-year-old international level concert pianist. They're going to Poland tomorrow to do mostly piano concerts but the violinist is playing as well. Suddenly I get this message at 10 o'clock last night to say, 'Just realised. Sasha hasn't got a spare A and D string. Any ideas?' So I go, 'Yes. I'll sort it'". Sorting it involved a trip to Dave's for Debbie. Today though, when she's on the phone, Debbie is in a bit of a flap. She's due to be playing a small ensemble quartet concert on a bass viol that evening, an instrument which she plays only intermittently. She's just got it out of its case and, of course, these being highly temperamental instruments, it needs tuning. She asks Dave if she can bring it in. "Yes! Bring it in" he says.

When Debbie arrives with it, there follows a pantomime on the shop floor of restringing the bass viol and trying to tune it. Dave's friend Ray Burns (Chapter One) had wandered into the shop in the interim, between Debbie ringing and arriving. He pulls out his harmonica and plays the relevant notes whilst Debbie and I are singing the notes that the gut strings need to be tuned to. Meanwhile, Debbie struggles to turn the pegs whilst singing, putting her whole bodily force behind the pegs and meeting nothing but resistance. Eventually, laughing at the spectacle of collective practical incompetence being played out in front of him, Dave shows Debbie how to use her thumbs rather than try to twist the pegs using her fingers. Et voila! A tuned bass viol, ready for a concert.

That same struggle with turning pegs figured on another day when I was in the workshop, this time in relation to an older amateur woman cellist. Janet Storrie is in her 80s and lives quite close to Dave's shop. On this day Dave suddenly said to me, "Oh! Got to go round and tune up this old lady's cello!" With that, he disappeared out of the shop leaving me in charge. When he came back, I asked him the backstory. Apparently, Janet had recently broken her wrist. Although recovered, she still didn't have the strength to turn her cello's pegs – so, this was Dave's 'community service' activity, tuning her cello for free. Some months later, I got to talk with Janet herself, about her house, her life, politics, activism and her family's connection to Dave's shop. Janet tells me: "I was a cellist at school. I wasn't really that good. But Catherine – daughter – by the time she came up here, she was 10/11 and she was already a very good cellist." So, I say: "two cellos in the house." Janet: "Yes, yes. And I don't quite know when Rob (her son) started playing the violin." I ask her if all these instruments have been maintained by Dave. Janet replies: "They've all been maintained by Dave's shop. Initially, Mr Archbold was there for some time, and then Nial was there. But since we moved to this house, Dave has done things like reposition the sound post and things like that. Nothing very extraordinary." I ask how she'd describe his work. Janet exclaims: "Oh, I mean it is perfection! Because if there's anything you want to question or come back with, he's always there, always interested in the issue that you're presenting to him. Always just lovely to talk with and about it." Then, confidingly, she goes on: "He's very, very modest in what he charges too, which sometimes troubles me because I say, 'We do want to keep you going Dave!' The last thing we want is for him to give up because we haven't been paying him enough!! But you see, he's a very generous person."

Talking with Janet shows how Dave's shop figures as a central node in the day-to-day everyday world of a family living with stringed instruments. It's their go-to place for strings, set-ups and the occasional MOT, nothing more. But it's this routine – what Dave calls 'bread and butter' luthier work – which keeps those instruments in good playing order, and not needing major repairs. Like all those living in the Hexham and Tynedale area, the advantage Janet and her family have is that this level of service is on their doorstep. Without Dave, their string playing world would be very different and certainly more inconvenient. But I'm also struck that Janet is as appreciative of the interactions she has with Dave as she is of his maintenance work. Accessories such as strings can certainly be purchased from online outlets, but that doesn't offer the same quality of encounter. Just as with buying a fiddle (Chapter Four), it's the holistic shop experience that matters for Janet. And that comes down to Dave.

*

Exactly the same combination of perfect repair and maintenance work and quality social interactions sits behind the geographical reach of the workshop. My first inkling of the extent of this reach came when I realised that, most weeks, long, reinforced cardboard tubes were arriving in the shop. The tubes contain bows for rehairing, and they come from all over the country, including from the far north of Scotland and the Isle of Man. But the more time I spent in the workshop and talking with people the more I realised that the workshop itself – and the wee guy at its centre – was actually the reason for the shop's geographical reach. What is known simply as "Dave's" is a magnet for violin and fiddle players. People travel, in many cases, long distances, not only to have their bows rehaired and their instruments serviced but also to spend time just sitting in the workshop talking with Dave.

An example: one morning Dave phoned me to tell me that the Arcus carbon-fibre bows he'd ordered for me to try had arrived in the shop. I drove through to Hexham and when I got to Dave's who should be sitting in the workshop chair opposite Dave but Gavin Marwick. Gavin is a very well-known fiddle player and composer who hails from Edinburgh. He now lives with his partner, the nykleharp player Ruth Morris, in Kirkcudbright, in Dumfries & Galloway in Scotland, not far from Dave's daughter Claire. He'd set off at 8-ish that morning, to bring three bows in for rehairs and

The Violin Shop

for his two fiddles to be checked over. The prompt for this is a set of gigs coming up, in Tunisia. One of these was to be on Burns' Night, so Gavin felt the need to find a pair of tartan trews. He was planning to stop off at the factory outlet shop at Gretna, an hour or so's drive from Hexham, which would also break the journey on the way back. Gavin offers to help me choose between the bows, so off both of us go into the shop, where we both play and listen to them. What joy! Whilst we're doing this Dave carries on with Gavin's bows in the workshop, and Gavin and I talk a bit, in between appreciating the bows (pictured).

Gavin tells me that he first started bringing his stuff through to Dave's during the first Covid lockdown in Spring 2020 – or, rather his partner Ruth did. Gavin wasn't at all well at that time and somehow or other, both of his fiddles also started to collapse on him. The neck fell off one of them, which had upset him no end, it seeming to be a metaphor for what was happening to him. Desperate to get the fiddles repaired, Gavin and Ruth started ringing around. During lockdowns Dave was working in the workshop, taking the opportunity to crack on with his backlog of commissioned fiddles. With few repairs coming into the shop, and little by way of maintenance work either, lockdowns meant that he for once had time to devote to making violins. Gavin tells me that Dave had said that if Ruth was willing to break the lockdown travel rules, then he'd do the work. She was – and she brought Gavin's bows to rehair as well. Gavin was so pleased with the quality of Dave's work that he's come back, even though this is a six-hour round trip in a day. More than an hour later, Gavin and I are still gassing, playing and listening to the bows, and comparing them. Eventually, his work complete, Dave comes through from the workshop and says to Gavin: "You need to get on the road, man, if you're going to get those trousers!!" A further exchange of CDs ensues, in which Gavin gives Dave a copy of his new CD to add to the collection in the workshop, and I buy one, before Gavin finally exits the shop, with his bows and fiddles.

Lauren MacColl has been bringing her Cain & Mann fiddle back to Dave's rather longer than Gavin: since 2012, when she purchased the instrument (Chapter Four). She says: "I usually tie it in with when I'm up and down the road." The habit Lauren had got into pre-Covid was that she would bring the fiddle in once every 18 months. Lauren: "I'm someone who can only go on sound. I'm not somebody who can see whether the bridge has moved half a mm. I don't kind of notice that so much". I ask Lauren if she's ever taken the fiddle anywhere else. She says that she has had to in order to have small repairs done, "but if it was an actual set up, or anything that was tweaking the measurements, no I don't think I could. He knows it literally inside out; the nuances; and how small a thing can just change it so much. But he'll always listen to you and get you to play it, and not go, 'Oh that's because the bridge's done that'. Rather than always going with the mathematical, he goes 'what is it that you're hearing and not enjoying?' So, he works in that much more musical way".

Dave also does Lauren's (Hill) bow re-hairs. "It's a beautiful bow and I love it; I'd got it a few years before the fiddle. I went to Dave's last year to buy a new bow but he wouldn't let me because he said it's a really good bow. He said: 'You don't need a new bow'. The last time I saw him he had it bent over his electric fire trying to fix it, which freaks me out no end, but he knows what he's doing. [To begin with} he would've probably seen my bow in a bit of a state – so he'd have said, 'That needs a rehair'. So, I'd have left it with him. And then I just talked about how it's hard to get back and forth. And he said, 'Just stick it in the post'. And yes, other people have rehaired my bows but I always go back to him because it's a very classy job that responds to my playing; it's strong; it lasts."

Having known Dave now for over 10 years, Dave's is not just a place Lauren goes to have her fiddle and bow maintained and repaired. It's also a place of quality social interaction. She reflects: "The moments I remember more about being in Dave's shop is when he'll suddenly start to talk about things, and that's because I don't see him from year to year, and you just have a two-minute chat on the phone when you're sending him your bow. It takes a long time to build up trust and build up a relationship with somebody and I suppose the last few times I've seen Dave, I'm getting a bit older, I've had more life experiences, and things have happened in Dave's life. I've got no interest in sitting and talking about my career – no interest; it's about life. Those are my memories of being there, you think 'Oh I've just got to know you a little bit better'. I suppose, 'cos I live so far from the shop, when I go, I actually find it quite hard to leave!"

Someone else for whom Dave's has been a major presence in their life is Aidan O'Rourke. Talking with Aidan, he tells me: "He's actually had to rebuild this fiddle you know. I came back from Canada once. I was in really humid Ottawa – really, really humid. Never seen anything like it. Got on the plane. And it must have retained a load of moisture in the case and then into air-conditioning and a long-haul flight. And I opened the case in Innerleithen [in the Scottish borders] – I'd flown home, slept, didn't check my fiddle for some reason. I opened the case to do the sound check, and the whole thing was a parallelogram! I didn't have a spare. I had to borrow someone's fiddle, someone else on the bill. I took it down to Dave and he said, 'Oh it's fine! The glue's come apart; there's nothing broken'. It was horrible. I've a photo of it somewhere – and I'd a terrible gig as well. Playing someone else's fiddle and traumatised; not knowing if my fiddle was salvageable at that point! So, I've been through that with him. It's almost like being brought back from the dead; resuscitated."

This story encapsulates both Aidan's relation to his fiddle, which is a living, breathing entity that's an extension of himself, and Dave's centrality in maintaining that relationship. Not only is Dave the fiddle's maker; here he's the equivalent of the intensive care consultant who not only has resuscitated it but who understands how central this fiddle is to life itself. Aidan's life. It's the same with Lauren, when she says: "when I think of that instrument, it's with me multiple hours of the day; it's what I use for my work, but it's also what I use for my social life; it's what makes me tick".

There are deep social ties too that connect Aidan and Dave. Aidan tells me: "There's a communication there for me that goes back decades. I trust him. He's more than a luthier. He knows what I want. I don't really have to say anything anymore; he just knows! I just walk in and make a cup of tea and he sorts it out!" With his Dave Mann fiddle, going to Dave's has become even more of an emotional journey. It's something Aidan describes as feeling like going to a haven. He says: "I feel as if I'm bringing the fiddle home. It's as if you're bringing the fiddle back to family; it's like going to visit family. It's similar to the feeling I get when I'm driving to Argyll to my parents. There's a familiarity, and taking it back to see its creator." That same sense of taking her fiddle back home is also felt by Lauren when she goes to the workshop. She says: "It feels to me quite a privilege to have an instrument whose maker is there to fine tune and tweak it, as well as to go back to and enthuse about. It's a comfort I guess to know that that connection is there".

Fiddle repair and maintenance, then, is a means to sociality and care amongst humans. The recursive work of repair and maintenance over the years builds deep social attachments. Perhaps inevitably, those attachments are at their strongest between Dave as the creator and maker of fiddles, and those who play his fiddles. Those who play his fiddles are part of his extended family; a fiddle family. But that level of warmth, care and generosity is not reserved exclusively for them. It extends to others that Dave lets in to his inner domain: the sanctuary that is the workshop. To people like Gavin Marwick. In this way, fiddle repair and maintenance become not just restorative of instruments and bows, ensuring their continued durability and playability, but also – through the conversations that take place in the workshop - of the humans who are their custodians and stewards. During my time in the workshop this was never clearer than a day I spent there just before Christmas 2022.

*

I'm sitting in the workshop in my customary seat opposite Dave watching him do a standard set-up on a customer's fiddle when the shop door buzzer sounds. Dave says: "That'll be Paul – the Vicar." In comes Paul Knox. Dave: "Do come in, we'll have a sermon! [To me – since this is the first time that I've met Paul] He's known as creeping paralysis 'cos he creeps up on you and tries to startle you. And the Vicar of Diddly, cos he plays Irish music. [To Paul] Do you want a cup of coffee?" So starts a day which shows the warmth, conviviality and generosity that Dave creates in his workshop, for the select few, and how this connects with the work of repair and maintenance.

Paul takes his coat off, introduces himself to me, and then sits down with the coffee Dave has made him, on the third chair in the workshop. Dave says: "So why aren't you vicaring today?" Paul: "I am preaching on Sunday. So, I'm thinking about it." Dave: "You did a funeral the other day didn't you?" Paul: "Yes. Bob Macklebeck's. It started at 11 and we didn't put him in the ground till 12.40." Dave: "He must've been getting cold!" Paul: "So many people talking. And I had to do another one at the Crem at Fenton at 2. So, I had to dash off; utter madness! The deceased lived in Bamburgh Castle, for many years – in a flat. There's plenty." Dave: "I'd like a one of them." Paul: "There's three available right now". Nicky: "Nice and canny, Dave; by the sea; it's a long way from Hexham mind". Dave: "Aye – but I could shift up there; find a little hut!" Paul: "I thought it'd cost a fortune to live in there but apparently it doesn't." Nicky: "Aye, but it must be cold – the heating system won't be that good". Paul: "Tourists! They came in their hundreds for the turning on of the Christmas lights – 300 we had in church. Then we went out and blessed the crib."

The Violin Shop

The shop buzzer rings again, and in to the workshop comes Carolyn Francis – or, 'The Lakeland Fiddler', as she is known, carrying a fiddle case. I realise that Dave has quietly orchestrated a workshop Christmas Party. Dave: "Do come in! [to Paul] Make her a cup of tea. [to Carolyn] Where've you come from, the Antarctic?" [Carolyn is dressed in multiple layers and a woolly hat] Carolyn: "I only believe there's two seasons – shorts and a t shirt or everything on; you've got to be prepared." Carolyn is on her way to a gig at Gamblesby. She says: "I spotted this gap to come over; I thought 'Hexham's half way there'." She's come over for a bow rehair but she also asks Dave to have a look at the bridge on her fiddle because she thinks it's looking "a bit warped and knackered".

Paul goes and finds another chair from the shop, and after removing all her outer layers, and handing over her fiddle to Dave, Carolyn sits down. She looks around the workshop walls and says to Dave: "You haven't got rid of any more violins, have you? It's three deep up there not one!" Dave though is inspecting her fiddle. He says: "The G's like twisted, but it's quite alright. Where's the bow?" Carolyn brings out what even I can see is a bodge of a bow rehair; it's wrecked! Dave exclaims: "Christ man! You caught him on a bad day!"

Carolyn laughs and says: "Only two-thirds' hair was put on it in the first place!"

Having whipped the strings off Carolyn's fiddle, Dave dips the fiddle's bridge in some water and then gets some tongs and warms one side of the bridge in front of the electric heater. The bridge is bent over at the top from being repetitively tuned on the pegs. Carolyn, Paul and I look on. Paul says: "It's like cooking toast." Dave, explaining to us, says: "What you do, the side that's curved, wet it; keep the wet side towards you and put it dry side towards the heat source, in front of something hot. Watch it straighten like that. It only takes a few seconds. Let it cool, and then it lasts for ages. So, if it does it again, you know what to do." Carolyn says: "I just thought it was knackered; I thought it was affecting my tuning." Dave replies: "Well it would do".

Then Dave turns to inspect the sound post. Anticipating problems in this direction, Carolyn says: "Is it in the wrong place?" Dave: "Wrong place?!!! It's been on a walk man!!!" Carolyn [laughing]: "I have observed that it's not sounding as good as it might do!!" Dave gets to work with his sound post adjuster and a new set of strings are put on the fiddle. He tunes it up and then hands it over to Carolyn, says "Help yourself to a bow" and with that she gives her revived fiddle a run out in the performance area that is the shop. This is accompanied by much general toe tapping and whistling from the workshop. "Dave, it's sounding fantastic!" she yells. Dave just smiles, and turns his attention to rehairing Carolyn's bow.

Happy with her fiddle, chat for the rest of the morning turns to what else people are up to in their lives and to folk music gossip, or who is playing with whom. With a lull in the conversation, Paul picks up an unfinished fiddle that has been languishing on the side bench in the workshop since I began the research. Dave tells us: "He started it before lockdown and it's still not finished! We call him Mastermind – "I've started so I'll finish". But – he can't be bothered." Paul replies: "I haven't got the time. I have to get back into it." Dave: "You need to get your mind back into it." Apparently, Paul has finished one fiddle previously. Dave tells us that he sold it to "some lassie". Paul exclaims: "Not some random lassie!" But then goes on to say "I wasn't bothered; I was more bothered by the process. I like making things." Dave tells us: "He makes Northumbrian pipes". Closer inspection of the unfinished fiddle, though, shows that Paul started making it well before Covid lockdowns. Paul, scrutinising his work, says: "I made this mould, in … 2014!! So, it's longer!!!". Paul rummages around the workshop and finds the wood he had earmarked for the back of this fiddle. Dave chides him: "That's yer back; and you haven't even started it!" Paul picks it up and points to the writing on it. It says 'Paul's, not Dave's!' I opine: "That's a nice bit of wood". Dave responds, with evident frustration: "Aye, it's a very nice bit of wood and it's sitting there!" To which Paul retorts: "It's not sitting there. I'm thinking about it!!!"

Carolyn talks a lot about her Lakeland Fiddlers projects. She's done this community project for 25 years. They're now 20 people; what she describes as "a fiddle group with a rhythm section". She gives Dave a copy of the *Happy Meeting* CD they've recently made – a gift to add to his workshop collection. She describes how she still has to catch herself from what she calls 'credentials envy'`: "I have to stop and re-examine my goals. They were to create a community, revive a tradition and have a good time. And I've done all of that, actually. I could've spent my time on the M6, worrying about who my next album was going to be with and bitching about everybody else." Dave laughs: "Well that's it!" Carolyn: "Instead I just do it in Dave's shop!" There's much laughter, for this is exactly the kind of talk that Dave gets to hear often in his workshop. Carolyn then goes on to talk about her desire to take on more solo and small-scale work. She describes touring Scotland with a puppet show: "I loved it; every time I made the music for it – those puppets are like real people; it was entrancing. We went to lots of tiny village halls. There's something very powerful about tiny, intimate shows. I think it's really worth doing those really small things".

    Talk then ranges to include jokes, stories and YouTube watching. Dave tells his Great Aunt Beattie Story, the punch line of which is 'It's nine months since Bene dicked us'. Carolyn tells a story about a saxophone-playing French monk who once lodged with her and, when charged by the abbot to grow stuff on a plot of land, chose to grow cannabis. Adopting a heavy French accent, she says: "Carolyn; they didn't like my cannabis; he wouldn't even sell it; he just burnt it!" At Carolyn's suggestion, we then all gather round Dave's PC to watch 'Mr Pastry' dancing on the Ed Sullevan Show.

    After some mighty ribbing of the marmite sandwiches which I've brought in a Tupperware box for my lunch, Dave then sends Paul out to get some lunches, giving him some cash. Later he tells me: "I'm aware they're coming a long way. So, I make a fuss of them; give them a cuppa, run down to get them a sandwich". Whilst Paul's away doing this, Tom McConville (Chapter Four) rings up. Tom says: "Aye what's going on; what's happening?" Dave: "Well I've got the vicar in. He's just gone down for pork pies". Tom: "Is he OK?" Dave: "Aye. And I've got Carolyn Francis in". Carolyn: "Hello Tom – good to hear you; I'm having all my instruments fettled up by Dr Mann". Dave: "And I've got Nicky in – who's writing the book. So, it's all going on today! Plenty excitement!" Tom rings off and Paul then returns: "Not a very successful trip I'm afraid. They don't do just sausages anymore. They just do the ones with this Christmas sandwich … with little sausages! Chipolatas! I think they're hiding inside!" Looking at the size of these sandwiches, Dave says to him: "Put it through the band saw and we'll share it! It's a Violin shop Christmas Party!! More teas and coffees?"

Lunch over, Paul says: "Is it quarter to one? I'll have to go soon to sort the place out. I have people coming tonight – Rosie and Jim. We've got a gig tomorrow, a ceilidh at Felton". He starts to begin to get his things together. Dave tells him: "Don't forget your pipes." Paul's Northumbrian pipes have been with Dave for some months, collateral against the loan Dave had given him to pay for his ordination robes. Reunited with them, Paul gets the pipes out for a play. He is the piper for the National Park of Northumberland. He tells us: "I opened The Sill". To which Dave adds: "So he got to meet [the then] Prince Charles". Paul mimics King Charles' voice, and their conversation: "Oh, I'm so pleased to see they've got a piper. They're not like Highland pipes, are they?" "No Sir". He was quite interested". Dave insists that Paul takes the sausage roll left over from lunch. Still in the throes of leaving the workshop,

Paul lights on the CD pile: "Any good CDs recently?" Dave: "Aye – Aaron's new one; Carmel Jones & Rachel Walker, Roland Leslie". Paul thumbs through them and says: "I'll take that then. Right, got me free CD; me pipes and me gloves – I'll be back!" And with that, after I've taken a few photos of him with Dave, he leaves the party.

Carolyn then buys some more strings and begins to gather her stuff together to leave. As she does this, she's thinking aloud, saying: "Now I'm not working in schools all the time I need to come over here more often. It's so nice to see you, Dave. I need to get over a bit more. It cheers me up no end. It's life. I need to get in the habit of having days out. Fridays a good day; it's me day for meandering. You go to so many places in the world where nobody gets you, and then you come in here and you don't feel like that anymore. It's the magic of the Mann!"

*

And that it is. Dave's workshop isn't just about the craft work of repairing and maintaining well, which rekindles violins and bows; in so doing re-forging an enchantment with a particular sound that is in turn central to a musicians' craft. It is that, of course. But it's also the site of generosity, hospitality and meaningful conversation; it's where the kind of human encounters happen that are a manifestation of care for, and about, particular people. The workshop, then, is not just a place where fiddles go to be repaired and maintained by a fiddle magician. It's a sanctuary and, often, a therapeutic space, from which people emerge feeling cared for and about, understood, and rejuvenated. That sense of human repair and restoration, ultimately, is "The Magic of the Mann", and it's why people keep returning to this place.

Nicky Gregson

CHAPTER SEVEN
The Lutherie Club

Many is the day when I was at Dave's when a customer would wander into the shop to buy minor accessories – spare strings, a shoulder rest, a mute – and then stay a while, attempting, not always successfully it has to be said, to engage Dave in conversation. The shop's ambience and atmosphere encourage this. Being simultaneously a step back in time and a suspension of time seems to invite a pause for thought and a degree of reflection. Typically, those reflections gravitate to the customer's thoughts on craft, and particularly what they see as a decline in craft working. Seeing in front of them the figure of an older man, people assume this to be a sign of lutherie as a dying craft; or, at least, this is the phrase that is frequently invoked. From there, thoughts typically drift to the general, societal-wide decline in the apprentice model of training, and to speculation on the theme of why, to paraphrase, "young people don't want to do this kind of craft work any longer".

It's easy to see how these understandings might be derived. They reflect living in a modern world, where most things are manufactured, often in faraway places; where hand-made goods produced in dedicated craft workshops are a rarity, and where the skills of repair, and particularly of repairing hand-made things, are widely portrayed as lost arts. Being a man of few words with strangers, Dave doesn't disabuse people of such notions. Typically, he volunteers little more than a few 'ayes', and with that the customer goes on their way. Yet, such understandings are a long way from the reality of lutherie. It's not just that lutherie as a craft skill is very much alive and well, as evidenced by the number of luthier-training schools internationally. It's also that behind the scenes at The Violin Shop is a world very much dedicated to luthier craft and to the passing on of knowledge and skills. But one needs to look hard to find it.

One day, a good while after I'd started coming to the workshop, Dave mentioned to me that "a bloke was in yesterday from Scotland, with a fiddle he'd made. He wanted me to criticise it, so I gave him a few tips. He'd come down for some advice". This was my first inkling of the workshop as a site of teaching and learning lutherie. Until then I'd assumed that Dave simply worked as a lone luthier, with only the occasional assistant – such as Paul Knox. I asked Dave if the guy's fiddle was any good. Dave: "Not bad for a first one, but his corners were naff. So, I advised him how to do his corners. He makes spinning wheels". I ask the obvious question: "So why did he decide that he wanted to do a fiddle?" Dave: "Well, he was a teacher, skilled craftsman, woodwork teacher like – and he's good at spinning wheels. He's retired. Spinning wheels are his passion but he thought he'd try a fiddle since his wife's a professional violinist."

This story is typical of how people – usually, but not exclusively, retired men with a passion for working with wood – start to dabble in lutherie by having a go at making a fiddle. What's also typical is that they will gravitate to luthiers like Dave – for the very same reasons that Dave himself embarked on Barry's evening classes back in the 1980s: because, whilst it's possible to make a violin with only Edward Heron-Allen (or nowadays, YouTube) as a guide, to begin to improve one needs to find a master craftsman.

In the ensuing months, I gradually began to piece together a barely visible and highly dispersed lutherie network consisting of hobby enthusiasts, professional musicians looking to increase their knowledge about fiddle maintenance, and professional and trainee professional luthiers, all of whom have either passed through Dave's workshop, learning from him, or who continue to seek out his knowledge and advice. Barely known to one another, they each have benefitted from one-on-one advice and tuition, always given freely and generously. Such free gifts – which stand in stark contrast to other luthiers who charge for their time - may seem reason enough for the journey. But that they've travelled the road to Dave's door in the first place is an indication of the level of skill and proficiency in this workshop; it's both a measure of Dave's reputation and a manifestation of the workshop's role as a hub for lutherie practice in the Northeast of England.

How does the hub work? What type of people come to it? How do they learn from and relate to Dave as a master craftsman? And how does all this connect with the perpetuation of lutherie as a profession?

*

An hour or so after The Violin Shop Christmas Party had dispersed (Chapter Six), and coincidentally as Dave and I are talking about his knife skills, the shop buzzer sounds again. "Who's this?" says Dave, with an air of resignation mixed with exasperation. The party being over, and it being near to Christmas, the last thing that Dave wants is more work coming through the shop door. We get up from our seats in the workshop and go through to the shop. Dave pronounces: "Why, it's Jim Bickel, cellist extraordinaire!" Jim plays in Durham Sinfonia and is a cello tutor for Durham University, a role he's done for 35 years. Already anticipating the answer to my question, I ask Jim if he's a frequent inhabitant of the shop. "Too frequent!" he laughs. What brings Jim to the shop today is an instrument purchase he's recently made. He says: "I've got a bass viol out there in the car. It's got a very interesting history. Shall I go and get it?" Cue an afternoon of instrument appreciation amongst lutherie enthusiasts, not as a sounding thing but as a fabricated craft object.

With the instrument in the shop and out of its case, Jim takes up the story of how it came to be in his possession. He tells us: "I've been looking for ages for a bass viol. I was bought up in Haslemere (in Surrey), and on my way home from school I used to go past a house called Jesses that housed the Dolmetsch family". Jesses House is an Arts & Crafts building dating from the early twentieth century. It was purchased by the Dolmetsch family in 1917. Arnold Dometsch and his son Carl played a foundational role in the revival of early music in the UK, through making period instruments, rediscovering old manuscripts and promoting the playing of early music. Jesses House itself became a centre of workshop production. Its output included viols, virginals, spinnets, harpsichords, clavichords and recorders. Jim continues with his story: "About two months ago a Dolmetsch tenor viol came up in an auction and I'm absolutely thrilled with it, but it's a tenor viol, not a bass viol. And it didn't come with a bow, so I started looking for a bow. About three weeks ago I was putting viol-bow into search terms, and I put in Dolmetsch – and it said 'Dolmetsch cello'. And I thought 'That's very strange', because they didn't make cellos. So, I looked at it and it was an auction over towards Liverpool who were selling it. Anyhow the long and the short of it is, I never saw it, except in terrible pictures. I got them to measure it. From the pictures I couldn't even tell the size of it; I couldn't tell whether it was a tenor or a bass viol. So, they measured it; all the measurements were wrong, so they had to measure it all over again. Eventually I bought it, and we went down to pick it up. And I said to the auctioneer, 'Would you mind – if you're prepared to - could you let me know something about its background, because it's in pretty good condition' - although it didn't look like this when I got it. 'Yes', he said. So, the story was that there was a house, which was really derelict; it had a garage, and somebody had been told just to clear the garage and put everything in a skip – and this was in the garage. And it went onto the skip outside their house. They just put it on top of the skip. Fortunately, they didn't put it underneath anything else; they put it on top. And it sat there for a week or two in the open air, and then it was driven to a tip. When it was driven into the tip, the tip proprietor happened to see this thing bouncing around. He keeps his eyes open. He picked it off, and he thought he'd bung it into an auction as a cello. Except it isn't a cello because it's got Dolmetsch inside. It's a bass viol. And not only this, it was made by the same guy that I used to go and see who used to repair my grandmother's mandolin: George Carley. Carley ran the Dolmetsch's viol workshop at Jesses House. He also repaired me and my brother's instruments. So, I knew him very well, and he's signed it inside."

Listening to the story, Dave says: "What an extraordinary find". Jim: "Yes, it's the find of a lifetime! Especially since I knew the guy who made it really well. I would think it's probably 1970s. That's my guess. But it hasn't any play wear at all; no fingerboard wear. That's skip damage but the back of the neck is pretty clean. I think someone bought it as a nice idea but it's quite difficult to play, so they stuck it in a corner and then in the garage. It's got a number; I'm using that to try to identify when it was made. I'm absolutely thrilled with it". With that Jim treats Dave and me to a demonstration, playing a passage of Bach on the bass viol, whilst Dave texts Ralph Plumb to come and see what Jim's got. Five minutes later, into the shop comes Ralph, who then gets the repeat story.

As well as being an instrument enthusiast and a bit of a collector, Jim does a fair bit of his own repair and maintenance work, "with a bit of advice from Dave!" He has his own workshop in his kitchen. Jim tells me: "Funnily enough, a long time ago, Dave and I had lessons from the same guru". Nicky: "Let me guess, that must be one Barry Oliver?" Jim: "The very same. We went for a while and then, this was going to be Dave's thing, and I was already busy playing, doing all that sort of thing." I suggest that being able to do DIY repairs is really useful. Jim: "That's really why I went. I did do a little bit of making with Barry, and it was fun. We learnt quite a lot." He pauses: "Well Dave learnt a lot and I learnt a little!" Turning to Dave he says, "But you did a proper apprenticeship with him". Dave: "Aye, more or less – I was his assistant". Jim: "Which I didn't. I just went for the evening classes." Remembering those times back in the 1980s, he continues: "And then there was what's his name, who did radiators and made violins". Dave: "Derek (Greener)". Jim: "Yes, Derek. He was very, very applied". Dave: "Aye, he could knock a fiddle out in 24 hours. That's because he was a plumber; that's the way it is in his trade". Jim: "He wasn't refined; you can't be refined in that trade, but he was very efficient. He had a good eye for making things and he was extremely applied, amazingly applied." Letting his thoughts run with him, Jim says: "When you think back to eighteenth century workshops, they'd have needed people like that. But I enjoy doing this. So, if a student has a problem with an instrument, or they're looking for an instrument, then I can help them in that. My view was that you can't teach someone if they're playing on an instrument that isn't working properly, so if I learn how to make an instrument work properly then it'll be easier for them to play it better. The schools, they don't encourage this but, if I was running a conservatoire, they'd be learning this. They'd be having classes on maintenance."

Given his repair and maintenance competences, Jim has started doing a bit of tinkering work already on his bass viol. There follows plenty of discussion between the two luthiers and an amateur enthusiast about the instrument, and what Jim is doing with it. Dave asks Jim: "Are you going to straighten the bridge?" Jim: "I am, slowly. I know your little techniques. I'm pulling it slowly, bit by bit. It was about here, and it was really, really, really bent – but it is the original bridge. It will straighten. I did it a little this morning. I haven't got the sound post quite right because the bridge isn't right yet – so the top strings are a little bit abrasive perhaps." Ralph admires the varnishing: "Nice texture in the varnish". He then suggests that Jim put gut strings on it – "that'll be a different sound". Jim remarks on the scroll: "It's beautifully done – beautifully graduated; the fluting, the chamfer. The most subtle chamfer all the way round". Ralph: "Yes; nice to get that continually smooth". Jim: "And the pegs have never been turned. They're sitting exactly on the peg board".

Jim tells Dave that he's already 'calmed down' some of the minor blemishes from the bass viol's time in the skip. He then says to Dave: "Do you think that (a scuff mark – pictured) can be improved or can you just leave it? I was wondering whether just to leave them and let them darken down." Dave tells him how to attend to the scuff mark: "You just touch with some colour, not varnish – and it won't dry glossy". Jim queries what he means: "Like water?" Dave: "No. Not really. You need to use colour with a dry brush. You dip your brush in, wipe it off, then you just gently spot it. Dry re-touching". Jim is evidently not sure about this. He says: "I've got some coloured varnish". Dave: "No. When you're ready, just bring it across. When the bridge is right, and then I'll show you". Jim is anxious not to make his efforts at retouching look bodged. He says: "Varnishing always scares me with these things because I've seen it go wrong". Dave asks him: "Have you tried walnut oil – that'll calm it down". Jim: "Is that very different from almond oil?" Dave: "Aye, it's better". Jim: "The reason I ask is because I have a bottle of almond oil and of walnut oil, and I knocked that over, so I've got a full bottle of almond oil".

A few months previously, I'd had a demonstration of the wonders of walnut oil with wood. Dave was then beginning to turn to finishing his latest commissioned fiddle, preparing it for the application of his ground. He'd explained to me: "You're trying to get the varnish to enhance the wood, not coat it. So, you've got to enhance the wood without hiding it, otherwise it'll look awful. It'll look dull and dead if you put too much colour and varnish on. Like, the more colour you put on the more you're hiding the flame. You're losing the qualities of the wood. The goal is to get a beautiful finish with as little varnish as possible, like the Italians did." He'd then used a test piece of wood to show me how his ground, walnut oil and varnish combine to produce a 3-D sheen effect in the wood. Smearing walnut oil onto the wood with his index finger he showed how it highlights the grain, shimmering in what appears to be three dimensions: "You see that, when you wave it in the light it shimmers. Then put some varnish on – it's a spirit varnish. And that holds the 3-D effect. See how it shimmers? It looks as if you can put your fingers in; it's an illusion".

Back in the shop, Jim then asks Dave if he has any old, dead gut strings. He wants to use these to make frets on the viol. Dave rummages behind the shop's counter and brings out a box of very old strings. He tells Jim "have a look through that lot". Jim sits down and starts methodically going through piles and piles of ancient string packets. Eventually he finds what he's looking for: very old gut strings. These strings are in packaging that looks like they're from the 1920s or 1930s. It's decided that they must be "Old Bob's stuff", for Dave hadn't a clue that they were even there. Having happened on these, Jim says: "Now Dave, I at least owe you a bottle of wine." Dave replies: "Oh come on, they've been sitting there for decades, and they'll just be binned, if I ever retire".

And there, in essence, in this one afternoon is the lutherie club in action. The shop is a place where a player, instrument collector and enthusiast like Jim comes to enthuse about his purchases with like-minded professionals, and to pick up tips and advice on how to return this find of a lifetime to pristine condition. But it goes beyond this in that also on offer is Dave's skill, knowledge and workshop resources. Dave offers his dry colouring skills and knowledge to Jim knowing full well that, as a classical player, Jim will only be fully satisfied when the bass viol's surface is returned to perfect condition. He also recognises Jim's concern that he lacks the competences to affect an invisible repair himself. As if that were not enough, the shop's legacy stock is also made available on a 'help yourself if it comes in useful' basis. Small wonder, then, that Jim felt the need to insist on a form of gift in return. But no. Such generosity, as ever, is Dave's way – at least for those, like Jim, whom he lets into what is tantamount to his informal lutherie club; membership strictly controlled.

*

A few months later I had the pleasure of meeting another member of Dave's amateur luthier club: Jeremy Scratchert – or, as Dave calls him, "Dr Jeremy", one of whose fiddles featured in Chapter Six. Jeremy tells me how he's been a keen amateur player all his life, spanning most genres: folk, jazz and classical. "I played front desk in the Tyneside Chamber Orchestra; I played jazz at the Sage at Gateshead. I played folk from my days as a student right through until 2008, when I had a rather nasty stroke, which rather encumbered my ability to play. But I played at the Cumberland Arms in Byker (in Newcastle); and I played for two folk bands; one of them was Lothlorien. One was a bluegrasss country and western band, and then I played with a local skittle band – Earl Grey and the Cha Wallers. But I found that genre wasn't for me – certainly not skittle".

As well as a player, Jeremy's a collector of instruments. After Dave has made some teas, we sit down in the workshop and begin talking about his instruments. Jeremy says: "I don't know how many violins I own. Have a guess, Dave". Dave: "Pfffh, 10?" Jeremy indicates more. "15?" "Keep going!" "20?" "Keep going". "30?" He nods. Dave: "Bloody hell!" Jeremy: "That includes the electric ones". I ask: "And how many came from here?" Jeremy: "Well he's made me two and he's restored several more. Andrea Pontedoro made me a violin and a viola, and I've acquired various other instruments from here and there, but Dave's done a lot of restorations for me. So, if I include the kiddie-sized ones and the electrics it must be about 30 by now." I ask Jeremy if he set out to collect this number. "No!" he replies. "They just came my way! I go to auction rooms and stick my arm up too much!" Later he describes his auction room habit as 'the opportunistic insanity of a true English eccentric'. It's a habit that extends beyond fiddles, for Jeremy confesses: "And not only that I've got a cello, two violas, about five 5-string banjos, an English concertina, two sets of Northumbrian pipes – one of which I made myself – and other bits and bobs". I ask if all these instruments get played. Laughing, Jeremy says: "They have to take turns!"

Like Jim Bickel, Jeremy has his own workshop at home, "the contents of which were guided by Dave". But again, much like with Jim, his repair and restoration projects tend to find their way to Dave's workbench. One such is one of the reasons for Jeremy's visit to the workshop today, for Dave has just finished working on it and it's ready for collection. The violin was made by a cabinet maker from Scotswood in Newcastle upon Tyne, near where Dave was born. Jeremy tells me: "And because it's made by a cabinet maker, not a violin maker, he's got the most intriguing way of joining the neck to the body of the violin. So intriguing that I had it X-rayed to find out what he'd done. The hammer price was about 60 or 70 quid".

Dave hands him the violin for his inspection. Jeremy exclaims: "Oh Dave, you've surpassed yourself here. Absolutely fabulous." He tells me, "I bought this at auction, in pieces. It must be a long time ago now. One of the curiosities about this fiddle is that instead of having a two-piece front it's made with four separate pieces of spruce." I ask: "So what's Dave done with it?" Jeremy: "Everything. Basically, we took the front off in the workshop here to see what was what inside. And it's all hand inscribed on the back, and it revealed the four-fold spruce at the front. When we took the front off to have a look inside, I never put it back on. It needed other bits and pieces done and, as one or two years went by, I decided that, despite all that Dave had taught me, I didn't feel confident in doing the whole job myself. So, I asked him as recently as 10 days ago if he'd be prepared to give it a go. And here it is! My word!" Continuing to inspect Dave's work, he says: "I've noticed that the previous impressions of the bridge feet don't line up with the f's. Is this the right scale length now?" Dave: "Yes". Jeremy: "So it was too short before. The edge work on this is really nice; the way he's brought that into the corners. I never noticed that it had no purfling!" Dave "That's because he's a cabinet maker". Jeremy: "I'm so delighted with this!"

Here is the same type of instrument appreciation talk that figured when Jim brought his newly acquired bass viol into the shop. The interest is in how the instrument has been made, or constructed, and in its unique qualities as a fabricated craft object, not in how it performs as a sounding instrument. And, just as with the bass viol, there is the same relation between an amateur luthier and Dave. For the informal amateur luthier club, Dave will always be 'the master craftsman', whose work is revered and admired. Yet the conjunction of the club with an auction house habit means that Dave keeps on acquiring unanticipated repair and restoration projects. The club keep buying up old, wrecked instruments either at auctions, or online; they then decide the restoration and/or repair job is beyond their capabilities, with the result that Dave gets another job for the workshop. There's a lesson here. An amateur luthier club generates work!

*

Jeremy explains to me how his interest in lutherie started to develop. He says: "Dave and I met about 20 years ago. I came in here to buy a violin and I mentioned that I'd been to Juliet Barker's summer school in Cambridge (this is a week-long course for luthiers). And Dave said, 'Well why don't you come in here?' So, I started coming in here as an unpaid apprentice – and I must have had some enthusiasm or ability for it because before long he was teaching me to do bridges; he taught me to do bass bars, and repair sound post cracks and neck grafts and stuff like that. I'd even look after the shop at times when he wasn't here".

We turn to discuss Dave's lutherie skills and learning from Dave. Jeremy opines: "He's tantamount to a genius!

He's incredibly modest but the talent is astonishing!" I ask Jeremy about Dave's style of teaching: "How did he teach you, do you reckon?" Jeremy: "By example. There are two ways of learning. Repetition and initial impact. You've got to watch him like a hawk. When he's cutting a bridge foot every single stroke of the knife is a lesson in itself. The blade takes a single curve across the whole foot, and that takes a lot of learning. Unless you learn that you'll start chipping away, and it'll never fit. And he doesn't think twice about it – it's just automatic for him!" Knowing what he means, I say: "I haven't seen anyone with knife skills like this". Jeremy agrees: "Exactly". Ever modest, Dave says: "Get away!" But Jeremy – reverting to professional mode - tells him firmly: "Dave, you're just being modest now; it's true."

*

It was on my very first visit to the workshop that I'd got to witness Dave's knife skills and, like everyone else who has seen him working a knife, I was blown away. At that time, he was carving the neck for the latest commissioned fiddle. The knife handle fitted his hand seamlessly, but it was the relationship between his thumb and what his fingers were doing that I was particularly interested in. Knife, hand and fingers were in perfect harmony; the one an extension of the other. Instinctively, I knew that I would never be able to hold a knife in this way, let alone get it to work with this degree of control. So, I got Dave to slow everything down so I could see exactly what was going on – even videoing the process. Initially he explained this action to me as "squeezing it; not pulling it". He described how most people's response to trying to work a knife initially is, as Jeremy describes, to pull with it or snatch it. The result is an irregular cut and taking chunks out of whatever is being cut. To hold the knife properly requires a careful placement of the thumb, such that it can act as both an anchor and guide, and free up the fingers to be able to control and squeeze.

Later, whilst demonstrating the chamfer process to me, Dave elaborated on knife control: "You've always got to be in perfect control. Guide with the thumb. Control with the index finger – then squeezing with the other fingers. And it's got to be a single bevel blade. Lots of violin makers use a double bevelled blade. But it's got to sit perfectly flat on there, and then you can judge your cut. You've got to keep that (the blade) pressed flat and then squeeze. If you go over, you rip chunks out. You've got to keep that pressed flat and squeeze it. And you've got to feel the pressure. The more you press the bigger the cut you're going to get; the lighter the less. And when you're coming into a curve, the grain changes – so you're going that way and that way. You've got to put enough pressure on so that the front cutting edge goes just under the surface as much as you're wanting it to."

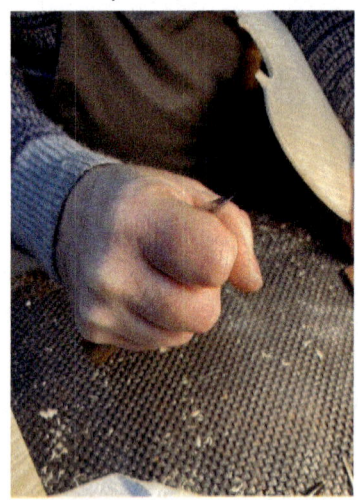

*

Back with Jeremy in the workshop, he says to me: "You know the best thing that Dave ever taught me? How to sharpen knives." As he's telling me this, I'm minded that he's repeating some of the very same key points of learning that Nial and Dave took from Barry. Jeremy continues: "Do you know, his favourite quip is 'Is your knife sharp enough?' This from a man who once, when replacing his glasses, didn't take the knife out of his hands and it went through his ear!" He goes on to tell me: "You can always tell a luthier because they've got a bald patch on their forearms (and yes, Dave has that!). That's what you do. It's got to be sharp enough to shave with." He tells me how he, of course, drew the inevitable comparisons with his life in the medical profession: "I used to think you could do this stuff with surgical scalpels, but you can't. Firstly, they're not sharp enough and secondly, they're not rigid enough – they're meant for cutting soft tissue, not hard curly maple. They may be OK for some work, like shaving a little bit off a bridge or something like that, but for really serious work, you can't do it."

When I ask Jeremy how he'd describe his relationship to Dave as a master craftsman he gave it some thought and then said: "I think the term would be amanuensis". It's a relationship that is particular to artistic, creative and craft work, whereby assistants are tasked with reproducing authentic copies, typically of a manuscript. Jeremy invokes Mozart's amanuensis to explain what he means: "Mozart lay in bed and dictated what should appear in the manuscript and Sussmayr wrote it down". What goes on in the workshop, I would say, is a little different to Mozart and Sussmayr. For sure, Dave shows how certain tasks should be done, and the task of the assistant or amateur enthusiast is to attempt to emulate this. But how successful they are in this is down to not just how closely they can observe what

Dave is doing but also their capacity to translate what they see into a form of kinaesthetic learning. This is about the combination of, often miniscule, bodily movement with the interface between a hand-craft tool and wood. There is no doubt that this is hard, even for people with a talent for lutherie and some years of experience.

Dave recounts to me how Andrea Pontadoro – who is now one of the top contemporary Italian luthiers – "was over for a few years. He lived in Edinburgh for five years; he was making nice fiddles and he'd take them into Stringers to sell them. Then he came down here. I said: 'Your fiddles aren't set up properly'. Eventually he was coming down here two days a week; he did that for two years. First off, I cut one side of the bridge, and then I told him to cut the other the same. He found that hard. Eventually he mastered it, and now he's renowned for doing the best set-ups and bridge setting in Italy!"

*

Most of the members of Dave's informal luthier club over the years have been amateurs, hobby enthusiasts. In that regard, Andrea Pontadoro, as a professional luthier, is an exception. Another exception is Anthony Pancke, who is the son of GPs, and from Whickham on the edge of the Newcastle conurbation. When I talked with Anthony, he was then in his second year at the violin-making school in Brienz, in Switzerland. He gave me a 360-degrees panorama of the location on his phone: "I'm by the lake here – it's very nice. Somewhere behind is the waterfall. It's great here; it's the right environment for violin making. You've got the right environment to focus; there's calm. If your eyes are getting tired from looking at something close-up for a long time you can just stare at the mountains for a few seconds". A more idyllic place is hard to imagine.

Before we talked, Dave had already given me his assessment of Anthony's potential: of all the people he's had through the workshop over the years, he is the one he singles out as having exceptional talent. "He's going to be world-class" is Dave's verdict. Keen to learn more, I began talking with Anthony by asking him how he got into making violins.

Anthony tells me: "So, I've played the violin since when I was about seven, I think. And my grandparents, they're also long-time enthusiastic musicians. So, I had that connection in the family. And, for as long as I can remember, I've been interested in making things. I did a lot of woodwork, origami; it was a bit of everything. I never did wood turning, but I did wood carving, like making elegant looking wooden swords or trying to carve the occasional figure out of wood. I tried working with metal as well, but that was difficult at home, and we did a tree house in the garden – so, that kind of thing. At some point it was a friend of mine who recommended that maybe I should try making a violin. I'd had the idea a couple of years previously, and I'd tried to figure out how it works, and then I realised that I kind of don't know how a violin is made. You can watch YouTube videos but it's difficult to get started. And then it was the dad of that friend of mine who knew Dave. I had one violin that needed a tiny repair – a missing corner; a new corner grafted on. So, we went to Dave with that, and we saw the workshop, and we saw someone else there who was learning violin making. We figured that that would pretty much be the ideal opportunity to start. So, I spoke to Dave about it. I was 13 at the time. And Dave kind of saw me, saw that I was interested, and that I'd done some woodworking stuff before. He sold me some tone wood and let me know where I could buy tools and resources, and I kind of just got started from there."

*

Tone wood, of course, is one of the reasons that hobby enthusiasts gravitate to luthiers. They are the obvious short cut to finding quality wood, and much as Barry's workshop was where Dave first acquired suitable wood for violin making, so Dave's now occupies the same niche for aspiring luthiers like Anthony. I see why when I find out that the shop is also a tone wood store.

Whilst the shop window display includes a few blocks of tone wood, artfully arranged by Paul and Charlotte, it's the counter which houses the main stash. One afternoon when I was in the shop, Dave opened the doors to the counter: et voila – cupboards stuffed full of the stuff. Laughing at my exclamations, Dave says: "Aye there's a canny bit! It's probably 50 instruments' worth!" The precipitate to this grand reveal had been not just my curiosity but also Dave's need to select wood for his next fiddle. What followed was the kind of lesson in reading tone wood which a keen amateur maker can only get from talking with, and standing alongside, a master craftsman. It's priceless knowledge.

Dave pulls out two pieces of maple and begins to compare them. He tells me: "That's a nice back. You look at the figure – tiger figure, on flame maple. That's an A; that's AA – because it's got more depth in it". Dave puts a small amount of walnut oil on each block of maple to bring out the figure, and the difference between the two blocks of maple that he's scrutinising: "See, the AA has a better 3-D effect. See – that's [the A grade wood] good, but this is super good. But this (the AA) is really hard to work, because of the grain and the figure. The figure's more 3-D but it's harder to work 'cos it pulls the curl. When you're working this stuff it's really hard and it makes your hands hurt. Your tools have to be really sharp because otherwise you're going to pull the curl out of it. And if you're nearly finished, and you've spent a lot of time on it, and you pull a curl out of it then you've knacked it." Knocking the AA block with his fist, he goes on: "This'll probably be a bright fiddle 'cos of the hardness. Hard wood you can get thinner, but it's hard work." Turning to another block altogether, he says: "This stuff I won't use – bird's eye maple. It can be troublesome. It has a slight 3-D effect. Some people love it. These are the bird's eyes – but they're like little, tiny knots, and sometimes, the knots can come loose in playing. I got this for nothing – for repairs, if I ever get anything in." Having selected his woods for the front and back he turns to the neck blocks: "That's nice; but it's a narrow figure. I'm looking more for a medium to broad flame effect – like fire. I'll use that for repairs". Eagle eyed, he identifies exactly the piece that matches his expectations, and with that – in less than five minutes - he's decided which wood will become his next fiddle.

*

Back to Anthony. He tells me: "I had like a small workshop in the cellar of the house – like a 4m^2 workbench. And I'd go to Dave's maybe like once or twice a month on Saturdays when I had some time or when I didn't have schoolwork, or when I needed help with something, I'd get my dad to drive me there." I ask Anthony specifically which stages of making a violin he needed help with: "Like doing the joints on the back and belly; you need a really good plane to get both parts right and for a long time I didn't have that. I had the small arching planes (used to shape the back and the belly) but those big planes are expensive. But Dave has one, so I'd go over to him. And for the bending iron, for bending the ribs. So, the things I couldn't do at home and the bits I was struggling with as well. I remember I had huge problems planing the ribs to the right thickness. I'd get all the way to a mm, and just above 1.1mm they'd snap. So, I went to Dave's, and he showed me how to do that."

*

In the workshop, I get to see Dave working on some of the stages which Anthony tells me gave him trouble. The week after Dave had selected the wood for his next fiddle, he began work on preparing the back and front. Each block is measured up by eye for cutting down a centreline to create two halves, which then need to be joined. The wedge-shaped maple back is cut through to open like a book. With the spruce block for the belly, the block is cut in half, and then Dave reverses the two halves such that the grain goes the same way on both sides.

Dave begins with the AA maple for the back. He tells me: "I've got to cut it down the centre; but I've got to get the cut right, otherwise it'll be wonky. I don't want to take too much out of there 'cos I can get the ribs out … Just do it by eye – a half – that's about halfway – ruler. I've got to trim this base up so that lines up straight with that, like that (he uses a set square for this). And now, I've got to plane it off that side until I get it level." He brings out a large plane , puts the maple block in a vice and begins planing the base. I get an immediate indication of what Dave had meant when he'd said that this quality maple is very hard to work. The resistance from the wood is considerable, and planing is very hard physical labour. As Dave works up a huge muck sweat, I'm holding the workbench with as much strength as I can muster to try to stop it moving right across the workshop floor. Yet at the same time as this is hard work, each pass of the plane is simultaneously an exercise in 'feel', for Dave explains that he is feeling 'the high points' off with the plane. Finally satisfied, he says: "Where's me big ruler?" He then draws a cutting line for the band saw, before cutting the maple block into half on the long side, thereby creating the two halves of the back.

He then exclaims: "Oh there's a bloody knot in it!!" He takes the two blocks back through from the machine room to the shop and puts both pieces on the counter, staring closely at them. There follows a lot of deliberation. Dave: "Should I use it, or not? 'Cos it's running right through. It might run out quick or it might go through the centre. Do you carry on with it or …" Realising that this is a $64k question, I ask Dave what his instinct tells him. He says: "Well you've got to weigh up – 'cos this is going to be the bottom, that's the top. So, you've got to think. It's coming out here – it's just about gone; so, I'm going to have plenty (of wood) to come out of the top where it's not going to be seen, and it's in the lower half nearer the base and it's coming out. So, I'm almost certain it's not going to affect anything, and you're not going to see it." I ask: "So, how far into the journey of making would you get before you'd get an answer?" Dave: "Well when you start the arching, and if it's starting to appear bad then you've got to think". I observe that there's a lot of work to get to that point. Dave: "Well that's it. I'll be a fair way into it. I'll have done the outlines and started shaving the arch work and probably purfled it. Or, it might appear straightaway, and then it's chuck it, or I could use it for repairs." I say: "I'm just so struck that you can't tell until you open it up like that."

Dave: "That's it – aye. When you buy wood, you don't get guarantees. So, if it's got a knot in it or a flaw in it in the middle that's tough – buyer beware! You can't send it back." I ask Dave how many blocks he's jettisoned over the years. Dave: "I can probably think of about six". Nicky: "I suppose that's not bad, but it's still a bit of a risk". Dave: "You just have to accept it."

Dave decides to give the wood the benefit of the doubt and to carry on, at least for the present. He proceeds to join the two pieces of maple using a technique called a rub joint. Rub joints are a fine woodworking skill, used in top-end cabinet making – which is also one of the reasons why cabinet makers over the years have dabbled in making fiddles.

On goes the glue pot and Dave pulls out a huge plane the likes of which I've never seen before. This is the expensive plane which Anthony referred to. Dave tells me: "It's German – Nievesen; a precision plane (pictured). The foot is accurate to 2000th of an inch across its length and width. That one (the one he'd used previously) is like a donkey's hind leg – it won't let you do it. ... It must be 20 years I've had this, 'cos when Nial was here we had a good one and we shared it, and then he took it, so I thought 'Christ I'll have to go and buy one!'" Dave places the two pieces of maple in the vice on his bench and repeatedly planes the long sides of them, where he's going to make the joint. Each few passes sees the wood released from the vice and them held together against the light, inspected for areas of daylight.

Dave then goes back to working with the plane, using feel, to remove the snagging points. It's a process that goes on until there's no daylight visible to the naked eye. Then he dons his magnifying goggles to inspect his work with more precision: "Yes, slight little line there – good, good, good, good, good – slight little line there. Check this one – good, good, good, just a little line there." He planes again. The surface completed to his satisfaction, he places one piece in the vice and then applies the rabbit hide glue. He tells me: "You've got to put it (the hide glue) on and then you put the two surfaces together and you've got to rub till it starts resisting or 'grabbing'." He rubs the joint backwards and forwards. "Right – let that settle there." He wipes the surplus glue off, and then after a short moment starts pressing down on the wood. He says: "I'm just doing that (a slight rotational twisting movement with wrists). If it starts spinning, it's no good; that should be perfect. So, that's both faces, perfectly level, all over. When you rub it together, like that, it closes the vacuum and sucks it in – 'schluk' – and there's no tension or strain on that joint at all." Satisfied, he declares himself "Happy with that!" – Dave's stock phrase for a job well done.

The task completed to his own exacting standards, Dave takes a rest in his chair. He tells me, other luthiers don't use rub jointing. Instead, they use polymer glue and clamps. Dave opines this is "'cos they don't trust themselves, they're not positive on what they're doing. For some reason they don't get it." He goes on: "they lack confidence on getting a good joint. The skill is in how you feel it. You hear them: 'I hate doing bloody joints; I know I shouldn't but I'm going to use it'. It's a short cut". Working with polymer glues means one can get away with doing just a quick visual check on the joint surfaces, for the polymer glues expand to fill any gaps. Whereas to produce a rub joint requires working to thousandths of an inch tolerances. In turn that requires being able to work with feel with a precision plane. It's a task not easily learnt. Dave tells me: "Anthony came in a few months ago. I was teaching him this technique I've shown you, of feeling the highs and lows with the plane in the vice (pictured). I was telling him, 'When it's resisting just feel it, and then do a quick sweep across the lot, using your back not your arms. It'll be perfectly smooth'. He couldn't believe it. They don't do this in Switzerland. It takes them hours back there. They haven't got it in a vice, so they can't feel the resistance. They're holding it instead on a bench."

*

I ask Anthony how Dave taught him as a teenager in the workshop. He tells me: "We'd be working on stuff in parallel. He'd set me working on something and I'd have a try at it whilst he was rehairing a bow, or doing some repairs, or whatever. He'd explain something to me and then, so long as I was coping, and not struggling, he'd be working on his own things in the background. I'd look at what he was doing, but I was mainly getting on with my own stuff." He goes on to tell me: "I was pretty motivated. At home I would be reading whatever I could find. My dad bought me books that I was interested in; I was reading whatever I could find on the internet. And then I would be trying those things out and taking them into Dave. And sometimes Dave would say, 'Yes, that's a pretty good idea'. And sometimes – I was reading about the whole plate tuning thing which Carleen Hutchins was doing in the 1980s, and I remember I emailed Dave about that asking him if this was how he tuned his plates. And I got the reply, 'Sounds good; doesn't work!'" Nicky: "That's so him!" Anthony: "That's him, and when you know him, you know it's not meant in an unfriendly way at all". Nicky: He's a man of few words! Blunt some would say!" Anthony: "But in a good way. And teaching me it was always great because I could come to him with questions and what he knew he would answer me. What was subjective, opinion based, evaluating the artistic styles of violin making, he was always very open minded, flexible. I remember with my second violin, I brought the finished-in-the white instrument to him, and I said, 'I've finished it, can I start varnishing?' And he said, 'Are you happy with the spruce texture on the belly?' And I said, 'Yes; I like it'. And no comment at all about 'I would sand that down a bit more'. There were a few things where it'd be obvious that it would not pass; say a joint that wasn't really closed in the centre. Then, he wouldn't say 'Are you happy with that?' He'd say 'That's not good enough. Let's work on this'. But this belly spruce texture; it's not going to ruin the violin. Actually, I still quite like it to this day. It's an aesthetic decision. He'd have done it differently but he's aware it's not a critical matter. It's a subjective matter. I'd do it differently nowadays, but it was a good experience seeing what it does. He saw that – if it goes well, fine. If it goes badly, it's a) not the end of the world and b) a learning opportunity."

As Anthony describes this, it is obvious that – even though he has never been Dave's formal assistant or apprentice – to all intents and purposes he has been exactly that all through his teenage years. Eschewing the standard assistant or apprentice model in favour of something less formalised is, at one level, typical of Dave. He's his own man and has never been one for following conventions. But it's also indicative of the decline of the assistant and apprentice model in lutherie, in favour of formalised training in an educational setting; the very setting that Anthony is currently in at the Swiss violin-making school. For any young person seeking to become a luthier, it is now essential to graduate from a school, and to be exposed to a wide variety of influences. Today, Anthony cites as his influences not just Dave but "Stefan-Peter Greiner. He's a world-famous violin maker and he taught me a lot of stuff. Roger Hargrave. He lives maybe half an hour's drive from my grandparents in Germany. So, both of those people and Andrew Finnigan and Pia Klaembt in Bremen as well."

That said, five years as an unofficial apprentice is inevitably foundational. I ask Anthony about Dave's influence. Anthony reflects: "He was there right from the start, so it's definitely central. It's not as if you can pinpoint a style that I've taken directly from Dave. If anything, it's got to be more of a mindset, of working to high standards but still being pragmatic about everything." He goes on: "A lot of violin makers they get very caught up in weird details. It's good to pay attention to the details but if you're obsessing over only using historical ingredients in your varnish to the point where you're overlooking the quality of the varnishes themselves then that's not so good. And Dave is pragmatic like that. And I'd say it's this mindset; being focused, but not stressing, and being laid back enough about the work."

Hearing Anthony talk in these terms about Dave's influence on him, I was minded of how Nial and Dave talked about learning from Barry Oliver. Years of being in the same workshop, working alongside a master craftsman, doesn't just teach particular skills and techniques. It's also a means to the transmission of the cultures and rhythms of craft working.

*

Mostly, on the occasions when I watched Dave working in the workshop, he was focused on demonstrating specific tasks, or skills and techniques to me – just as he does with his luthier club. Except, unlike the club, I wasn't being tasked with the unenviable challenge of reproducing what was being demonstrated to the skill level on display! Inevitably, such an emphasis highlights particular skills and techniques. What it struggles to convey, though, is one of the defining qualities of a master craftsman at work, which is the rhythm, or flow, of craft work. This can only be learnt through osmosis, by working in the space of a workshop alongside, or in the vicinity of, a master craftsman over many hours.

My first inkling of the importance of rhythm and flow came on the occasions when Dave would sit at his bench and recount to me how the problem-solving facets of lutherie never really stop. Dave tells me: "Your subconscious is working all the time and some of the things come to you in the middle of the night. You wake up and think 'Oh, I'll do that'." Minded of the parallels with writing as a craft, I ask Dave: "What kind of things drop into your head?" Dave: "Like when you're working the wood say, but you're not quite happy about the way it's flexing, and you think 'Well, I'm down to my thicknesses, but it's still not right'. And then you forget about it and go home, and then subconsciously you must be thinking about it because It'll come in the middle of the night. 'Oh, just take a bit out of that area; take it down to 2.2mm in there'. And then you cannot wait to get in in the morning to try it."

Richard Sennett identifies recursive problem-identification and problem-solving as one of the defining characteristics of craft work, along with what he calls slow time. Slow time is fundamental to making things well. It's most immediately obvious in the schedule of fiddle making, or rather its lack. Rather than producing fiddles to a predetermined schedule, Dave's fiddles emerge in their own time – only when he is entirely satisfied with them and the quality of the work. So, if he's not happy with the flexing of the back of a fiddle, to take just one example, he'll not proceed until he is. At times, though, slow time is more than this, for working with wood also demands from Dave that he works in a particular way; it insists on working in a flow state.

The nearest I got to seeing this happened one afternoon, when Dave had started to rough shape the arching on the back of the latest fiddle (pictured). Dave says: "I'll use a massive, big gouger. We'll have a cup of coffee and I'll show you. This is a couple of days work – and then three days to finish it off with the purfling, but I'll just show you the basics. I'm going to set me first height for the edge; so, when I'm gouging, I mustn't go past that line. The finished thickness will be thinner, but this is just a guide, so I don't go over." He then starts rough shaping with the big gouger. Big, deep gouges. Dave is working the gouger from the shoulder and putting his entire body weight behind it. This is hard physical work, for the resistance from the AA grade maple is there to hear with every gouge, but it's also subtle work, for it involves the play of light and shade. Dave tells me: "You've got to use the light to create shadows to see what you're taking off. If the light is in the wrong place, it looks flat. I need to see what I'm taking off." He explains: "If you have the light so that it's casting shadows, you see. It lets you see. The shadows show everything, and anyone who doesn't work with shadows – well, they don't know what they're doing. Sometimes though I switch the light off, and just use the natural light." He tells me, "If you come round here and see the little bit I've done – you can see it. (I nod) Right, you can see it now.

The Violin Shop

But if you've got your light on top (he moves the angle of the light to demonstrate) you cannot see it. You've got to create the shadow, and then you get the sharp detail of it."

He then starts working methodically with the gouger around the back bouts: "I'm roughing it out – forming the arches. This early stage is exploratory, just to see which way it's going to let us work. Press and twist. If you just push like that you're not going to get anywhere. Once you get in the groove of it, you're on your way. Now, I've learnt which way it's letting us carve it; it's that way and with a twist, and once I've learnt that then it's more rapid see." Nicky: "So, that's you reading it." Dave: "Exactly, you read it. You alter what you do according to what the wood will let you do." Now Dave has worked out how to work the maple, the gouges become finer and faster, and more rhythmical. Dave: "See that; there's the curl. If you catch the curl the wrong way, you'll cut a massive big chunk out of it. Little is more really. It lets you find your flow. I'm now quite happy to potter along like this." Watching him work, it's obvious that Dave's now in a groove, or flow state, and that, just like that, the flow state has taken over. What's suddenly happened in front of me is not

235

just the kinaesthetic connection between a master craftsman and their tools, and wood. Rhythm has taken over entirely; it's choreographing Dave's work, shaping and defining it as a task space, outside the world of clock time. Instinctively, Dave recognises this. He tells me: "If it's quiet and stuff and I come in at nine, I can just sit here doing it – and then I might stop for a cup of tea at one o'clock, but the time has gone in five minutes. Something clicks and it just takes over; you're lost in a different world."

*

A few weeks later I'm sitting in the workshop, opposite Dave, drinking tea. We're talking about tools. He tells me: "I've got two good gougers; now where are they?" Rummaging, he finds the very same two gougers I'd seen him working with previously. Looking at them, he says, "Aye. Harris. They're one hundred plus years old; maybe 150. Harris of Gateshead – shaped to your hand." He demonstrates. The gougers fit his hand perfectly. "Not like the modern stuff; it's too bulky." He then picks up his copy of a reference work he refers to as "the bible" (*The Universal Dictionary of Violin & Bow Makers*). Finding the relevant entry, he says: "There you go. 'Harris of Gateshead'. From Staffordshire originally; studied with Chanot, in London." I realise that these two gougers link the very workshop where Edward Heron-Allen learnt to make a violin and Dave's workshop in Hexham where we're currently sitting. Dave continues: "They could be used for anything, but they were part of his violin-making kit. He died in 1951." Then, he tells me, "I got them off Barry. I think Barry got them off Harris' son. He had two sons; they carried on with the tradition, but they weren't very good. They'd be old men when Barry got them."

Dave goes on to show me some of the rest of the tool collection that he has built up over the years. Then he tells me: "I had a big box of tools given to me a few years ago, full of violin makers' stuff. They were from Derek Greener". This is the very same Derek Greener, the plumber who'd attended Barry's evening classes back in the 1980s. "He was in his 90s then. 'Dave, do you want these?' They sat there for a few years, and then Anthony was going off to Switzerland. So, I said, 'Do you want that big box of chisels?'

'Oh yes'. He emailed me from Switzerland and says, 'the chisels are really good'."

In such a way tools connect luthiers and workshops across generations. They do this by moving through the social networks of luthiers. In the gifting of Derek Greener's box of chisels we see how connections are forged between lutherie clubs separated, in this instance, by four decades – between Barry's evening classes in Washington in the 1980s and Dave's informal lutherie club in Hexham in the 2000s and 2010s. Clubs which comprised and have continued the Cremonese diaspora in Northeast England. Yet, what is at one level a straightforward act of generosity on Dave's behalf, of passing on tools that are surplus to his requirements, is also, more symbolically, a passage of tools from one hand to another. In the typically understated way that is a marker of the man, it signals the transmission of quality tools to an identified successor, the next master craftsman.

CHAPTER EIGHT
The Last Commission

Dave is sitting at his bench scrutinising the fiddle-in-the-white he he's been making for the months in which I've been visiting the workshop. He says: "All the fine details are in now. All the chunks have gone; where I was chasing, but I need to make sure the edges are smooth". He checks them. Ever the perfectionist, there's an area, imperceptible to me, which doesn't pass to his satisfaction. Water, from chasing, has got into the end grain in one tiny area. "I need to do a bit more 'detail' work. Take the nibs off here. Just correct it 'cos I don't want it uneven. The end grain's swollen; so I've just got to nibble it off". On go the magnifying goggles for what he calls 'microsurgery'. "Don't make a mistake" he chides himself, "or it'll look awful!"

Finally satisfied, Dave shows me the start of the finishing process. He's preparing the fiddle-in-the-white for varnishing. He tells me: "Me ground is tea; tea bags. Yorkshire tea; it's got to be Yorkshire tea. Tetley's is too weak. I tried Ringtons – no good. So, it's just Yorkshire tea bags from Presto's (a cheap, local convenience store); that plus walnut oil. So, its 10 tea bags in a mug, half fill it; mulch it down. Put it on the white wood and it's a biscuit colour, then put the colour on." The tea bags safely stewing in a mug, I ask Dave how he settled on tea. "Eeeh, well", he says, "A lot of people in the old days used tea – or what's the name of it? Eeh, me brain! The acid; tannic acid! I've got a jar full of that. I could use that – or wood bark and stuff, boiled up. But tea bags are quicker and easier!" With the Martin Hayes Quartet playing in the background, courtesy of "Alexa", Dave starts applying the heavily stewed tea to the fiddle with an artist's paint brush. He's in his happy space, and we both whistle along. Two coats later, Dave hangs the treated fiddle up in the shop window to dry in the sunlight. I ask Dave about colours. They are artists' materials – yellow, burnt ochre, mahogany. They're stored in the cupboard on the workshop wall. Those who commission fiddles, like this one, get a choice of colour. But thereby hangs a tale. For, as Dave says, "Mostly they haven't got a clue. I have to tell them, 'Look around – what do you like?'"

A week or so later, one Monday I'm back in the workshop. In my absence, Dave has had a push on to finish the fiddle. This has been prompted by his own impending annual pilgrimage to Miltown, County Clare, in Ireland for the Willie Clancy Festival, where he indulges his passion for Irish dancing and Irish music. When I arrive he shows me the fiddle with a flourish, proclaiming "it's finished!" Three coats of varnish went on in the previous week and he'd set it up the previous Saturday, to leave it under tension over the weekend, ready for playing in today, and collection on Tuesday. In appearance the fiddle is a bright, bright glossy golden brown; it's so shiny it's like a mirror. Along with the flame in the grain, I can see my own reflection in it. It's completely different to my fiddle's antique finish – but then I didn't get a choice, and anyway finish is all about the buyer's personal preferences.

"Off you go, then" says Dave as he hands it to me; "Let's hear it. You're the first person to play it!" The fiddle is very tight. Because it's been made on a Guadagnini model, there's a lot of power but it's also very bright, a complete contrast to the darker, mellower tone of my own Dave Mann Guadagnini. It's also on Dominant Pro strings, not what I'd usually use. All that notwithstanding, I'm not happy. The fiddle is not what I was expecting in sound. Or, perhaps more accurately, accustomed as I am to hearing how a Dave Mann fiddle generally sounds, it's not what I was expecting it to sound like. By way of confirmation, for he's hearing similar things, Dave asks me to compare it with another Dave Mann Guadagnini commission that is back in the workshop (Chapter Four). And that throws up an unwelcome problem: both Dave and I prefer the sound of this other fiddle. To comply with the commissioner's request means that Dave has made considerable adjustments to what he would normally do with the table in the making. He tells me: "there's more arching 'cos he wanted it brighter. The flatter it is the more the resonance".

After five minutes of my playing, though, the fiddle starts to change. Initially, I'd been playing the kinds of modal tunes that I'd normally gravitate to on my fiddle, and – to my ears at least - it really was not happy being asked to play in those keys straight away. I then twigged: 'bright fiddle – try it in bright major keys'. I started in G and then switched quickly to playing in A. Doing that meant that it started to open up. Dave: "That's it starting to open up now, and you've only been going five minutes. Now it just needs to be played, which you're doing ... cup of tea?!"

Dave's suggestion of a cup of tea is his relief signal. He's much happier now. His worries over sounding are set at ease completely when Martin Hughes comes in to subject it to the test pilot regimen (Chapter Five). Yet, as we all sit talking in the workshop, it's clear that Dave's worries haven't entirely dissipated. Rather, they've switched from the fiddle itself to the ability of the player who has commissioned it to actually play it. During a pause in the conversation, Dave says to Martin and me: "I may have to drop the action on it". Martin asks: "Why's that?" Dave: "Well he's an Irish fiddle player. He won't be able to play it." He goes on to explain to us how he's set it up at exactly the professional measurements. Then he says: "Both of you have played it and said absolutely nothing. But he'll come in here and he won't be able to play it. It'll be too high. The string height will be too high for him. I'll have to drop the height of the bridge – and that'll affect the sound. It'll be less bright." Obviously worrying about this, he continues to 'go round the houses' with this concern: "Maybe it'll be all right but most of the Irish players are really low. One guy has it so low it's like that much off the fingerboard, literally millimetres. They just like to touch the strings; they don't want to come down on it like you two do. He might say it's OK. But if I drop the bridge height it'll be less bright and more the way you like it. But he's got to be comfortable playing it." In retrospect, I realise that this whole morning has been a worry for Dave. The to-and-fro between the two instruments which he asked me to do initially is an indication that he wasn't entirely happy with the sound was hearing. The fiddle may look beautiful as an object, but playing it is the moment of sounding truth. And this being a commissioned fiddle means that it's a double-edged moment of truth.

The question at stake here is not just the perennial one that faces all violin makers, of 'Have I made a good one?' It's also how well the fiddle fits with the brief of the commission. As with all commissioned creative works – be they art, architecture, or music – this is a challenge, but the challenges of making a musical instrument to a brief are particularly acute.

*

There are two issues at the heart of the challenge of commissioned instruments. On the one hand, there's the ability of the commissioner to describe what they desire in sound; on the other, there's the capacity of the luthier to fabricate an object to that brief. The first is highly problematic. Many of those who decide to commission a fiddle don't know what they're seeking, or – if they do – they struggle to put this into words. This is because sound is aural and personal. It's what we hear, each of us, individually – and ears hear sound differently. Words, by contrast, are standardised. Their meaning is shared within language groups and widely recognised. The descriptors 'bright', 'dark' and 'mellow', then, might sound consistent but they might not be consistent across different people, whilst beyond them is an immense complexity of tonal colour which is almost impossible to convey in words. Yet it is this very complexity which is central to finding a violin which sounds in such a way that it forges a connection with a person. The effect is huge: it means that commissioned fiddles may never connect with the commissioner. Then there are the considerable challenges facing the luthier. Even if a commissioner can pinpoint with a degree of accuracy the sound that they're seeking, typically by playing a violin whose sound they wish to be emulated, the luthier faces the challenge of replicating that with wood that will be uniquely different to that instrument.

For a master craftsman like Dave, as their reputation for making quality fiddles grows, so demand for commissioned fiddles increases. With that comes the headache of repeatedly trying to satisfy a brief, for inevitably, orders pile up. Very quickly, making becomes less a source of pleasure and more a source of endless anxiety, as no luthier can guarantee the sound which will emerge from a fiddle; only that they will have made well, to the best of their abilities. The rest is down to the wood and the way it wants to resonate. With such uncertainties, I wanted to know more about who commissions Dave Mann fiddles, and why. I was also intrigued by the stories of the two commissioned fiddles that had been a constant backdrop to my time in the workshop; the shiny, glossy one that had just emerged and the one that had been returned.

*

Kevin (Chapter Four) and Jeremy Scratchert (Chapter Seven) are just two of the people who have commissioned fiddles from Dave. I asked Kevin why he'd decided to commission one: "Two reasons – one I came into some money and could afford it; the other – I think it's very special to have an instrument that you know who made it. I don't always meet the people. Like my flute. I bought one from Sam Partridge and I've got two made by George Ormiston. And some of the whistles; one is made by Malcolm Bushby's father. I think it's particularly good to have instruments where you know, or at least have a connection with, the maker". It's the same with Jeremy who, alongside his self-confessed auction habit, has collected quality fiddles with a connection to Dave's workshop – two from Dave and one from Andrea Pontedoro. For both Kevin and Jeremy, their Dave Mann fiddles are testimony to their connection to Dave's workshop and their friendship with Dave himself. Commissioning is a marker of those dense social ties. I encountered exactly the same sentiments when I talked with another shop regular, Roddy Matthews.

Like Jeremy, Roddy is a talented amateur player. Unlike him, his professional career has been spent as a partner in a successful estate-agent business based in Hexham. Despite living in Northumberland, Roddy describes himself as a Scottish musician. He tells me: "I've played mainly Scottish dance music all my life, from being eight or nine years old". The inspiration was a family holiday to Lochailort, south of Mallaig on the west coast of the Highlands of Scotland, where Roddy met Farquhar Macrae. "He was very inspirational to me; never read a note but played a lot of pipe marches and things on the fiddle. It made the hairs stand up on the back of my neck". By the time he was 14, Roddy was in the David White band, a six-piece he describes as the premier Scottish dance band on Tyneside. They were based in Whitley Bay but did gigs as far afield as London, Leeds and Edinburgh. Roddy also describes a Scottish dancing scene in the 1970s which extended to Wallington Hall in Northumberland. "Jack Armstrong, who did lots of BBC recordings, had moved from Wideopen (on Tyneside} to Wallington, and the bands used to come in to have tea with Jack in the corner before they used to go on. That's how I started playing Scottish dance music".

Jack Armstrong's band turns out to have been the original point of connection between Roddy and Dave. Roddy: "So, in Jack's band there was an old guy called Roy who lived in Ponteland (west of Newcastle). He was an ex-military musician. Dave used to play the drums with him. You're talking at least 30 years ago. Roy was a good accordionist. So there were the three of us". Dave comes through from the workshop to the shop, where Roddy and I are talking. Roddy says to him: "I seem to remember we were down in that old hall down by the Quayside, the Merchant's Hall". Dave: "Aye, that's it". Roddy: "Remember we were in the old Town Hall. That's the first time". I ask Dave how he ended up in this ceilidh band. Dave: "I don't know" but Roddy tells him: "You just ended up in a lot of ceilidh bands at that time." He tells me: "He was just nice company. So we did things at Otterburn, in the old Percy Arms. I remember Dave, me and Roy doing that". Dave: "Aye – early 90s that you know" – and then jokes, "He'd just left school!!" Roddy: "No, no – I was late 20s when I was doing that stuff!"

Warming to his resume of his musical career, Roddy tells me how he played multiple fiddle and accordion clubs in Scotland with all sorts of different bands; of being a guest artist in Shetland, "where anyone who is between five and 95 plays the fiddle", and of his continued playing in and around the Fort William area, as well as for BBC Scotland, with his band The Roddy Matthews Trio.

I ask Roddy about his fiddles. He tells me that his first came from Tom Alexander, another luthier, who had a shop on Simonside Terrace in Heaton in Newcastle. The shop has long since disappeared. Then he got what he describes as "two very good fiddles" from Jack Armstrong. One was "a nice German one; dark, with a head on it. Jack thought it was a very good fiddle but Dave said it was just a good trade fiddle! After that I got another fiddle – quite light, bright orange, but a very good fiddle; very easy to play, quite strong. I've still got it. I don't play it much but it's quite good in a Scottish dance band because you've got two accordions and they make a lot of noise!" Then Roddy turns to the fiddle case he's brought with him to the shop; it's a double.

He opens it. Inside the case are two fiddles. One is a Ewan Thompson and the other is a Dave Mann. The two are the most revered of contemporary luthiers in the Scottish traditional music scene. Roddy tells me: "I needed to get a fiddle that was a bit better. There's a very good fiddle player in Shetland, Bryan Gear. He lined this fiddle (the Ewan Thompson) up for me. He was going to keep it himself but he said 'I'd like du to have it – You need to have it.' So 'Raddy' got this fiddle, which was made by Ewan Thompson who was in Fair Isle at the time. And Ewan says, although he's made better looking fiddles, this is one of the better sounding fiddles he's made. It's a very good fiddle – good at the top and the bottom, which is good for what I do. This was 2000. But I wanted another fiddle to match it. Dave had made a couple of nice fiddles and I said, 'Well how about making one for me?' I had to wait two years, because there's a waiting list. He knew the sort of thing I wanted. So I got this eventually in about 2005." Later, Dave tells me that Roddy's fiddle is on a Degani model. Roddy goes on to compare the two fiddles: "With these two, the action's very, very similar. That's the way Dave sets the two up. The Ewan Thompson one moves quicker; you can get round the reels very quick on it; the Dave Mann is a slightly more woody sound. I like it and they both play very well for different stuff".

I ask Roddy what he likes to play on his Dave Mann fiddle. He tells me: "I like to play pipe marches on the Dave Mann. I've just done a BBC broadcast in Aberdeen, last week with Ian Cruickshank and his dance band. I did a solo on it." Roddy then consults a tune-book of his compositions, a pile of which lie in the shop window and which Dave has already given me a copy of. About half a dozen of these tunes are well known tunes, but the two standouts are *Leaving Lordenshaw* and *The Kirk Stack*. Roddy tells me something of the backstories to these tunes: "When I'd got the fiddle made, Ewan Thompson took me round the Kirk Stack on his boat. It's the most amazing place. There's a spire and an arch and all the seabirds; it's the most inspirational place, so I wrote this tune called *The Kirk Stack*. It's been played by loads of fiddle players". I push Roddy a bit more on what he plays mostly on his Dave Mann fiddle. Roddy thinks about this and says: "I would say Dave's is really nice for minor stuff. It's beautiful on the top; if you go into position it's really lovely and sweet. Whereas a lot of fiddles they can get quite harsh. A tune like *Bonnie at Morne* – now that sounds great on Dave's fiddle." Then I ask him if any of the tunes in his tune-book were inspired by Dave's fiddle. "There's a tune called *The Eternal Tears of Love*. That goes right down onto the bottom A and then it has some position work".

Roddy's summary of the sound world of his Dave Mann fiddle and the soundscape that suits it is one which accords with many others who play Dave's fiddles. Reflecting further on this, though, I'm minded that the tune Roddy wrote which is inspired by his Dave Mann fiddle is itself testimony to the deep social connection Roddy feels to Dave and his shop. Inspired by the sound of this fiddle - a fiddle that was made in this place – the composition is a means of acknowledging and reciprocating the gift which Dave has given him. This is not just the gift of a making him a fiddle; it's the gift of sociality and companionship. Roddy tells me: "I come down here for a chat. I enjoy that because as you get older it's just about friendship. Maybe sometimes I'll miss a few weeks but then I'm in again." He continues: "And Dave's not allowed to retire or die until we've all died. He's totally irreplaceable! He's allowed to have time off; he's allowed to go down to three days a week".

Hearing this, Dave calls through from the workshop, "Lord, Have Mercy!"

*

Whereas Kevin, Jeremy and Roddy are all amateur players, there are professional musicians who've commissioned fiddles from Dave. Some of these, like Carly Bain and Peter Tickell, are people who have had a long and close personal connection to Dave and the shop. So, in that regard, whilst they might earn their living through music, their reason for commissioning an instrument is exactly the same as Kevin, Jeremy and Roddy.

Peter tells me: "Dave has known me since I was a boy really. He always looked after me. He was encouraging. He'd come and see me play and that sort of thing. He's always been a family friend." Peter grew up being classically trained, but as a member of the world famous Tickell family he was steeped in folk music from an early age. He played for a while in his sister Kathryn's band before joining the Scottish band The Peatbog Faeries, playing on two of their albums – *Live* (2009) and *Dust* (2011). At the same time he started to do a bit of session work for Sting, which led to him being asked to join Sting's Back to Bass World Tour, from 2011 – 13, which led on to another world tour with Paul Simon.

Peter has two Dave Mann fiddles. One he plays all, or most of, the time; the other is a spare, and it lives mostly in a cupboard. I ask him how he came by the first. Peter tells me: "I must've been 21 when I got it." He goes and gets it to check the date it was made. Showing it to me, he says, "I like this one so much that I got a second one off him, but I don't play it that much, because I love this one so much; that one's more of a spare." I ask why he loves this one so much. Peter: "Possibly because I've played it so much – it feels natural to me. My wife played it and she said there's almost like grooves on the fingerboard which fit my fingers. 2009 it says. So I'd have been 22." This is the fiddle which has accompanied Peter throughout his professional working life.

I ask Peter how he'd describe the one he favours. Peter: "I'd say it's powerful. I can give it my full power, because I'm quite strong; I'm not waif like, so I can really give it some wellie and it'll take it". I say: "It'll take strong playing won't it; do you think it needs that? It's like if you give a lot of yourself it gives back, and if you just approach it (I mime very reserved, cautious playing) it just goes a bit 'Meh.'" Peter: "Yes, yes! And I do have this strong emotional attachment too to it; I'm really attached to it." I ask: "How would you describe that?" Peter: "I've never really considered it before – it's my sound; and it might sound like a cliché but it's intricately connected to me. I can't imagine ever playing anything else. I'd never consider having another instrument."

Playing mostly highly technical, experimental music and jazz, Peter puts considerable demands on his instruments. He says: "It's quite technical a lot of the stuff that I do. I remember there being a sort of reticence when I started doing the Sting stuff. Is the instrument, me, up to this, and am I going to be able to make this sort of sound? It's not a saxophone or a trumpet or that sort of thing. It was a jump into the unknown. The practice that I'd done – it's one thing practising on your own in a room trying to perfect your technique but it's another thing trying to use the big PA system. It becomes a whole other thing. I started to think, I'm almost not playing the violin. I'm using the violin to play the PA system. And then, you're never privy to what it's sounding like out front. All you can hear is what it sounds like on the stage." I ask Peter what that sounds like. "Kind of haunting I guess. The sound on stage is quite bass-y and meaty. And the range of the instruments meant that I'd sit above it. It's quite a difficult thing to describe – though I'd communicate quite regularly with the sound engineer. And he'd tell me what worked, what didn't work, and how I might improve it. So there was a process there."

Taking my cues from Peter's description of his own uncertainties about the musical transition he made in moving to play with Sting's band, I ask him, "How did you trust that this instrument was going to go there with you?"

Peter: "That was the sort of gamble for me. I'd a month to prepare for it. I locked myself away for three weeks, and got fit as well – because I knew I needed to look quite good to be a part of it, because image is a big thing. So I was training on my fitness, and practising Sting's back catalogue. I got sent like 50 songs – 'it could be like any 20 of these, but nudge-nudge, these ones are definitely going to be there', and you could pretty much guess which ones those were going to be. So I worked my way through his back catalogue; listening to them." I ask: "Had he had a violin in the band before?" Peter: "Not really, not like this, no. There'd been a saxophone player, Branford Marsalis. I'd learnt a lot of what he'd done – but it's a different instrument. But I learnt the key, crucial melody lines. They're unchangeable and then I'd try to find my own interpretation on some songs as well. And that also helped me develop my improvisational skill, to take that to the next level. There was a musician called Nigel Hitchcock who played saxophone in the Peatbogs – himself and Rick Taylor they'd done all the stuff that I was about to do; the rock touring in the 1980s. They'd worked with Elton John and Wet, Wet, Wet." I comment: "But those, how to say this, they're quite constrained by comparison, and here it's like there's a great big space when the bass stops and you've got to fill that..." Peter: "And there were world class improvisers in the band as well. David Sancious who's a world class keyboard player, and then I'd have to go after that! You know, just after he's brought the house down with this great big solo to rapturous applause and I'd have to go after that! Pause – now it's you son! The band that I used to use for inspiration was Mahavishnu Orchestra." Nicky: "Yeah, yeah, yeah – John McLaughlin" Peter: "Yeah – John McLaughlin, Jean-Luc Ponty, Jerry Goodman – they were the guys. They were my benchmark. I was trying – not to lift but

The Violin Shop

to add elements of the folk stuff that I was doing to add to that."

If one searches YouTube, there are plenty of clips of Sting's Back to Bass World Tour, with Sting introducing "And on violin, Mr Peter Tickell!" The violin is always his Dave Mann fiddle. Peter: "And when I was doing these gigs far away from home, and there'd be a moment when I wasn't playing, and I'd be standing statuesque, so as not to draw attention to myself when I was on stage with these like superstars, and the lights on the stage would shine at all sorts of different angles and I could be in Indonesia or wherever, and I'd look at the violin and I'd see the label 'David G Mann, Hexham, England'! That was a real sense of homeliness; it's the place I'm from."

*

Such is Dave's reputation for producing quality violins that by the 2010s orders had begun to stretch beyond the social network of the shop and the Northeast region of England.

With professionals of the standing of Aidan O'Rourke, Lauren MacColl and Peter Tickell all playing Dave Mann fiddles, commissions started to come in from other professional musicians, and particularly from players in the Scottish traditional music scene. Jack Smedley is one.

Jack is a Scottish traditional musician who plays with the bands Rura and Staran and as a duo with David Foley. We begin talking with Jack showing me his Dave Mann fiddle: "This is the one, here. I picked it up in 2014. So, I've been playing it since then." I ask Jack whether it's made on a Guarneri model, like Peter's, or a Guadagnini. Jack: "I probably should know the answer to this. There is a certificate somewhere, but we moved house earlier this year and I've no idea what it is." Hearing this, I suggest: "But then, it probably doesn't matter to you, does it? It's more what it sounds like." Jack: "Yes — and that's something. When I got this fiddle it was just so much better than anything that I'd used in the past that it was almost irrelevant what it was."

Jack expands on his playing history in instruments. "I'm from the North East of Scotland originally and I grew up in a place called Cullen. It's near a place called Fochabers, and there's a maker – actually I don't know if Charlie is still making fiddles; he's getting on a bit. But Charlie Armour was the guy who made the very first actual violin that I had. And I've still got a Charlie fiddle knocking around the house somewhere. So, that was – obviously for the stage I was at and a young teenager and all of that, it was more than enough. By the time I went to the Glasgow Conservatoire I had a different Charlie Armour fiddle that I bought, either early on in uni or half way through or something. I was actually laughing with Megan Henderson the other day, because I have a fiddle of hers upstairs at the moment, because I needed two fiddles for something recently. And we were laughing about how we don't know how we got through with the instruments that we had back then, because – with the greatest respect to Charlie in particular – lovely sounding fiddles and great to play at a certain level, but to go and play them now they're just so heavy and so much work. I actually can't believe how I used to play them, and with relative ease. I must have just been compensating so much with my muscles to make certain sounds and to move to certain places but as soon as you get an instrument at this level it's just a different kettle of fish altogether."

I ask Jack how he came to commission an instrument from Dave. "In all honesty, I think at the time, some people go on quite long journeys getting instruments don't they, and I'm maybe a bit more pernickety these days but I've never been someone who's been particularly – I've never really bought into this world of minute adjustments to this and tiny little differences and having one E string from one kind of set and the rest from another. I've just never really thought like that. So, in all honesty when I was looking for a fiddle I was like 'well who are the key makers that lots of people I know and respect are working with?' One was

Ewan Thompson in Shetland – Megan plays one of them, and I know a few people who play those fiddles and I think they're amazing, and if I was being completely honest it was just – well Dave's so close to Glasgow. And I've always loved Lauren's sound – I think her playing is so beautiful and the sound of her instrument's been so nice, and obviously, Aidan as well. At the time, when I was at uni, Peter Tickell was also kicking around a bit and I think I'd heard his. I don't know Peter but I think I'd definitely heard him playing his at one point. Carly Blain as well – I knew she had one. So I thought, 'well if all these great players are using them then they can't be that bad!'"

Jack's journey to Dave's door is effectively a toss of a coin and down to convenience. Of his time at the shop, Jack tells me: "I thought I'd just go down and spend some time with Dave. At the time he did have one on the shelf that was an older one he'd made. I just played it and I thought it was great. Like I said, anything he was going to put in front of me was going to be so much better than what I was using. So it was like, 'You know what, I don't really know what I want'. I was going round the shop and I was trying beautiful fiddles that had these amazing mellow, deep sounds that would be amazing if I was just doing albums of slow airs all the time but then you'd play another fiddle that had really great response in reels or really faster music. So I was like, at the end of the day, maybe at that point in my career I needed a bit of a workhorse; something that was a good all-rounder. So I thought 'well why not just get him to make me one and see what it's like?' I guess one thing that I did push him on was getting the one-piece back. He offered me a two or a one. At the time he said that the one-piece tends to be slightly mellower. So that's what I said, 'I really do want a warm, deep sound if possible, but within reason.'"

The story, as Jack tells it, is one of not really knowing what he wanted and of drifting into commissioning an instrument – and of the challenges of finding what is the holy grail of an instrument, one that'll play equally responsively in slow airs and the fastest of reels. What's also eminently visible here is the difficulty Dave has with commissioned work. Players, even players as accomplished as Jack, struggle to describe what sound and responsiveness they're looking for. It's as if they can't quite work out what they want when confronted with an array of an already made instruments – but then think, 'Oh, get him to make me one instead', without realising how open the potential is in that.

The luthier world, and the world of wood and craft work within that, is a complete unknown to many players. A consequence is that there's always the risk that, having commissioned something, a player will turn out not to like it. That has not turned out to be the case with Jack's fiddle. "I picked this instrument up in November or December of 2014, and drove straight to the studio to record Rura's second album. So, I recorded that album on this fiddle, and the fiddle was like days old." I ask: "And it played immediately as you wanted it to? There was no kind of sense of 'I need to get to know this fiddle'?" Jack: "There was a bit of that. But I guess it was like the perfect kind of album to be doing this because Rura's second record is quite different from all the others, because of the producers that we were working with and the engineers we worked with. All the instruments are very processed; like very highly edited. So I could get away with it. And you've got like bagpipes in there. If I was going in to do a more intimate or exposed record – I wouldn't have taken that risk on something like that. But for that album in particular it was almost as if it was the perfect excuse to just have to sit and play it for hours and break it in."

I begin to talk with Jack about how his relationship and connection with this fiddle has evolved over the years, and about what I see as the pull of Dave's fiddles towards certain registers and keys. Jack says: "I would totally agree with that. Like when I play slower more mellow music on this fiddle, that's when it's at home. And it's great for playing faster tunes and such on, but I would say that's not where it's at home. Though I'd say this fiddle sits really comfortably in A major and like really major major. It almost has that nice 'Scandi' thing going with it. It really sits well in that place. I do a lot of my writing in like D major and A major on the fiddle. Even if I want to change the key down the line I'll maybe start in that place and get some sounds up and running. There's probably a couple of reasons why. One is very obvious – because I've done so much playing with Rura over the years, so much of our music is in that tonality. So D and A – even if you're heading in a different direction and going down a more minor route, D and A are the bedrock of so much of the music that we've played over the years. But then I think also, I've been hugely influenced in terms of my writing by a lot of 'Scandi' sounds. I went through a period maybe 10 years ago or so where I was immersed in bands like Frig – and Chris Stout's playing to a certain extent. I grew up listening to Fiddler's Bid and all that too. So I tend to head in those directions when I'm writing. I guess that's just where I feel comfortable as a player and a writer, and my fiddle probably feels the same. I've heard people say that an instrument will almost grow with whatever's playing it."

Warming to this theme, Jack says: "My instrument does lend itself to a certain style of playing and a certain sound. There've been moments in recording where I've had the chance to explore that a bit more. Megan Henderson's solo album (2021) has a few moments on it where it's just us doing our thing and I think that's great. I'd never claim to be an improviser in the sense of a jazz musician. But I do love exploring different sounds and tones on my instrument. Often that opens the door to where I want to exist. That might be the only reason I pick up my fiddle that day, to just chill out you know. Initially I'll sit in this kitchen and just play some nice long notes, just because they sound so nice. I just like do different shapes, different motifs, different ideas or whatever and maybe one of them will stick."

I ask Jack specifically about his collaboration with fellow Rura band mate, the wooden flute player, David Foley. I do so because, at least to my ears, this is where his fiddle sounds most at home. Jack: "Through the process of having written quite a bit for Rura, David and I have pushed out random tunes. You'll spend a bit of time developing a jig or a reel or whatever and you get to the end of it and they're nice but it doesn't fit what you're trying to write for. But you've got it out of your system. And you've got it down on the page or recorded it. We both had a lot of that stuff lying there. Tunes that we liked, that we enjoyed but there wasn't a place to perform that. That's exactly why David and I decided to do that record. It was a bit of craic more than anything else. *Drift* – David wrote the guitar line for that. He had that – and he was saying how he thought that was a really cool sound, a really cool progression. So he was like 'Can we write a tune over it?' And I just started improvising over the top. I can't remember but I think I wrote the first half on the fiddle and then David wrote the second half on the flute. I think one of the reasons people enjoy that track is because it's so organic. It's honest. And you might not be into instrumental music, but because it's coming from such a genuine place it's not like you've sat down and said, 'Here are the bars, here's the tempo here's the key'. It came from an improvisation space. And I guess that is one thing I will do on this fiddle. I will just sit and improvise for ages. I like doing that on this violin."

A marker of Dave's fiddles is this quality; they have what I would call fiddle agency. It's not just that they seemingly pull their players towards a certain tonality and modality, and to certain tune types more than others, but almost as if they want to be played like this; that they want to be a co-partner in an improvisation space. These fiddles almost insist that their players develop as musicians to become more than tunesmiths, to develop as improvisers and composers. And more than this, they seem to insist that this compositional space is a sparer, instrumental space – a space which allows the fiddle to be heard in all its complexity. It's an idea which resonates with my conversations with both Lauren MacColl and Aidan O'Rourke.

*

Although they both play fiddles which emanated from Dave's workshop, neither Aidan nor Lauren actually commissioned the instruments they play. Lauren's Cain & Mann fiddle has been with her since 2012 (Chapter Four); "it's on all my recordings". For her, there is an intimacy of connection between this fiddle and what she calls 'her sound', which extends beyond playing to now encompass composition. Her first venture in the direction of composition was *The Seer* (2017), a commission for Feis Rois, focused on the life of a Black Isle mystic. More recently there has been *Heal & Harrow* (2022) with Rachel Newton, and *Haar* (2023), both of which exemplify the sound world of a Dave Mann fiddle.

Lauren begins by talking about her connection with this fiddle as a player. She says: "If I was doing a solo gig tomorrow and it was sold out but my fiddle went missing I would not do the gig, because I don't feel it would be like a representation of me." The fiddle is an extension of herself and inseparable from her performing self. But it's also integral to how she produces sound, and the sound that she gravitates to compositionally. She says: "Whenever I've composed, it's been for myself and others. So, I suppose my sound would be at the centre of that, yes." I ask her how she would describe her sound. Lauren: "That's very hard; I'm so attached to it. I feel my sound is a collaboration; between me and the music that I have within me and the way I feel about that music and the instrument that I play. It's the combination of that."

Lauren's Cain & Mann, then, is integral to her life as a musician. It's not just expressive of her, a representation of her as a player and a musician. It's also a conduit - a channel through which composition emerges. She describes her relationship to this fiddle as organic: "It grows and develops. Like any relationship, it has its ups and downs, but it teaches me an awful lot about music. Like sometimes a melody that I have in my head – it might be a traditional melody or something I'm trying to write – but it's often the way the instrument responds, whether that's like a little harmonic thing that happens or the way that the strings ring. It's like it writes the music with me" Nicky: "So, the unique sounding qualities of this instrument are there in your composition?" Lauren: "Absolutely. I wrote a couple of tunes for *The Seer* on my mandolin --- my noodling instrument. Then I tried to put them onto the fiddle. I knew immediately I've not written it on my instrument; it said; 'it's not me'."

I ask Lauren about her fiddle's 'happy space'. Lauren: "I know immediately when it's unhappy. I'll play it for like 30 seconds and just put it down because I don't want to get into an argument with it. 'Let's just leave it; we'll go back to that'. To me – when I'm playing slow music and I'm really getting into the tone, it responds so well. And it's really responsive to being in different tunings. It really responds and starts ringing in different ways. I just feel it's got this inquisitive quality itself. When it's – I don't know that there's certain things or music that it's not happy. I wouldn't say that it likes being just thrashed away. If I have to do gigs where I'm having to play in that way, I don't know if I'd really bother on that instrument. I think it really responds when it gets to ring and resonate in a bigger way, that's not just about playing really fast. But that's my playing as well."

The connection between how a Dave Mann fiddle communicates that it wants to be played, and how a player, musician and composer develops is something that emerged strongly in two conversations with Aidan O'Rourke.

Aidan: "I don't like shrill, solo-istic, like leader-tone instruments. I've tried like really expensive Stradivaris and Amatis, and stuff like that. These instruments shout in a way; they're for projecting to a 2000-seater concert hall and over an orchestra. I'd never need that. I'd never, ever need that. Over the years I've spoken to Dave about tone and he's adjusted the fiddle to suit. Partly it is about adjusting the fiddle to suit the tone I want." I ask: "So how do you describe the tone to him?" Aidan: "I never want a loud fiddle but words like 'mellow' and 'warm' and 'dark'. I like a dark sounding fiddle, not at all shrill. And I spend a lot of time on the bottom two strings and a lot of time doing double stops. But I think my style has changed because of the sound of the fiddle." I suggest that's where these fiddles are really happy. Aidan: "They are. It's almost like we've grown together."

We begin to explore the dynamic, dialogic relationship that Aidan has with his Dave Mann fiddle. Aidan: "So, I got this fiddle in 2006. There are huge leaps of development in music making I think, between starting, aged seven or eight up to age 12; there's amazing leaps. And then I think I spent a lot of my mid and late 20s trying to be a bit flash, trying to absorb as much as possible and not really thinking. I had so much respect for the tradition and I wanted to be really fluent in that tradition. So for me that was about absorbing tunes and styles. My style was all over the place. And (Dave's daughter) Claire had a huge influence on my style; listening to her beautiful ornamentation on that fiddle [the red fiddle of Chapter Two}. I can still vividly hear and see that and that fiddle sounding a million times better than my Lamy, and it making me want to work a million times harder.

"I was 30 when I got this fiddle. I moved to Edinburgh when I was 23 and I'd been exploring sound and extended composition; spending time with jazz musicians in Edinburgh – you know serious musicians. I was recording on the Lamy then and I was already exploring stuff, but it's almost like – it wasn't till I got the Mann that I felt I had the tools for the job really. I remember really clearly the leap; that I'd stepped up really two or three gears and that it took me two or three years to catch up with that. It was almost as if the instrument was ahead of me and I had to then grow into it; it was such a leap off. The agility of this new fiddle; I'd been used to this average, decent enough, fiddle, but nothing great. Yeah – I think because of the quality of the instrument and because of the depth of tone and the feel of the whole thing. It accelerates whatever route one's on. And it coincided with the start of Lau." I ask Aidan if he feels he would have developed with Lau in the same way with the Lamy. Aidan: "Probably not. I don't think I'd be the player I am now without that fiddle."

I ask Aidan where in sound terms he thinks his fiddle's happy home is. Aidan: "I naturally gravitate to D or D minor, or E minor. It's interesting – I actually did used to play a lot in D major and A major, but I guess I was playing a lot with bagpipes back then! But that was my old fiddle. As soon as I got this Dave Mann fiddle my playing changed. My articulation changed; my thinking about sound changed – and I was writing a lot more; I was thinking about tonalities and a lot about orchestration; working with instruments with different timbres. I was starting to think not just about the notes but about the sound."

Aidan then shifts back to trying to capture his relation with this instrument: "I do feel now though that I've spent enough time with this instrument that I've embodied it or it's embodied me." I say: "It's an extension of you." Aidan: "Wholly. I play it so innately. I've had 17 years with it. And actually I remember having a bit of a slump about four years ago and thinking 'maybe I should change my instrument?'" I ask: "What triggered that out of interest?" Aidan: "I dunno. We all have peaks and troughs and just thinking I felt like I needed a change. I fell out of love with how I was playing for a while. It was pre-pandemic and just before I did the 365 thing. And then I did 365 and spent more time with the instrument than ever before! I wrote every single one of those on this instrument; I'd get the book out, make sure everything was ready to record. I'd meditate for 10 or 20 minutes, or half an hour if I had the time, to just clear everything, and then the fiddle would be there and ready to go. And I'd go, harness whatever feeling I got from that story and immediately just play an unfiltered response. And without having that deep connection to the instrument I wouldn't have been able to do that. I totally trusted the instrument; I totally trusted my inner conduit for the way I was feeling that day, or what I took from the stories. The fiddle was the creative conduit between my emotion, the story and what I put down. Every tune was the same and I didn't muck about either."

For me, the album 365 is the soundscape of Aidan and his Dave Mann fiddle. It is pure, unadulterated; a supreme example of a fiddle's capacity to channel the compositional impulse and to create a distinctive sound space. Aidan: "So that journey started with this instrument and it's continued with this instrument. I think it would be very hard for me to part with it. I mean some fiddle players have three or four fiddles and I'm in a position where I could buy another instrument but I don't want to. I don't want to mess with it. I really don't want to. This instrument is my sound. And my sound is this instrument.

"And all that's tied to Dave's personality as well. You just want to do the best for him – you don't want to let him down, after you've acquired one of these instruments. There's an extra element there." I ask: "Do you feel he's in them Aidan, in any way?" He replies: "Well I think it's just the same as I'm in every single tune I've ever written. Regardless who plays it; I'm the sinew in that tune; it's the same with him – he's in every fiddle he's ever made."

*

Back in the workshop, the atmosphere of distress and pain that surrounds the returned Dave Mann Guadagnini fiddle is now explained. These fiddles, like all craft objects, are personal; they're invested with the personhood of their maker. So, to have one returned is tantamount to a personal rejection. It's heartfelt. More than that, this fiddle is recognised to be an example of the work of a master craftsman at the peak of his capacities; at the point where expertise, skill levels and experience coincide in a peak, or crescendo, of activity and before there is any decline in physical capabilities. As Dave himself says, "Strad's best work was when he was in his 80s". Whilst being far too modest and humble to compare himself to the ultimate violin luthier, Dave has little doubt that his fiddles made on a Guadagnini model are the best he's ever made. "Not that I've made a bad one", he says, "except for the ones that went in the bin!" Martin, who has played every single one of the Guadagninis, concurs: "They're all good. And some of them are exceptional", he says. To have one of these fiddles rejected, then, is doubly painful.

Yet rejection is always the risk of commissioned work; even when commissioners can describe what they're seeking with pinpoint accuracy. Difficulties are compounded when commissioners have little to no knowledge of violins as fabricated objects. In the Scottish traditional music scene, players' reputations have ensured that a Dave Mann instrument has acquired an aura. They've become fiddles to be desired, but they're seen simply as "a Dave Mann." And yet, a Dave Mann Guadagnini is not the same thing as a Dave Mann Guarneri or a Dave Mann Degani. Reflecting on my own Mann-Guadagnini, I wonder what Aidan might make of its power and projective qualities.

And then, difficulties are further exacerbated when fiddlers change the strings on a fiddle to what they're used to, or think that they like. What this does is to alter the sound, or colour, of an instrument. It also seeks to impose a player's learnt preferences from playing an earlier, typically inferior quality, factory-made instrument onto another far higher quality, hand-made craft produced instrument, rather than experiment with that instrument to see where its sound world lies.

In the face of such trouble, is it any wonder that on the day when I'd taken my fiddle in for its annual visit, and when this book project was about to be borne, Dave had declared to me: "This is the last commissioned one!" With a mix of exasperation and frustration, he'd gone on to explain: "I've had it; I'm fed up with it. I've decided, I'm just going to carry on making them and then I'll just let everyone know when one's ready and then they can just fight over it."

*

So what are the stories behind the two commissioned Dave Mann Guadagnini fiddles, the glossy, shiny one and the one that had been returned? As is so often the case with instruments that come into the shop or the workshop, it's Martin who inadvertently comes to the rescue with the returned Guadagnini, facilitating the passage of the violin to somebody else through his extensive networks.

It's that network which brings Ali Kyle to Dave's shop door one day. Ali tells me: "I suppose I'm a high-level amateur player; I'm not professional – I'm second violin in Lakeland Sinfonia. I started playing when I was eight. I'm classically trained and I started playing traditional music when I was 22 and living in Cambridge. I accidentally found out about a session. I'd been to see some buskers in a pub and everyone got their instruments out – it was a session, and I'd never heard of sessions. So I started playing Irish music when I was in Cambridge and met my husband who's also a musician. I resurrected the classical side while we were still in Cambridge, where I was in an orchestra like Lakeland Sinfonia, where you have a professional conductor, leader and soloists, four rehearsals and a concert kind of idea. When we moved up to the Lakes I wasn't doing anything for a while because it takes ages to find out what's going on. But I set up a traditional session here in Ulverston. And I go out to play sessions in Windermere and Lancaster. I do Scottish and Shetland, and I go up (to Shetland) most years for the festival."

Ali's playing is spread between different violins. She has had her French Darazy since she was 18 or 19; it's her classical instrument. Over the years, however, there have been a number of folk/traditional instruments. The first was Hungarian, found by her teacher. Then along came an early Ewan Thompson instrument which had been given to her husband, a personal friend of Ewan's, who knew him when he was studying at the Newark Violin Making School. Her husband gave it to her for her 30th birthday. But Ali felt neither instrument to be properly hers; instead, they'd been selected for her. So she decided to set about a quest to choose her own instrument. Initially this took her to a shop in nearby Dalton in Cumbria, where she bought one which she liked. Then the Covid-19 pandemic happened and she started playing jazz violin at home. At this point, the limits of her violins started to become very apparent.

Ali: "My husband plays guitar and banjo and stuff. We played over an internet connection with a pianist who lives in town, and then we got together when we were allowed. So I was starting to play jazz up the neck; I was using my French violin – but it has a very pure sound. It does not work at all for a session. It's too pure; you can't hear it; it hasn't got that cut through that you need. And I was playing traditional on my other violin, and I was having intonation problems up the neck. I'd had it set up when I bought it and it had a really high bridge. So I'd heard about Dave from Martin. And at that point I took the two violins to him; I wasn't looking for one then. He looked at the bridge for me. And while I was there he got me to try two of his violins. One was the one I've ended up with and the other was one he was doing some work on for someone. So he asked me to play them to get my opinion on them. Then he said to me that the string length on my traditional violin is different to my French violin. I didn't really think too much about it. Went away happy and then I looked at the two violins; I was still having these issues. And I thought I'd just measure and see what the difference in string length was and it was

5mm. I thought, 'Hmm, maybe that's why I've been having these issues!' Switching between the two instruments on a regular basis; it was really messing me up. So my husband said, 'Why don't you get another violin?' So I got in touch with Dave and he said to me that the one that I'd tried was for sale.

"So I made an appointment. And when I went through the only violin that he had on the counter was that one! He'd asked me my budget – but I'd said I don't really want to set a budget because I don't want to constrain things but I did have in my mind that this was probably going to be more than my French violin is worth. So I spent all afternoon trying – it must have been 10 or 12 violins. I kept saying 'Can you get another one out'; 'Can you get another one out?!' I tested them all; tested them against my current one and ended up – well to be fair his was standing out but I was thinking budget. I took three away. I had a friend who was staying because we had a gig at Folk Fell at Holker Hall. She was up for the weekend – so I did a blind testing with her and my husband. And Dave's; it was no contest basically. It was the absolute standout. The other two didn't cut it at all. And the workmanship as well is so lovely.

"I bought it to play folk specifically, and the reason I got it is it's got a good volume and it's got an amazing sound; the tone's fantastic. It's even. We had a bit of a play around on strings. Dave had got the new Dominant Pros on it, but the E string was sticking out. Dave got Martin down. He suggested an Obligato E."

I ask Ali to describe its sound: "It's really – it's full, and it's got that cut that you need. So if you're playing in a session you can really hear yourself. Now it's got the Obligato E on it it's really good over its whole range. You can go right up the neck; the sound doesn't crack at all. You can play really loud and really quiet. It'll play anything – it has that beautiful sound; it's sweet but rich. It's not a thin sound; it's an all-round sound. You can really dig into those bottom strings and it just keeps giving."

Ali tells me: "It's made a massive difference. In the jazz I was using my French violin and my husband said 'Why don't you try Dave's violin?' And it was like 'Oh right!' So now I use it for jazz as well and the French one I keep for just classical. The reason I don't play Dave's in Lakeland Sinfonia is that I don't want to stand out. Dave's would work perfectly if you're Martin and doing a solo – but it's too big a sound for a second (violin). So I won't be taking it to Lakeland rehearsals! But I will play it at home; it goes out to do ceilidhs; any folk stuff; any jazz gigs. And I'll be taking it to Shetland. It's usurped my folk ones – the one with the wrong string length and the Ewan Thompson. I need to sell both of them. It hasn't usurped my French violin; that's gorgeous. I'm never getting rid of that. But I will never be looking for another violin. I just feel so lucky because I could've spent a long time looking. So whoever it was has really lost out quite a lot! Their loss my gain! I've just been raving about it since I got it!"

*

And what of The Last Commission itself? The bright, super glossy, shiny Guadagnini. Some months after the fiddle has left the workshop, I eventually get to meet its commissioner. Conor is an amateur player who comes from a family of Irish fiddlers. He tells me: "I grew up in a household where there were lots of fiddles hanging on the walls. My father was quite an accomplished fiddler in the Tyrone tradition. He was known in his community as a fiddle player but the tradition was dying really; there were very few people playing it in Ireland. So a lot of people had fiddles in their houses that weren't being used. When I say lots of fiddles, there were probably five in the house. They were all French and German fiddles, from the nineteenth century. My father bought them. I still wonder how that happened because you're talking about poor people, rural poverty. I think these fiddles were just like the factory fiddles of today. They were cheap fiddles that came from France and Germany that were churning them out. I've got one of them sitting here. It's beautiful – French. I played similar ones as a child, and then I played this one, and then work took over and I had a gap.

"So I retired and I'd always said I'd start again when I retired. A year went past and I just couldn't get myself organised to go back to the fiddle. And then I took it to Stringer's and said, after 20 years sitting in a box kind of thing, could they look at it and get it all set up to play? It was a bit awkward because by then it was 2020; we were into lockdown and travel was restricted. But eventually I got the fiddle back. Then I thought if I could find a teacher they'd be able to teach me things that I didn't learn when I was younger. I looked to see if there was a teacher and found someone living literally a few minutes from the house."

Conor's teacher liked the fiddle that went to Stringer's. But Conor has always been very conscious that it is a family fiddle. He doesn't have children, so he wanted that fiddle "to find its home in the next generation. I wanted it to move on. And I was saying to my teacher that I was keen to move up a level in terms of the quality of instrument I was playing and thinking about looking into perhaps commissioning a fiddle. And he just said immediately, 'if you're going to do that you want to get a fiddle from David Mann'".

Conor and I talk about how his teacher knew about Dave's fiddles. Conor: "He knows people who have David's fiddles. I think that someone had given him the opportunity to pick one of his up – I remember he said, 'You only have to pick one of his fiddles up and put the bow to it and then you know that he can't make a bad instrument'".

So, in the gap between lockdowns when travel was possible, off Conor went to Dave's. Conor: "I spent only about an hour, an hour and a half in the shop with him. There were a couple of things that I said to him. I wanted it to be loud; if I'm going to play I want to hear it myself, I want other people to be able to hear it; I don't want to be working to get volume out of it. But I also wanted it to be sweet and bright – a bright sound. So he just came out from the back with this fiddle, and said 'Take what you can from that fiddle'. And as soon as I touched that fiddle it started to play on its own. It was almost like having a live creature in my hand; like it had its own life. And it had this really deep, mellow sound. I stopped quite quickly and I said, 'I don't want that sound. That's not what I want'. It's a bit like whisky. This was like a 32, 33 year old malt. I prefer a whisky that is seven or eight years old and doesn't have a dark colour. I'd also brought my own fiddle, and I played that for him to hear. I explained to him that I wasn't changing from this one because I needed to; it was more a longer term concern about seeing it on within my family. And that there was no point in commissioning another fiddle unless it could be better than the one that I was playing. He had someone there working with him. He asked him to come out and play my fiddle. And then David said, 'the question is can I make one that's better than this one?' And this guy said, 'Of course! If you buy a fiddle from David you'll get a better fiddle than the one you have'. And then David asked me, 'what did I want it to look like?' I really didn't know what he meant, so I said 'What would you do?' And he said, 'Well it's what would you do that I'm asking – it's not what I would do that's relevant here'. So I said something about the wood itself and that being a natural colour. And I remember having to really pull this out of him. I couldn't work out what he meant by this question. Eventually he said, 'Some people, particularly classical people playing in orchestras don't want their fiddle to stand out so they will ask for it to be made to look old'. Well that just horrified me. The idea of the aesthetic being made to look what it isn't. I was saying 'it's a new fiddle; I want it to look like a new fiddle. If someone's playing it in 200 years' time and its colour has changed and it looks like an old fiddle then it is an old fiddle'. So I left it with him, and I didn't know what colour it was going to be."

Conor continues: "One of the rules I gave myself was that once I'd left the shop I would never go back to him to ask how he's getting on with it. I didn't hear from David for months and months and months. And he had said to me 'I'll get it done'. I think it would have been by February 2021. But I was determined I wouldn't ring him up and say 'Where's this fiddle?' I was worried I'd panic him and that he'd work faster on it than he wanted to do. And then eventually I got this text and it said, 'So far so good'. Full stop. That was it! There might have been a photograph of the wood being worked. So I just texted back and said 'thanks'. Nothing about when's it going to be ready? My teacher had told me that there was a two-to-three year waiting list, so from my point of view, with him starting it, I'd already cut two years off. I was thrilled – to me this was superfast, compared to what I'd been told to expect."

And then, in July 2022, Dave rang Conor to tell him it was ready to collect. Conor picks up the story: "it was just really lovely. My partner came with me. He wanted to come along as well. He wanted to be there. And the first note I did with it, well it was just – the immediate word that came to mind was 'responsiveness'. You just touched it and yeah! So David said, 'that's what I wanted to hear from you – that's all I need to hear'. And that was just literally one note. One of the things David did say though was 'I've spent a lot of time thinking about getting it right; what you wanted'. The ever understated Dave Mann!

*

Like Dave, I too have spent a lot time thinking in relation to Conor's fiddle; and not just about the making of it, how that connects with the commissioning brief and what the brief might mean for arching and carving. Rather, a large part of this book has emerged in thinking through its making. The making of Conor's fiddle has been the primary means by which I've witnessed the craft practices of violin making, its skills and techniques, its problem-finding and solving, and its rhythms and flow. Watching Dave make this fiddle has been not just a window on the various stages of violin making – the visualisation of a manual, or practical 'how-to' guide, if you like - but a privilege, of being able to spend many hours just watching a master craftsman at work; deep in the flow of that work. It's also been the means to deepening my own understanding of my own fiddle. I now know what it means to be playing a Dave Mann Guadagnini and how what first drew me, unknowingly, to this instrument - its tonal colour, complexity, power and projection - relates to the fabrication of a sounding object. I know what makes it a

Dave Mann Guadagnini, and not just a Dave Mann fiddle. Perhaps most importantly, though, Conor's fiddle has been an opening. Dave's workshop takes on many guises. But one of them is a therapeutic space, a sanctuary, where people go just to sit and talk with Dave; they take immense comfort from that. I'm in no doubt that the making of Conor's fiddle has provided the same opportunity for Dave. It's in its making, through its making, that the kind of trust that's essential to tell a semi-biographical life history emerged – and it's in that making that Dave and I found the capacity to connect across our differences. In such a way, Conor's fiddle isn't just a violin; it's been a means to give voice to a luthier's world. And to give voice to a unique luthier at that – an accidental luthier, a working class lad, a professional drummer and a panel beater from Benwell.

Nicky Gregson

EPILOGUE

20 February 2024. I'm walking along the familiar street of Hencotes in Hexham, with my fiddle, on my way towards Number 27. The sun is shining. There's warmth in it, the crocuses and daffodils are starting to bloom and people are smiling. It's been a long, wet winter. But there's more than the weather that's brightening the mood, for today is a homecoming. Not just for my fiddle but for me.

The period from the summer of 2023 was a hiatus in the life of the violin shop; one keenly felt, and tangibly, by all connected with it. This was a period of closure and goodbyes and uncertain futures, for that summer Dave had received an offer for the business. He accepted it, promptly ceasing trading. This marked the end of an era and seemingly a resolution to the question that had hung in the air throughout the researching and writing of this book. What was going to happen, to the shop and to Dave?

Although agreeing to keep Dave on in a consultancy role, the new business owner immediately set about finding, and employing, a new luthier, Stephen Ramsey.

With a curious symmetry, Steve's trajectory into the luthier world is remarkable for its affinities with Nial Cain's. Born in Gosforth in Newcastle in the North east of England, he played classical guitar as a teenager, before going to study at Art College in Newcastle. But art wasn't really his thing; just like Nial, guitars were – or so he thought. Steve dropped out of Art College in the early 1980s and headed to London to do a City & Guilds in Musical Instruments Technology at Merton College. The course was wide ranging. It included guitars but also woodwind instruments and the instruments of the violin family. And that was where Steve's love of the guitar as an object of instrumental technology met its challenge. On being introduced to violins, that was it with guitars for Steve. Not interesting. Violins, and their relatives, became a lifelong passion.

Clearly talented as a luthier, Steve's subsequent career took him to working at one of the iconic violin dealers in London: JP Guivier's in Mortimer Street in the heart of the violin quarter. From there he moved to Bristol, to work at Caswell Strings – until, on the proprietor's retirement, that closed, at which point Steve migrated home to his native North east, along with a cello given to him by Hamilton, the proprietor.

Like Nial, Steve is a self-taught string player – but in his case he's a cellist, not a violinist. At Caswell's Steve also had the role of the cello assistant, demonstrating cellos' sound for prospective buyers. As he says, he didn't mind doing that when the buyer was an amateur but it was a different ball game when serious professionals came in, as they did – such was the global reputation of this shop: "Playing a bit of Bach for an amateur's ok, but when a top soloist comes in and wants to hear how an instrument sounds from across the room, well that's a different level of pressure!"

Twenty plus years on from when Nial had left for Wales, Dave therefore found himself back having to share 'his' workshop space with an artsy and cello playing luthier. Not only that, the working class drummer from Benwell was now sharing 'his' workshop, the place that he had frequently referred to me as "me sanctuary", with a lad from Gosforth. It wasn't just class differences that once more were playing out and being negotiated in the atelier; Newcastle's micro social geographies and distinctions were being played out! Not only that, a shop that had defined itself against the exclusivity of the classical violin world now had in its midst a luthier from that very world. The shop was being remade and its place in the violin world redefined.

Throughout the summer, Steve and Dave continued to work in the atelier, learning to accommodate to working alongside and with one another, whilst the new owner sought new premises in Hexham; 27 Hencotes having been deemed not fit for purpose. The new location was found in the late summer, and in September of 2023, after saying their goodbyes to the Hencotes community, Dave, Steve and the shop's contents moved the best part of a mile, to a terraced property. With an interior aesthetic of wooden floors and Persian rugs, and including a small performance space, the ambience of the new premises conveyed fundamental change.

*

Less than six months later, I'm back sitting in the old atelier in 27 Hencotes. Steve and Dave are back sitting at the benches they'd settled on as their preferred working layout the previous summer. It's as if they've never been away. Steve – looking at Dave – acknowledges, more as a statement than a question, "He never really left, did he." Business differences between the two luthiers and the proprietor had led to a parting of the ways. In early February 2024, Dave and Steve left the new venture, returning to 27 Hencotes, with Steve as the new business proprietor.

Sitting in the workshop, it's palpable that everyone is happy – and not just the humans. This is a workshop where violins have been made, repaired and restored for well over 50 years. The legacy of that craft work is in the brickwork of the place; you can literally feel it. Taking the workshop apart the previous summer had felt as if the very soul of the place was being destroyed; abandoned. Now, reassembled, with luthier work returned to it, and with violins on the workbenches, there's an all pervasive sense of calmness and tranquillity. Order has been restored.

Yet, quietly, seamlessly, amidst all the tranquillity, a major transition has occurred. After some 35 years, Dave is clearly taking more of a back seat. The shop has fashioned its own transition. In agreeing to sell up, Dave had inadvertently set in train a chain of events which led to the shop finding its new proprietor and luthier. Steve feels that lineage acutely, just as he does the shop's place in the community. We talk of cementing that lineage in portraits on the shop wall – of Bob, Nial, Dave and Steve. A marker of a special place and the people who, collectively and sequentially, have made it this.

As I sit in the workshop talking and thinking, another transition happens seamlessly in front of my eyes. I'd brought in both my viola bow and the fiddle that morning – not because I thought there was much wrong with the fiddle, but because I needed a case to carry the viola bow in.

Steve admires the craftsmanship on display in my fiddle (again – for he's seen it before), and then we get talking about some decay in the A string. He scrutinises it closely and detects a slight flaw in the nut ebony, which means that the nut needs to be replaced – and the strings. This is going to be interesting, I think to myself. Who is going to do this? Straight away, Dave sets to work on my viola bow, in so doing effectively passing the responsibility of working on my fiddle, which will also forever be Dave's fiddle, to Steve. Having this fiddle on his workbench is a further opportunity for Steve to appreciate and admire the skill of its maker, who is sat opposite him, but to my mind there can have been no better illustration of Dave's acknowledgement of Steve's skills than entrusting that work to him. In such a way, a violin which thus far in its life has only been worked on by its maker now has a new custodian.

Having finished the necessary work on the viola bow, Dave asks if anyone wants a sausage roll from Greggs. We laugh – for, true to form, I've bought marmite sandwiches. Yet, as Dave disappears out of the shop, to beat a familiar pathway to Greggs, the humour subsides and Steve says to me: "I hope he carries on working here for as long as he wants to". So do we all – for once a luthier always a luthier; it's a way of life, not a job. This is what makes retiring so hard for everyone in the trade. Yet, in this place, in this workshop, that transition is being made in a way which, rather than casting someone out, continues to recognise the capacities of the older skilled craft worker and the life affirming nature of putting those skills to work, most days but not every day. Much as one of my first visits to the atelier opened up its role as a confessional space amongst men of a certain age, where they felt comfortable talking about health issues, on this occasion, when writing this book was coming to its point of final closure, the shop had more to offer and to say. In showing the possibilities for post-retired work, it is a beacon for how to think differently about work in later years.

ACKNOWLEDGEMENTS

This book owes everything to the generosity of Dave Mann, who welcomed me into his atelier for the best part of 18 months, from May 2022 to December 2023. I spent a day a week there, most weeks – much like many others who have come to learn the lutherie craft. Except, I wasn't trying to learn lutherie; rather, I was seeking to make that world – and particularly the world of this shop – more visible, by turning a practical craft and a place into words. To that end, Dave didn't just demonstrate to me the craft work of making, restoring and repairing violins; he also had to put up with my endless questioning and multiple lines of enquiry. Often, this required him, a man of few words, to put into words a lifetime's tacit knowledge. I hope in that translation that I've done justice to what is, without question, the working life of a master craftsman.

To Dave's daughters: Sarah Wilson and Claire Mann, for their support for this project, for their willingness to talk about Dave's first experiments in violin making and their younger playing days, and for digging out some of the photographs of their younger lives.

To three luthiers: Stephen Ramsey, 27 Hencotes' new proprietor, who embraced this project and the book that resulted; Nial Cain, Dave's former business partner, who shared with me so much of the previous life of the shop, and Anthony Pancke, for his recollections of being taught lutherie by Dave.

To the many people who, notwithstanding being busy professional musicians, gave so freely of their time to be interviewed for this project. Their enthusiasm and commitment to it is the biggest testimony to the importance of 'Dave's' and Dave in their careers: Lauren MacColl, Aidan O'Rourke, Jack Smedley, Peter Tickell, Magdalena Loth Hill, Alistair Vennart, Rebecca Howell, Abigail Tickell, Carly Bain.

To the community of 27 Hencotes, who found themselves part of a book project, and who invested in that in their own inimitable ways: Martin Hughes, Paul Knox, Charlotte Hawes, Ralph Plumb, Jim Bickel, Freddie Thompson, Deborah Thorne, Ray Burns, Roddy Matthews, Jeremy Scratchert, Mickey Hutton, Kevin Jones and Janet Storrie.

And last, but by no means least, my thanks to those other members of what I dubbed 'the Hencotes diaspora' – the professional, semi-pro and amateur musicians who, whilst they don't live locally, are nonetheless part of Dave's wider fiddle family. Some of you were interviewed, others of you have 'walk on parts' but each and every one of your appearances helps to capture the essence of this place: Carolyn Francis, Ali Kyle, Rhiannon and Clemmie Germaine, Gavin Marwick and Des Dillon.

My hope is that something of what we all recognise to be the magic of 27 Hencotes comes across in these pages.

Nicky Gregson – June 2024

Nicky Gregson is Emerita Professor in the Department of Geography at Durham University. She writes at Nicky Gregson Substack. She's also a keen amateur fiddle player, who has had the immense good fortune to be taught by two of the finest exponents of Scottish fiddle, Lauren MacColl and Patsy Reid. She lives in Durham.

FURTHER READING

The Violin Shop is based on primary research conducted from May 2022 through December 2023. I describe that work in more depth in the Preface. It's been supplemented by archival research and wider reading. For those readers who may be interested in delving further into various issues and topics raised, I provide an indicative list here together with a brief description.

Chapter One

On the fire at Callers department store, see 'How Newcastle city centre was hit by its largest fire for years in the run up to Christmas' – *Evening Chronicle*, 30 November 2021. Newcastle's club scene in the 1960s and 1970s is meticulously curated by Roger Smith on his website, Readysteadygone.co.uk. The film *Get Carter* has recently celebrated its 50-year release and is widely available in multiple formats. For a review, see Domeneghetti R (2021) Get Carter at 50: the movie that transformed the North East, *The New European*. For a discussion of the background to how the film came to be made, see Jakubowski W (2020) A conversation with writer/director Mike Hodges – mulhollandbooks.com. There is considerable material available in the public domain on the Angus Sibbert murder, which continues to be a focus of fascination and speculation. On this, The Murder of Angus Sibbert: Neil Jackson True Crime Podcast 163 is a particularly good listen.

On working men's clubs, two books stand out: Ruth Cherrington's (2012) *Not Just Beer and Bingo: A Social History of Working Men's Clubs* (Authorhouse) and Pete

Brown's (2023) *Clubland: how the working men's clubs shaped Britain* (Harper Collins).

Chapter Two

Although understandably somewhat dated now, the standard reference work on contemporary violin luthiers in Britain is Alburger M (1978) *The Violin Makers: portrait of a living craft* (Victor Gollancz Ltd). Nial and Dave's mentor, Barry Oliver, features as a chapter in this.

On Edward Heron-Allen, the original text is Heron-Allen E (1884) *Violin-making, as it was and is – being a historical, theoretical and practical treatise on the science and art of violin-making for the use of violin makers and players, amateurs and professionals* (Ward Lock Ltd, London). It is still available in print. For a contextualisation of the man himself, the Heron-Allen Society is a good starting place – see heronallensociety.co.uk. On London's violin quarter at this time, see Navarre J – 157 Wardour Street – themuseumofsoho.org.uk

Richard Sennett's (2008) book *The Craftsman* (Penguin) is one of the best discussions available of craft working practices. Sennett is an academic, and the book has a philosophical underbelly, but it is open and accessible to wider audiences. There is a section in this on the Stradivari workshop in Cremona – but then Sennett is also a cellist, so that probably explains his fascination with stringed instruments. A different tack is taken by Toby Faber's (2004) book, *Stradivari's Genius* (Random House), which traces the history of six famous Strads.

Chapter Three

On guitars, and particularly guitar making, Chris Gibson & Andrew Warren's (2021) *The Guitar: tracing the grain back to the tree* (University of Chicago Press) is an accessibly written, if primarily academically-oriented book, which does just what the title suggests. Its concern is with the sustainability (or not) of guitar lutherie, but along the way there's much on how different guitars are made and the history of guitar making. The book which so fascinated Nigel Forster and Nial Cain is Robert (Bob) Bernadetto's (1996) *Making an Archtop Guitar* (Centerstream Publishing). The interview with Nigel Forster can be found on guitarbench.com – Interview 2008 with Terence Tan.

Helena Atlee's (2021) *Lev's Violin: an Italian adventure* (Random House) is an odyssey in search of the backstory to a violin whose sound bewitched her. Along the way, she gives the reader a primer in the history of violin making in Europe. Recommended for those who don't know much about this but would like a story to help shape that narrative.

Chapter Four

Des Dillon's work includes *Me & Ma Gal* (1995); *Singin I'm No a Billy He's a Tim* (2005) and *My Epileptic Lurcher* (2008). For more details, see his website, desdillon.com

Chapter Seven

For more details on the Dometsch family and Jesses House, see The Haslemere Society - Arnold Dometsch, Carl Dometsch – www.haslemeresociety.org